The media's watch...
Here's a sampling of our coverage.

VAULT GUIDE TO THE
TOP FINANCE
FIRMS

VAULT GUIDE TO THE
TOP FINANCE
FIRMS

CHRIS PRIOR, TYYA N. TURNER AND HANS H. CHEN

ACKNOWLEDGEMENTS

Vault would like to take the time to acknowledge the assistance and support of Matt Doull, Ahmad Al-Khaled, Lee Black, Eric Ober, Hollinger Ventures, Tekbanc, New York City Investment Fund, American Lawyer Media, Globix, Ingram, Hoover's, Glenn Fischer, Mark Hernandez, Ravi Mhatre, Tom Phillips, Carter Weiss, Ken Cron, Ed Somekh, Isidore Mayrock, Zahi Khouri, Sana Sabbagh, Esther Dyson and other Vault investors, as well as our loving families and friends.

This book could not have been written without the extraordinary efforts of Ben Adler, Alex Apelbaum, Michael Erman, Jayne Feld, Maggie Geiger, Anita Kapadia, Tom Lott, Corrie Moore, Brook Moshan, Kathleen Pierce, Rob Schipano, Ed Shen, Jake Wallace and Angela Williams. Thanks to Todd Kuhlman and the helpful folks at FIRM (especially Basil Petrov and Per Arne Moi) for providing technical support for the surveys. Thanks also to Tom Petner, Marcy Lerner, Dan Stanco, Kristy Sisko, Jennifer Sloan and Kate Carey for their support.

Special thanks to all of the recruiting coordinators and corporate communications representatives who helped with this book. We appreciate your patience with our repeated requests and tight deadlines.

The *Vault Guide to the Top Finance Firms* is dedicated to the finance professionals who took time out of their busy schedules to be interviewed or complete our survey.

THE VAULT TOP 25   63

BEST OF THE REST 237

WHY WORK FOR US 283

APPENDIX 287

Visit the Vault Finance Job Board — one of the best job boards on the
Internet exclusively for finance professionals. Go to www.vault.com.

VAULT xi

Introduction

Everyone deals with money, but few people really know what a career in finance entails. Though virtually every adult has some contact with a company in the finance sector — perhaps through a checking account, a loan, a brokerage account or a mutual fund investment — many people find it difficult to differentiate between the kinds of companies with which they do business.

This confusion hasn't stopped careers in the finance industry from being among the most coveted. According to the Bureau of Labor Statistics, commercial banks employed approximately 2 million people in 1998 while securities firms employed close to 650,000 that same year. The BLS projects that the employment in these industries will grow by 3 and 40 percent, respectively, through 2008, as compared to 15 percent for all industries. That's close to 3 million jobs before the end of this decade.

Why the stampede toward finance jobs? For one thing, the finance industry is relatively stable. Though some areas are susceptible to economic slumps (one example is loans, which decrease in times of recession), the finance industry is less likely than, say, manufacturing to see significant layoffs when the economy struggles. Though businesses and individuals may have less cash to put away, the need for both commercial and consumer bank accounts doesn't abate when the economy slows. And more American households than ever are involved in the stock or bond markets, and that number is expected to grow. That means more brokerage accounts, more 401(k)s and more IRAs — and, of course, more people to manage them.

But the greatest lure of the industry is its generous compensation. In commercial banking, entry-level jobs pay base salaries that start at $45,000 — a pretty good haul, by most standards. In investment banking, college graduates at large firms can pull down $55,000 to $65,000 in base salary, plus thousands in signing and relocation bonuses, plus yearly bonuses equal to approximately 60 to 70 percent of the base salary. All together, first-year analysts (as they're called) at Wall Street firms can make between $75,000 and $90,000. Asset management, another stable and lucrative field, isn't too shabby, either. Junior-level employees at investment management firms can pull down $40,000-$50,000 per year.

Visit the Vault Finance Job Board — one of the best job boards on the Internet exclusively for finance professionals. Go to www.vault.com.

VAULT   1

Because of the high demand for jobs in investment banking, asset management and commercial banking, this guide will focus on careers in those industries. Basically, investment banking is the business of raising money for companies through public markets. Commercial banking is the loaning of money to businesses. Asset management, meanwhile, involves handling money and investments for both businesses and individuals.

If this is all a little confusing, don't worry. What follows is a basic guide to those industries — what they do, what separates them from the others, what it means to work in those industries — as well as trends that affect the finance industry in general. You'll also know who the players are in each industry, what their employees think about the firms and what it's like to work at these companies. You'll also find the Vault Top 25, which lists the 25 most prestigious finance firms according to Vault's independent survey of finance professionals.

THE VAULT
PRESTIGE
RANKINGS

METHODOLOGY

In attempting to compile a ranking of the top 25 finance firms, Vault first decided to focus on three core finance industries — investment banking, investment management and commercial banking. Vault chose those sectors because they are the most competitive industries in terms of recruiting in the finance industry. Additionally, because companies in these industries often perform comparable functions, the skills required of employees are often similar.

Vault invited 94 companies in these industries to participate in our employees survey. The survey included a prestige rating and questions about life within the firm. We chose 44 investment banks, 25 investment management firms and 25 commercial banks. We chose these firms based on previous Vault surveys that gauged the opinions of industry insiders as well as some factual data, including size in terms of revenues and/or assets and standing in league tables. Employees who took the survey were asked to rank the firms in terms of prestige on a scale of 1 to 10. They were asked to rate only the companies with which they were familiar and were not allowed to rate their employer.

Five companies — Robertson Stephens, Salomon Smith Barney, TD Securities, Thomas Weisel Partners and Wit Soundview — agreed to participate. All surveys were completely anonymous. For those companies who refused our request, Vault sought contacts at the firm through other sources. These finance professionals took the same survey as the employees at firms that participated.

All told, 241 finance professionals filled out Vault's 2001 finance employees survey. Vault averaged the prestige scores for each firm and ranked them in order, with the highest average prestige score being our No. 1 firm. That firm was investment bank Goldman Sachs, which received a score of 9.721, far outdistancing competitor Morgan Stanley, which received a 9.264.

Six of the top 10 companies were investment banks, three were investment managers and one, J.P. Morgan Chase, has significant operations in both investment banking and commercial banking. For the top 25 as a whole, 12 companies can be classified investment banks, 11 can be called investment managers, one (Citibank) is a commercial bank and one is a hybrid. The highest ranking investment manager is Fidelity Investments at No. 6 (with a 7.690 prestige score) and the highest (and only) commercial bank is Citibank at No. 15 (with a 6.711). Profiles of all firms begin on page 63.

Visit the Vault Finance Job Board — one of the best job boards on the Internet exclusively for finance professionals. Go to www.vault.com.

VAULT 5

why your best

self-employment
opportunity

might involve some teamwork

As a Financial Representative of the Northwestern Mutual Financial Network, you'll be in business for yourself, but you won't be alone. You'll work with a network of specialists to help clients achieve their financial goals. You'll help clients build and preserve wealth. And you'll become a trusted financial confidant—known for your expert guidance and innovative solutions. We offer a proven training program and unlimited income potential. Call us today to arrange a no-obligation meeting.

SES Considering Self-Employment? Take the Self-Employment Profile at **www.doprofile.com/ses.htm** Password: **nmfn**

Northwestern Mutual
FINANCIAL NETWORK™

The Vault 25 • 2001

[The 25 most prestigious finance firms]

RANK	FIRM	SCORE	HEADQUARTERS
1	Goldman Sachs	9.721	New York, NY
2	Morgan Stanley	9.264	New York, NY
3	Credit Suisse First Boston	8.448	New York, NY*
4	Merrill Lynch	7.843	New York, NY
5	J.P. Morgan Chase	7.725	New York, NY
6	Fidelity Investments	7.690	Boston, MA
7	Salomon Smith Barney	7.519	New York, NY
8	Putnam Investments	7.270	Boston, MA
9	Janus Capital	7.218	Denver, CO
10	Lazard	7.084	New York, NY*
11	Lehman Brothers	7.054	New York, NY
12	Vanguard Group	6.923	Malverne, PA
13	Pequot Capital Management	6.861	Westport, CT
14	T. Rowe Price	6.800	Balitmore, MD
15	Citibank	6.711	New York, NY
16	Deutsche Bank	6.665	New York, NY*
17	CalPERS	6.225	Sacramento, CA
18	UBS Warburg	6.165	New York, NY*
19	Charles Schwab	6.144	San Francisco, CA
20	Alliance Capital Management	6.118	New York, NY
21	Gabelli Asset Management	6.029	Rye, NY
22	Robertson Stephens	6.028	San Francisco, CA
23	Thomas Weisel Partners	5.990	San Francisco, CA
24	Franklin Resources	5.815	San Mateo, CA
25	Bear Stearns	5.710	New York, NY

Source: Vault 2001 Finance Industry Survey

*U.S. Headquarters

Visit the Vault Finance Job Board — one of the best job boards on the
Internet exclusively for finance professionals. Go to www.vault.com.

VAULT 7

Ready. Aim. HIRE!

Target the quality candidates you want with Vault's Recruiting Solutions

- **Finance Job Board**
  Cut through the clutter by reaching the exact candidates looking to work in your industry.

- **Finance VaultMatch™ Resume Database**
  Quickly search, screen and view the exact candidates you want and move to hire within minutes.

- **Why Work for Us™ Recruitment Marketing**
  Appeal to potential hires by placing your online recruiting brochure alongside Vault's award-winning company profiles.

To request more information about our finance recruiting solutions, please email us at recruitingsales@staff.vault.com or call 1-888-562-VAULT x257.

Vault users are a rare breed.

- **AMBITIOUS:** 94% of Vault users visit Vault to "manage my career" or "keep on top of options."

- **EXPERIENCED:** Nearly 60% have 5+ years of work experience.

- **SMART:** 1 in 3 graduated from a top 50 university.

VAULT
> the insider career network™

OVERVIEW OF THE FINANCE INDUSTRY

VΛULT

Equity and Debt

Companies seeking capital have two options: equity (selling part of their business) and debt (borrowing money). Equity options include selling shares of stock on the open market or agreeing to be acquired by another firm. Debt options include the sale of bonds through an investment bank or arranging a loan from a commercial bank.

Section 1: Equity markets

The stock market

If you've ever watched with bemusement as the Dow fell and rose 100 points in a single day, or pounded your head on your desk after watching stock in your pet dot-com shrivel into unprofitable dust, you're familiar with the stock market. If you're not, suffice it to say that the stock market is where shares of stock — pieces of ownership in companies — are traded every day. The stocks are actually traded on exchanges, physical locations where trades take place. The oldest and best-known exchange is the New York Stock Exchange (NYSE). Another well-known exchange is the Nasdaq, which is a computerized trading system. Both exchanges are headquartered in New York. There are smaller, less-renowned exchanges all over the United States and exchanges all over the world.

Measuring the markets

The Dow Jones Industrial Average (DJIA) is one widely known metric of the stock market's performance. Created in 1896 as a yardstick to measure the performance of the U.S. stock market, the Dow Jones originally consisted of 12 stocks and started trading at 41 points. Today, the index consists of 30 large companies and traded over 10,000 points for the first time in March 1999. (The DJIA exceeded 11,700 in January 2000 but has slid back since then.) The Dow Jones is picked by the editors of *The Wall Street Journal* and is periodically updated to reflect changes in the economy. For example, in November 1999, four companies (including tech giants Microsoft and Intel) were added, while several "old

Visit the Vault Finance Job Board — one of the best job boards on the Internet exclusively for finance professionals. Go to www.vault.com.

VAULT   11

economy" companies like retailer Sears and chemical company Union Carbide were unceremoniously kicked to the curb.

While the DJIA is widely quoted as an indicator of the overall stock market, there are some flaws in tracking the index too closely. Because the Dow Jones is made up of only 30 stocks, it's only a small sample of all the businesses in the world. Additionally, the index only tracks very large companies. When gauging the health of the stock market, analysts often factor in other indexes as well. The Standard & Poor's 500 tracks the 500 largest companies in the world (like the Dow, this index has its limitations). The NYSE Composite Index measures the performance of every stock traded on that exchange, a much broader field than the Dow or the S&P 500. Finally, the Russell 2000 tracks 2000 small companies.

What moves the stock market?

Not surprisingly, the factors that most influence the broader stock market are economic in nature. Among equities, Gross Domestic Product (GDP) and the Consumer Price Index (CPI) are king.

When GDP slows substantially, market investors fear a recession. And if economic conditions worsen and the market enters a recession, many companies will face reduced demand for their products, company earnings will be hurt and, hence, equity (stock) prices will decline. Thus, when the GDP suffers, so does the stock market.

When the CPI heats up, investors fear inflation. Inflation fears trigger a different chain of events than fears of recession. First, inflation will cause interest rates to rise. Companies with debt will be forced to pay higher interest rates on existing debt, thereby reducing earnings. And compounding the problem, because inflation fears cause interest rates to rise, higher rates will make investments other than stocks more attractive from the investor's perspective. Why would an investor purchase a stock that may only earn 8 percent (and carries substantial risk), when lower risk CDs and government bonds offer similar yields with less risk? These inflation fears are known as capital allocations in the market (whether investors are putting money into stocks vs. bonds), which can substantially impact stock and bond prices. Investors typically re-allocate funds from stocks to low-risk bonds when the economy experiences a slowdown and vice versa when the opposite occurs.

What moves individual stocks?

When it comes to individual stocks, it's all about earnings, earnings, earnings. No other measure even compares to earnings per share (EPS) when it comes to an individual stock's price. Every quarter, companies must report EPS figures, and stockholders wait with bated breath, ready to compare the actual EPS figure with the EPS estimates. For instance, if a company reports $1.00 EPS for a quarter, but the market had anticipated EPS of $1.20, then the stock will be dramatically hit in the market that day. Conversely, a company that beats its estimates will rally in the markets.

It is important to note at this point that in the frenzied Internet stock market of 1999, investors did not show the traditional focus on near-term earnings. It was acceptable for these companies to operate at a loss for a year or more, because these companies, investors hoped, would achieve long-term future earnings.

The market does not care about last year's earnings. Investors maintain a tough "what have you done for me lately" attitude and are unforgiving towards a company that misses its numbers.

Mergers and acquisitions

In the 1980s, hostile takeovers and LBO acquisitions were trendy. Companies sought to acquire others through aggressive stock purchases and cared little about the target company's concerns or long-term viability.

The 1990s were the decade of friendly mergers, dominated by a few sectors in the economy. Today, mergers in the telecommunications, financial services and technology industries have been commanding headlines as these sectors go through dramatic change, both regulatory and financial. But giant mergers have been occurring in virtually every industry. M&A business has been consistently brisk, as demands to go global, to keep pace with the competition and to expand earnings by any possible means have been foremost in the minds of CEOs.

When a public company acquires another public company, the target company's stock often shoots through the roof, while the acquiring company's stock often declines. Why? One must realize that existing shareholders must be convinced to sell their stock. Few shareholders are willing to sell their stock to an acquirer without first being paid a premium on the current stock price. In addition, shareholders must also capture a takeover

Visit the Vault Finance Job Board — one of the best job boards on the Internet exclusively for finance professionals. Go to www.vault.com.

V/\ULT   13

premium to relinquish control over the stock. The large shareholders of the target company typically demand such an extraction. For example, the management of the selling company may require a substantial premium to give up control of their firm.

M&A transactions can be roughly divided into either mergers or acquisitions. These terms are often used interchangeably in the press, and the actual legal difference between the two involves minutiae of accounting procedures, but we can still draw a rough difference between the two.

> **Acquisition** — When a larger company takes over another (smaller) firm and clearly becomes the new owner, the purchase is called an acquisition. Typically, the target company ceases to exist post-transaction (from a legal corporation point of view) and the acquiring corporation swallows the business. The stock of the acquiring company continues to be traded.

> **Merger** — A merger occurs when two companies, often roughly the same size, combine to create a new company. Such a situation is often called a merger of equals. Both companies' stocks are tendered (or given up), and new company stock is issued in its place. For example, both Chrysler and Daimler-Benz ceased to exist when their firms merged, and a new combined company, the euphoniously named DaimlerChrysler, was created.

M&A advisory services

For an investment bank, M&A advising is highly profitable, and there are many possibilities for types of transactions. Perhaps a small private company's owner/manager wishes to sell out for cash and retire. Or perhaps a big public firm aims to buy a competitor through a stock swap. Whatever the case, M&A advisors come directly from the corporate finance departments of investment banks. Unlike public offerings, merger transactions do not directly involve salespeople, traders or research analysts. In particular, M&A advisory falls onto the laps of M&A specialists and fits into one of either two buckets: seller representation or buyer representation (also called target representation and acquirer representation).

Representing the target

An I-bank that represents a potential seller has a much greater likelihood of completing a transaction (and therefore being paid) than an I-bank that represents a potential acquirer. Generally speaking, the work involved in finding a buyer includes writing a selling memorandum and then contacting potential strategic or financial buyers of the client. If the client hopes to sell a semiconductor plant, for instance, the I-bankers will contact firms in that industry, as well as buyout firms that focus on purchasing technology or high-tech manufacturing operations.

Representing the acquirer

When advising sellers, the I-bank's work is complete once another party purchases the business up for sale. Buy-side work is an entirely different animal. The advisory work itself is straightforward: The investment bank contacts the firm its client wishes to purchase, attempts to structure a palatable offer for all parties and make the deal a reality.

However, sad to say, most of these proposals do not work out. Few firms or owners are willing to sell their business just because an investment bank thinks it's a good idea. And because the banks primarily collect fees based on completed transactions, their work often goes unpaid. Deals that do get done, though, are extremely profitable for the buy-side bank. Fees depend on the size of the deal but generally fall in the 1 percent range.

Private placements

A private placement, which involves the selling of debt or equity to private investors, resembles both a public offering and a merger. A private placement differs little from a public offering aside from the fact that a private placement involves a firm selling stock or equity to private investors, rather than to public investors. Also, a typical private placement deal is smaller than a public transaction. Despite these differences, the primary reason for a private placement — to raise capital — is fundamentally the same as a public offering.

Why private placements?

Firms wishing to raise capital often discover that they are unable to go public for a number of reasons. The company may not be big enough, the markets may not have an appetite for IPOs or the company may simply prefer not to

Visit the Vault Finance Job Board — one of the best job boards on the Internet exclusively for finance professionals. Go to www.vault.com.

VAULT   15

have its stock publicly traded. Such firms make excellent private placement candidates. Often, firms wishing to go public may be advised by investment bankers to first do a private placement, as they need to gain critical mass or size to justify an IPO.

Private placements, then, are usually the province of small companies hoping to go public. The process of raising private equity or debt changes only slightly from a public deal. One difference is that private placements do not require any securities to be registered with the SEC, nor do they involve publicly flogging the stock. In place of prospectus, I-banks draft a detailed private placement memorandum (PPM for short), which divulges information similar to a prospectus. Instead of a road show, companies looking to sell private stock or debt will host potential investors as interest arises and give presentations detailing how they will be the greatest thing since sliced bread. The investment banker's work involved in a private placement is quite similar to sell-side M&A representation. The bankers attempt to find a buyer by writing the PPM and then contacting potential strategic or financial buyers of the client.

Section 2: Debt Markets

What is the bond market?

The average person doesn't follow the bond market and often doesn't even hear about it. Stocks are sexy. Bonds aren't. Because of the bond market's low profile, it's surprising to many people that the bond markets are approximately the same size as the equity markets.

Until the late 1970s and early 1980s, bonds were considered non-thrilling investments, bought by retired grandparents and insurance companies. They traded infrequently and provided safe, steady returns. Beginning in the early 1980s, however, Michael Milken essentially created the high-stakes world of junk bonds, making a fortune. (Junk bonds, also called high-yield bonds, are bonds with more risk than classic government or corporate bonds.) And with the development of mortgage-backed securities, Salomon Brothers also transformed bonds into something exciting and extremely profitable.

To begin our discussion of the fixed-income markets, we'll identify the main types of securities:

- U.S. Government Treasury securities
- Agency bonds
- High-grade corporate bonds
- High-yield (junk) bonds
- Municipal bonds
- Mortgage-backed bonds
- Asset-backed securities
- Emerging market bonds

Bond market indicators

The Yield Curve

A primary measure of importance to fixed-income investors is the yield curve. The yield curve (also called the "term structure of interest rates") depicts graphically the yields on different maturity U.S. government securities. To construct a simple yield curve, investors typically look at the yield on a 90-day U.S. T-bill and then the yield on the 30-year U.S. government bond (called the Long Bond). Typically, the yields of shorter-term government T-bill are lower than Long Bond's yield, indicating what is

Visit the Vault Finance Job Board — one of the best job boards on the
Internet exclusively for finance professionals. Go to www.vault.com.

VAULT   17

called an upward sloping yield curve. (We've heard of the question "What is the long bond?" being asked in finance interviews.)

Bond Indices

As with the stock market, the bond market has some widely watched indexes. One prominent example is the Lehman Government Corporate Bond Index. The LGC index measures the returns on mostly government securities, but also blends in a portion of corporate bonds. The index is adjusted to reflect the percentage of assets in government and corporate bonds. Mortgage bonds are excluded entirely from the LGC index.

U.S. Government Bonds

Particularly important in the universe of fixed-income products are U.S. government bonds. These bonds are the most reliable in the world, as the U.S. government is unlikely to default on its loans (and if it ever did, the bond market would be the least of your worries). Because they are virtually risk-free, U.S. government bonds, also called Treasuries, offer low yields (a low rate of interest), and are standards by which other bonds are measured.

Spreads

In the bond world, investors track spreads as carefully as any single index of bond prices or any single bond. The spread is essentially the difference between a bond's yield (the amount of interest, measured in percent, paid to bondholders) and the yield on a U.S. Treasury bond of the same time to maturity. For instance, an investor investigating the 20-year Acme Company bond would compare it to a U.S. Treasury bond that has 20 years remaining until maturity.

Bond ratings for corporate and municipal bonds

A bond's risk level, or the risk that the bond issuer will default on payments to bondholders, is measured by bond rating agencies. Several companies rate credit, but Standard & Poor's and Moody's are the two largest. The riskier a bond, the larger the spread; low-risk bonds trade at a small spread to Treasuries, while below-investment grade bonds trade at tremendous spreads to Treasuries. Investors refer to company specific risk as credit risk.

Triple-A ratings represents the highest possible corporate bond designation, and are reserved for the best-managed, largest blue-chip companies. Triple-A bonds trade at a yield close to the yield on a risk-free government Treasury. Junk bonds, or bonds with a rating of BB or below, currently trade at yields ranging from 10 to 15 percent, depending on the precise rating, the company's situation and the economic conditions at the time.

Companies continue to be monitored by the rating agencies as long as bonds trade in the markets. If a company is put on credit watch, it is possible that the rating agencies are considering raising or lowering the rating on the company. When a bond is actually downgraded by Moody's or S&P, the bond's price drops dramatically (and therefore its yield increases).

Factors affecting the bond market

What factors affect the bond market? In short, interest rates. The general level of interest rates, as measured by many different barometers moves bond prices up and down, in dramatic inverse fashion. In other words, if interest rates rise, the bond markets suffer.

Think of it this way. Say you own a bond is paying you a fixed rate of 8 percent today, and that this rate represents a 1.5 percent spread over Treasuries. An increase in rates of 1 percent means that this same bond purchased now (as opposed to when you purchased the bond) will yield 9 percent. And as the yield goes up, the price declines. So, your bond loses value and you are only earning 8 percent when the rest of the market is earning 9 percent.

You could have waited, purchased the bond after the rate increase and earned a greater yield. The opposite occurs when rates go down. If you lock in a fixed rate of 8 percent and rates plunge by 1 percent, you now earn more than those who purchase the bond after the rate decrease.

Why do interest rates move?

Interest rates react mostly to inflation expectations. If it is believed that inflation will be high, interest rates rise. Think of it this way. Say inflation is 5 percent a year. In order to make money on a loan, a bank would have to at least charge more than 5 percent — otherwise it would essentially be

Visit the Vault Finance Job Board — one of the best job boards on the Internet exclusively for finance professionals. Go to www.vault.com.

VAULT 19

losing money on the loan. The same is true with bonds and other fixed income products.

In the late 1970s, interest rates topped 20 percent, as inflation began to spiral out of control (and the market expected continued high inflation). Today, many believe that the Federal Reserve has successfully vanquished inflation and has all but eliminated market concerns of future inflation. This is certainly debatable, but clearly, the sound monetary policies and remarkable price stability in the U.S. have made it the envy of the world.

Bank loans

The most well-known form of debt is the loan. A loan, also called commercial credit when it involves a business, is an arrangement between the lender (for our purposes, a commercial bank) and the borrower to repay the principal amount plus interest over a set period of time. The terms of the arrangement are laid out in the loan commitment, a contract between the lender and borrower.

Though loans are the more famous form of debt, companies turn to them only when they have few or no other financing options. Interest rates on loans are usually much higher than bonds. Only companies that have a poor credit rating — too poor to sell bonds — will seek a bank loan, unless it's for the short term.

What's What?
Industry Overviews

Section 1: Investment Banking

Investment banking is the business of raising money for companies. Companies need capital in order to grow their business; they turn to investment banks to sell securities to investors — either public or private — to raise this capital. These securities come in the form of stocks or bonds.

Generally, an investment bank is comprised of the following areas:

Corporate finance

The bread and butter of a traditional investment bank, corporate finance generally performs two different functions: 1) mergers and acquisitions advisory and 2) underwriting. On the mergers and acquisitions (M&A) advising side of corporate finance, bankers assist in negotiating and structuring a merger between two companies. If, for example, a company wants to buy another firm, then an investment bank will help finalize the purchase price, structure the deal and generally ensure a smooth transaction. The underwriting function within corporate finance involves raising capital for a client. In the investment banking world, capital can be raised by selling either stocks or bonds to investors.

Sales

Sales is another core component of the investment bank. Salespeople take the form of: 1) the classic retail broker, 2) the institutional salesperson or 3) the private client service representative. Brokers develop relationships with individual investors and sell stocks and stock advice to the average Joe. Institutional salespeople develop business relationships with large institutional investors. Institutional investors are those who manage large groups of assets, for example pension funds or mutual funds. Private Client Service (PCS) representatives lie somewhere between retail brokers and institutional salespeople, providing brokerage and money management services for extremely wealthy individuals. Salespeople make money through commissions on trades made through their firms.

Visit the Vault Finance Job Board — one of the best job boards on the Internet exclusively for finance professionals. Go to www.vault.com.

VAULT   21

Trading

Traders also provide a vital role for the investment bank. Traders facilitate the buying and selling of stock, bonds or other securities, such as currencies, either by carrying an inventory of securities for sale or by executing a given trade for a client. Traders deal with transactions large and small and provide liquidity (the ability to buy and sell securities) for the market. (This is often called making a market.) Traders make money by purchasing securities and selling them at a slightly higher price. This price differential is called the "bid-ask spread."

Research

Research analysts follow stocks and bonds and make recommendations on whether to buy, sell or hold those securities. Stock analysts (known as equity analysts) typically focus on one industry and will cover up to 20 companies' stocks at any given time. Some research analysts work on the fixed-income side and will cover a particular segment, such as high-yield bonds or U.S. Treasury bonds. Salespeople within the I-bank utilize research published by analysts to convince their clients to buy or sell securities through their firm. Corporate finance bankers rely on research analysts to be experts in the industry in which they are working. Reputable research analysts can generate substantial corporate finance business as well as substantial trading activity and thus are an integral part of any investment bank.

Syndicate

The hub of the investment banking wheel, syndicate provides a vital link between salespeople and corporate finance. Syndicate exists to facilitate the placing of securities in a public offering, a knock-down drag-out affair between and among buyers of offerings and the investment banks managing the process. In a corporate or municipal debt deal, syndicate also determines the allocation of bonds.

Section 2: Investment Management

Investment management, also known as asset management, is a straightforward business. A client entrusts his money to an asset manager, who then invests it to meet the client's objectives. Still, outside of the relatively small circle of money managers, the profession is little understood.

The potential employers of an asset manager can vary widely. Asset managers who work for mutual funds, for example, manage money for retail clients, while asset managers at investment banks often invest money for institutional investors, like companies or municipalities. Asset managers can also work for hedge funds, which combine outside capital with capital contributed by the partners of the fund, and invest the money (using complex and sometimes risky techniques) with the goal of receiving extraordinary gains.

Insiders say that investment management is a misunderstood field. "So many people think it's investment banking; they think it's capital markets," says Michael Weinstock, a recruiter with Manhattan-based Advisors Search Group. Essentially, says Weinstock, "The industry is built around people who would like to have their money managed, whether it's for pension funds, 401(k) plans, endowments, foundations, high-worth individuals, families or trusts." Investment management relies on customers who feel comfortable "giving money to a professional and saying, 'You're on the pulse of the market. Watch my money for me. Manage it for me.' We have the autonomy to do this without clearing every trade with our clients."

Buy side versus sell side

To manage the assets under their purview, investment managers buy stocks, bonds and other financial products from salespeople at investment banks, who are on what is called the "sell side." Because sell-siders earn commissions on every trade they facilitate, they provide research and ideas to the buy side — along with perks like prime seats to sporting events, sold-out concerts and expensive dinners at fancy restaurants — in hopes of making their securities look especially appealing. "In general, if the sell-side person is with you, there's no limit on what he can spend," says an insider at Lazard, an international investment bank and money manager.

Back on the "buy side," asset management firms build their business around supporting the people who manage portfolios, including analysts,

Visit the Vault Finance Job Board — one of the best job boards on the Internet exclusively for finance professionals. Go to www.vault.com.

VAULT   23

administrative support staff and marketers who drum up the business and educate clients about their investments.

Although asset management firms exist virtually anywhere there's money to invest, New York and Boston are buy-side centers. The largest firms employ several hundred professionals to manage total assets upwards of hundreds of billions of dollars, covering both institutional and individual clients. Smaller mom-and-pop shops may employ three of four professionals to handle $300 to $800 million in institutional money. Firms serving high-wealth clients use about the same number of people to manage slightly less money. Major firms also have roots in Los Angeles, San Francisco and Chicago. Other cities considered up-and-coming include Baltimore, Minneapolis, Atlanta, Denver, Dallas, Fort Worth and San Diego.

Section 3: Commercial Banking

"Neither a borrower nor a lender be," Polonius advises Laertes in *Hamlet*. Good thing commercial banks haven't taken Shakespearean bromides to heart. (It didn't get Polonius anywhere either.) Commercial banks, unlike investment banks, generally act as lenders, putting forth their own money to support businesses, as opposed to investment advisors who rely on other folks — buyers of stocks and bonds — to pony up cash. This distinction, enshrined by fundamental banking laws in place since the 1930s, has led to noticeable cultural differences (exaggerated by stereotype) between commercial and investment bankers.

Commercial bankers (deservedly or not) have a reputation for being less aggressive, more risk-averse and simply not as mean as investment bankers. Commercial bankers also don't command the eye-popping salaries and elite prestige that I-bankers receive.

There is a basis for the stereotype. Commercial banks must carefully screen borrowers, since the banks are investing huge sums of their own money in companies that must remain healthy enough to make regular loan payments for decades. Investment bankers, on the other hand, can make their fortunes in one day by skimming off some of the money raised in a stock offering or invested into an acquisition. While a borrower's subsequent business decline can damage a commercial bank's bottom line, a stock that plummets after an offering has no effect on the investment bank that managed that IPO.

We'll take your money

Commercial bankers, who far outnumber any other type of financial service professionals, make money by their legal charter to take deposits from businesses and consumers. To gain the confidence of these depositors, commercial banks offer government-sponsored guarantees on these deposits on amounts up to $100,000. But to get FDIC guarantees, commercial banks must follow a myriad of regulations (and hire regulators to manage them). Many of these guidelines were set up in the Glass-Steagall Act of 1933, which was meant to separate the activities of commercial and investment banks. Glass-Steagall included a restriction on the sale of stocks and bonds (investment banks, which could not take deposits, were exempt from banking laws and free to offer more speculative securities offerings). Deregulation — especially the Financial Services Modernization Act of 1999 — and consolidation in the

Visit the Vault Finance Job Board — one of the best job boards on the Internet exclusively for finance professionals. Go to www.vault.com.

VAULT 25

banking industry over the past decade have significantly weakened these traditional barriers, however.

The lending train

The typical commercial banking process is fairly straightforward. Since commercial bankers typically work alongside retail bankers, the lending cycle starts with consumers depositing savings or businesses depositing sales proceeds at the bank. The bank, in turn, puts aside a relatively small portion of the money for withdrawals and to pay for possible loan defaults and then loans the rest of the money to companies in need of capital to pay for, say, a new factory or an overseas venture. A commercial bank's customers can range from the dry cleaner on the corner to a multinational conglomerate. For very large clients, several commercial banks may band together to issue "syndicated loans" of truly staggering size.

Commercial banks lend out money at interest rates that are largely determined by the Federal Reserve Board (currently governed by the bespectacled Alan Greenspan). Along with lending money that they have on deposit from clients, commercial banks lend out money that they have received from the Fed. The Fed loans out money to commercial banks, that in turn lend it to bank customers in a variety of forms — standard loans, mortgages, and so on. Besides its ability to set a baseline interest rate for all loans, the Fed also uses its lending power to equalize the economy. To prevent inflation, it raises the interest rate it charges for the money it loans to banks, slowing down the circulation of money and the growth of the economy. To encourage growth, it will lower the interest rate it charges banks.

Making money by moving money

Take a moment to consider how a bank makes its money. Commercial banks in the U.S. earn 5 to 14 percent interest on most of their loans. Since commercial banks typically only pay depositors 1 percent — if anything — on checking accounts and 2 to 3 percent on savings accounts, they make a tremendous amount of money in the difference between the cost of their funds (1 percent for checking account deposits) and the return on the funds they loan (5 to 14 percent).

Trends in the Finance Industry

Glass-Steagall reform

By far, the biggest change in the finance industry has been consolidation. The last decade has seen an unprecedented wave of mergers both within individual industries and across several industries. The most glaring example of merger prowess is Citigroup, the financial services giant that includes a large commercial bank (Citibank), insurance company (Travelers) and investment bank (Salomon Smith Barney). The behemoth was formed in 1998 when Travelers, which had purchased Salomon Brothers and combined it with its own Smith Barney unit in 1997, agreed to merge with Citibank. The new company has not slowed the acquisition juggernaut. Salomon Smith Barney announced the acquisition of London-based Schroders plc in January 2000 and Citibank added consumer loan specialist Associates First Capital in September 2000.

The Citigroup story is especially interesting, as it reflects a fundamental change in how the U.S. government has viewed the finance industry. During the Great Depression, Congress passed the Glass-Steagall Act, which was designed to prevent the kind of collapse in the financial services industry that was such a large factor in the Depression. In the late 1980s and early 1990s, regulators chipped away at the regulation and finally repealed it in 1999.

The history of Glass-Steagall

The Glass-Steagall Act, enacted in 1933, erected barriers between commercial banking and the securities industry. Glass-Steagall was created in the aftermath of the stock market crash of 1929 and the subsequent collapse of many commercial banks. At the time, many blamed the securities activities of commercial banks for the banks instability. Dealings in securities, critics claimed, upset the soundness of the banking community, caused banks to fail and crippled the stock markets. Therefore, separating securities businesses and commercial banking seemed the best solution to provide solidity to the U.S. banking and securities system.

In later years, a different truth seemed evident. The framers of Glass-Steagall argued that a conflict of interest existed between commercial and investment

Visit the Vault Finance Job Board — one of the best job boards on the Internet exclusively for finance professionals. Go to www.vault.com.

VAULT   27

banks. The conflict of interest argument ran something like this. A bank that made a bad loan might try to reduce its risk of defaulting by underwriting a public offering and selling stock in that company. The proceeds from the IPO would be used to pay off the bad loan. Consequently, the bank would shift risk from its own balance sheet to new investors via the initial public offering.

Academic research and common sense, however, have convinced many that this conflict of interest isn't valid. A bank that consistently sells ill-fated stock would quickly lose its reputation and ability to sell IPOs to new investors.

Walking on broken Glass

In the late 1990s, before legislation officially eradicated the Glass-Steagall Act's restrictions, the investment and commercial banking industries witnessed many intrepid commercial banking firms making forays into the I-banking world. The mania reached its height in the spring of 1998 when NationsBank bought Montgomery Securities, Societe Generale bought Cowen & Co., First Union purchased Wheat First and Bowles Hollowell Connor, Bank of America acquired Robertson Stephens (and then sold it to BankBoston), Deutsche Bank bought Bankers Trust (which had bought Alex. Brown months before) and Citigroup was created in a merger of Travelers Insurance and Citibank.

What took so long?

So why did it take so long to enact a repeal of Glass-Steagall? There were several logistical and political issues to address in undoing Glass-Steagall. Remember that the FDIC and the Federal Reserve regulate commercial banks, while the SEC regulates securities firms. A debate emerged as to who would regulate the new "universal" financial services firms. The Fed eventually won, with Alan Greenspan defining his office's role as that of an "umbrella supervisor." A second factor was the Community Reinvestment Act of 1977 — an act that requires commercial banks to re-invest a portion of their earnings back into their community. Senator Phil Gramm (R-Tex.), Chairman of the Senate Banking Committee, was a strong opponent of this legislation, while then-President Bill Clinton was in favor of keeping and even expanding the CRA. The two sides finally agreed on a compromise in which CRA requirements were lessened for small banks.

In November 1999, President Clinton signed the Gramm-Leach-Bliley Act (also known as the Financial Services Modernization Act of 1999), which repealed restrictions contained in Glass-Steagall that prevent banks from affiliating with securities firms. The new law allows banks, securities firms and insurance companies to affiliate within a financial holding company (FHC) structure. Under the new system, insurance, banking and securities activities are "functionally regulated." Incidentally, the players in the Citibank/Travelers merger were active in the passage of the Financial Services Modernization Act. John Reed, former Citibank CEO and Sanford Weill, former Travelers CEO and current head of Citigroup, lobbied President Clinton for change while the merger was being negotiated. According to *Crain's New York Business*, Weill has as a memento the pen Clinton used to sign the Act into law.

One-stop shopping? Not so fast

When Glass-Steagall fell, many predicted a flood of financial services combinations like Citigroup. Though there has been some cross-industry consolidation, to date there has been no deluge of financial service supermarkets. Why? For one thing, companies in different sectors of the financial services sector aren't similar. An insurance company has little in common with an investment bank. The two companies have different management styles, different kinds of investors and, in some ways, different goals (though both companies are trying to make a profit). Therefore, investors and management aren't always eager to pair up.

Additionally, there's no evidence that individuals or businesses are desperate to get all of their finance products from the same company. For example, a business gets some benefit from buying insurance, having bank accounts and raising capital from one source, but competition and the ease with which many transactions can be handled minimize the benefit of one-stop shopping. Some companies are unwilling to put all their eggs in one basket, worrying that having too much business with one financial services firm takes away the incentive to give them the best prices and service.

The dot-bust

In early 2000, it seemed dot-coms could do no wrong. Professionals at established companies — especially analysts and associates at investment

Visit the Vault Finance Job Board — one of the best job boards on the Internet exclusively for finance professionals. Go to www.vault.com.

VAULT   29

banks — were rushing to Internet companies for finance and business development positions. Finance companies recruiting at undergraduate and MBA schools faced stiff competition from dot-coms.

The Internet crash of April 2000 changed that. As the prices of Internet stock plummeted and dot-coms went dot-gone, jobs at dot-coms looked less and less enticing. Suddenly, banks were having an easier time recruiting on campus. Bankers who had left the industry fled dot-coms and headed back to the finance sector.

One positive side effect of the Internet bubble: an improvement in working conditions at finance firms, which raised salaries to compete with the dot-coms and relaxed their dress codes. While dot-coms are no longer fierce competitors for top finance candidates, it's safe to say that some Internet-inspired perks will remain a permanent fixture at finance firms.

Pink slip party

As the New Economy tumbled, the old economy slumped. The end of 2000 saw a torrent of bad economic news and falling corporate profits. Those dropping profits, along with a handful of mergers among large firms, led to a number of layoffs. For example, in commercial banking, First Union cut approximately 2,300 workers in June 2000 when it closed the Money Store, a consumer lending unit. In August 2000, Bank of America announced the elimination of 10,000 jobs, and Wachovia Corp. trimmed 1,800 from its payroll. (Bank of America cut approximately 60 investment bankers in January 2001, 6 percent of the investment banking staff at its Banc of America Securities unit.)

In investment banking, J.P. Morgan Chase laid off 5,000 workers after the September 2000 union of J.P. Morgan and Chase Manhattan. Credit Suisse First Boston also slashed staff, cutting 2,000 jobs after it purchased Donaldson, Lufkin & Jenrette. On a smaller scale, Prudential Securities virtually eliminated its investment banking operations, putting more than 150 I-bankers out of work, while Bear Stearns and Merrill Lynch cut a handful of staff members. The investment management industry didn't escape unscathed, either. Janus Capital laid off more than 500 workers in early 2001.

THE JOBS

Investment Banking

By far, investment banking careers are the most coveted in the finance industry. But, *Wall Street* aside, what is it that investment bankers do? Employees in the four groups — corporate finance, sales and trading, research, and syndicate — have very different roles.

Section 1: Corporate Finance

Stuffy bankers?

The stereotype of the corporate finance department is stuffy, arrogant, white, male MBAs who frequent golf courses and talk on cell-phones incessantly. While this stereotype isn't completely true, corporate finance remains the most white-shoe department in the typical investment bank. The atmosphere in corporate finance is, unlike that in sales and trading, often quiet and reserved. Junior bankers sit separated by cubicles, quietly crunching numbers hour after hour after hour.

Depending on the firm, corporate finance can also be a tough place to work, with unforgiving bankers and extremely high expectations of performance. Stories of analyst abuse abound, and some bankers come down hard on new analysts to scare and intimidate them. The lifestyle for corporate finance professionals can be a killer. In fact, many corporate finance workers find that they literally dedicate their lives to the job. It is not uncommon for analysts and associates to pull back-to-back all-nighters; many say that their personal relationships suffer. Fortunately, these long hours pay remarkable dividends in the form of six-figure salaries and huge year-end bonuses.

Bankers tend to be highly intelligent, motivated and not lacking in confidence. Money is important to corporate bankers, and many work in the field in the hopes of retiring early.

The deal team

Investment bankers generally work in deal teams that, depending on the size of a deal, vary somewhat in makeup. Because the titles and roles really do not change between underwriting to M&A, we have included both in this explanation. In fact, at most smaller firms, underwriting and transaction

Visit the Vault Finance Job Board — one of the best job boards on the Internet exclusively for finance professionals. Go to www.vault.com.

VAULT   33

advisory are not separated, and bankers typically pitch whatever business they can scout out within their industry sector.

Analysts

Analysts are the grunts in the corporate finance world. They often toil endlessly with little thanks, relatively low pay (when calculated on an hourly basis) and barely enough free time to sleep four hours a night. Typically hired directly out of top undergraduate universities, this crop of bright, highly motivated kids does the financial modeling and basic entry-level duties associated with any corporate finance deal.

Modeling every night until 2 a.m. and not having much of a social life proves to be unbearable for many an analyst, and after two years, many analysts leave the industry. Unfortunately, many bankers recognize the transient nature of analysts and work them to the bone. The unfortunate analyst that screws up or talks back too much may find himself subject to particular torture. Such disfavored analysts are seldom called to work on live transactions, and do menial work or just put together pitchbooks all the time.

Location has a big influence on first-year associate pay. In New York City, pay for first-year analysts often reaches $45,000 to $60,000 per year, with an annual bonus of approximately $30,000. While this seems to be a lot for a 22-year-old with an undergrad degree, it's not a great deal if you consider that analysts routinely work more than 80 hours a week. There are some (albeit slight) advantages to this grueling schedule: Analysts often get free dinner while working late, and the lack of free time to spend money means most analysts can save a fair amount.

At regional firms, pay typically is 20 percent less than that of their New York counterparts. At the same time, regional analysts often work shorter hours and live in areas where the cost of living is much lower. Be wary, however, of the occasional small regional firm that pays at the low end of the scale but still demands New York City-style hours. While the salary generally doesn't increase much for second-year analysts, the bonus can double for those second-years with demonstrated high performance. At this level, bonuses depend mostly on an analyst's contribution, attitude and work ethic, not the overall performance of the company.

Associates

Much like analysts, associates work very hard, up to 100 hours a week and rarely less than 80. Associates stress over pitchbooks and models all night and become true experts in financial modeling on Excel. These tasks aren't entirely unlike the typical responsibilities of the analyst. Unlike analysts, however, associates gain exposure to clients more quickly. Most importantly, they're not quite at the bottom of the totem pole. Associates quickly learn to play quarterback and hand off menial modeling work and research projects to analysts.

Associates, who typically come straight from top MBA programs, usually only have a summer's worth of experience in corporate finance. They must learn the business (almost) from the beginning. The overall level of business sophistication an MBA possesses, however, makes a tremendous difference, and associates quickly earn the luxury of more complicated work and better bonuses.

Associates are much better paid than analysts. They typically start in the $80,000 range, and bonuses normally hit $25,000 in the first six months. (At most firms, associates start in August and get what's called a stub bonus in January.) Newly minted MBAs benefit from signing bonuses and forgivable loans as well, especially on Wall Street. These can amount to another $25,000 to $30,000, depending on the firm, providing total compensation of up to $130,000.

Vice presidents

Upon attaining the position of vice president, those in corporate finance enter the realm of real bankers. The lifestyle becomes much more manageable once the associate moves up to VP. On the plus side, weekends free up, all-nighters drop off and the general level of responsibility increases — VPs are the ones telling analysts to stay late on Friday nights. In the office, VPs manage the financial modeling/ pitchbook production process in the office. On the negative side, the wear and tear of traveling that accompanies banker responsibilities can be difficult.

As a VP, one begins to handle client relationships and thus spends much more time on the road than analysts or associates. You can look forward to being on the road at least three to four days per week, usually visiting clients and potential clients. Don't forget about closing dinners (to celebrate completed deals), industry conferences (to drum up potential business and build a solid

Visit the Vault Finance Job Board — one of the best job boards on the Internet exclusively for finance professionals. Go to www.vault.com.

VAULT   35

network within their industry) and, of course, roadshows. VPs are perfect candidates to baby-sit company management on roadshows.

The formula for paying bankers varies dramatically from firm to firm. Some adhere to rigid formulas based on how much business a banker brings in, while others pay based on a subjective allocation of corporate finance profits. No matter how compensation is structured, however, when business is slow, bonuses taper off rapidly. For most bankers, typical salaries may range from $100,000 to $200,000 per year, but bonuses can be significantly greater. Total packages for VPs on Wall Street often hit over the $500,000 level in the first year — and pay can skyrocket from there.

Directors/Managing directors

Directors and managing directors are the major players in corporate finance. Typically, MDs work their own hours, deal with clients at the highest level and disappear whenever a drafting session of a prospectus takes place, leaving this grueling work to others. MDs mostly develop and cultivate relationships with various companies in order to generate corporate finance business for the firm. MDs typically focus on one industry, develop relationships among management teams of companies in the industry and visit these companies on a regular basis. These visits are aptly called sales calls.

Top bankers at the MD level might be pulling in bonuses of up to $1 million or more a year, but slow markets (and hence slow business) can cut that number dramatically. It is important to realize that for the most part, MDs act as relationship managers, and are essentially paid on commission. For top performers, compensation can be almost inconceivable. For example, in 1999, Warburg Dillon Read (now UBS Warburg) hired health care banker Benjamin Lorello away from Salomon Smith Barney with a reported package of $70 million over five years.

Section 2: Sales and Trading

The war zone

If you've ever been to an investment banking trading floor, you've witnessed the chaos. There's usually a lot of swearing, yelling and shouting: a pressure cooker of stress. Sometimes the floor is a quiet rumble of activity, but when the market takes a nosedive, panic ensues and the volume kicks up a notch. Traders must rely on their market instincts, and salespeople yell for bids when the market tumbles. Deciding what to buy or sell, and at what price to buy and sell, isn't easy with millions of dollars at stake.

However, salespeople and traders work much more reasonable hours than research analysts or corporate finance bankers. Rarely does a salesperson or trader venture into the office on a Saturday or Sunday, making the trading floor completely void of life on weekends. Any corporate finance analyst who has crossed a trading floor on a Saturday will tell you that the only noise to be heard on the floor is the clocks ticking and the whir of the air conditioner.

The players

The players in the trading game depend on the firm. There are no hard and fast rules regarding whether or not one needs an MBA. The degree itself, though less applicable directly to the trading position, tends to matter beyond the trader level. Managers (heads of desks) and higher-ups are often selected from the MBA ranks.

Generally, regional I-banks hire clerks and/or trading assistants (non-MBAs) who are sometimes able to advance to a full-fledged trading job within a few years. Other banks, like Merrill Lynch and others on Wall Street, hire analysts and associates just as they do in investment banking. Thus an analyst job on Wall Street in trading includes a two- to three-year stint before the expectation of going back to business school, and the associate position begins after one earns his or her MBA. The ultimate job in trading is to become a full-fledged trader or a manager over a trading desk. Here we break out the early positions into those more common at regional I-banks and those more common on Wall Street.

Entry-level positions

Regional Frameworks — Traditional Programs

Clerks: The bottom rung of the ladder in trading in regional firms, clerks generally balance the books, tracking a desk or a particular trader's buy and sell transactions throughout the day. A starting point for an undergrad aiming to move up to an assistant trader role, clerks gain exposure to the trading floor environment, the traders themselves and the markets. However, clerks take messages, make copies, go get coffee and are hardly respected by traders. And at bigger firms, this position can be a dead-end job: clerks may remain in these roles indefinitely, while new MBAs move into full-time trading positions or top undergrads move into real analyst jobs.

Trading Assistants: Typically filled by recent graduates of undergraduate universities, the trading assistant position is more involved in trades than the clerk position. Trading assistants move beyond staring at the computer and balancing the books to become more involved with the actual traders. Backing up accounts, relaying messages and reports to and from the floor of the NYSE and actually speaking with some accounts occasionally — these responsibilities bring trading assistants much closer to understanding how the whole biz works. Depending on the firm, some undergrads immediately move into a trading assistant position with the hope of moving into a full-time trading job.

Clerks and trading assistants at some firms are hired with the possibility of upward advancement, though promoting non-MBAs to full-time trading jobs is becoming more and more uncommon, even at regional firms.

Wall Street Analyst and Associate Programs

Analysts: Similar to corporate finance analysts, trading analysts at Wall Street firms typically are smart undergraduates with the desire to either become a trader or learn about the trading environment. Quantitative skills are a must for analysts, as much of their time is spent dealing with books of trades and numbers. The ability to crunch numbers in a short time is especially important on the fixed-income side. Traders often demand bond price or yield calculations with only a moment's notice, and analysts must be able to produce. After a two- to three-year stint, analysts move on to business school or go to another firm, although promotion to the associate level is much more common in trading than it is in corporate finance. (Salaries mirror those paid to corporate finance analysts.)

Associates: Trading associates, typically recent business school graduates, begin in either rotational programs or are hired directly to a desk. Rotations can last anywhere from a month to a year, and are designed to both educate new MBAs on various desks and to ensure a good fit prior to placement. As in other areas of investment banks, new MBAs begin at about $80,000 salary with about $25,000 bonus at major Wall Street banks. Second-year associate compensation also tracks closely to that of the second-year corporate finance associate. Associates move to full-fledged trading positions generally in about two to three years, but can move more quickly if they perform well and there are openings (turnover) on the desk.

Full-fledged trading positions

Block trader: These are the folks you see sitting on a desk with dozens of phone lines ringing simultaneously and four or more computer monitors blinking, with orders coming in like machine-gun fire. Typically, traders deal in active, mature markets, such as government securities, stocks, currencies and corporate bonds. Sometimes hailing from top MBA schools, and sometimes tough guys named Vinny from the mailroom, traders historically are hired based on work ethic, attitude and street-smarts.

Sales-trader: Sales-traders essentially operate in a dual role as both salesperson and block trader. While block traders deal with huge trades and often massive inventories of stocks or bonds, sales-traders act somewhat as a go-between for salespeople and block traders and trade somewhat smaller blocks of securities. Different from the pure block trader, the sales-trader actually initiates calls to clients, pitches investment ideas and gives market commentary. The sales-trader keeps abreast of market conditions and research commentaries, but unlike the salesperson, does not need to know the ins and outs of every company when pitching products to clients. Salespeople must be thoroughly versed in the companies they are pitching to clients, whereas sales-traders typically cover the highlights and the big picture. When specific questions arise, a sales-trader will often refer a client to the research analyst.

Visit the Vault Finance Job Board — one of the best job boards on the Internet exclusively for finance professionals. Go to www.vault.com.

VAULT 39

Structured product trader: At some of the biggest Wall Street firms, structured product traders deal with derivatives, a.k.a. structured products. (Derivatives are complex securities that derive their value out of, or have their value contingent on, the values of other assets like stocks, bonds, commodity prices or market index values.) Because of their complexity, derivatives typically require substantial time to price and structure and so foster an entirely different environment than that of a block trader who deals with heavy trading flows and intense on-the-spot pressure. Note, however, that common stock options (calls and puts) and even Treasury options trade much like any other liquid security. The pricing is fairly transparent, the securities standardized and the volume high. Low-volume, complex derivatives such as interest rate swaps, structured repurchase agreements and credit derivatives require pricing and typically more legwork prior to trading.

Note that in trading, job titles can range from associate to VP to managing director. But the roles as a trader change little. The difference is that MDs typically manage the desks, spending their time dealing with desk issues, risk management issues, personnel issues, etc.

Sales: the basics

Sales is a core area of any investment bank, comprising the vast majority of people and the relationships that account for a substantial portion of any investment banks' revenues. This section illustrates the divisions seen in sales today at most investment banks. Note, however, that many firms, such as Goldman Sachs, identify themselves as institutionally focused I-banks and do not even have a retail sales distribution network. Goldman does, however maintain a solid presence in providing brokerage services to the vastly rich in a division called private client services (PCS for short).

Retail brokers: Some firms call them account executives and some call them financial advisors or financial consultants. Regardless of the official designator, they are still referring to your classic retail broker. The broker's job involves managing the account portfolios for individual investors — usually called retail investors. Brokers charge a commission on any stock trade and also give advice to their clients regarding stocks to buy or sell and when to buy or sell them. To get into the business, retail brokers must have an undergraduate degree and demonstrated sales skills. The Series 7 and Series 63 examinations are also required before selling commences. Having connections to people with money offers a tremendous advantage for a starting broker.

The players in sales

For many, institutional sales offers the best of all worlds: great pay, fewer hours than in corporate finance or research, less stress than in trading and a nice blend of travel and office work. Like traders, the hours typically follow the market, with a few tacked on at the end of the day after the market closes. Another plus for talented salespeople is that they develop relationships with key money managers. On the downside, many institutional salespeople complain that many buy siders disregard their calls, that compensation can vary according to performance and that constantly entertaining clients can prove exhausting.

Sales assistant: This position is most often a dead-end job. It is extremely difficult to move into institutional sales without an MBA, so sales assistants take on a primarily clerical role on the desk. Handling the phones, administrative duties, message taking, letter writing — there's nothing glamorous about being an assistant.

Associates: The newly hired MBA is called an associate or sales associate. Like analogous associates in other investment banking departments, a sales associate spends a year or so in the role learning the ropes and establishing himself. Associates typically spend one to two months rotating through various desks, ensuring a solid fit between the desk and the new associate. Once the rotations end, the associate is placed on a desk and the business of building client relationships begins.

Most sales associates out of business school pull in the standard package on Wall Street: $80,000 base, plus bonuses of $25,000 in the first six months. Pay escalation in the first year depends on the bonus, which often ranges from 50 percent of salary to 90 percent of salary. Beyond that, compensation packages depend on the firm — most firms pay based on commissions generated for the firm.

Salesperson: The associate moves into a full-fledged salesperson role extremely quickly. Within a few months on a desk, the associate begins to handle "B" accounts and gradually manages them exclusively. A salesperson's ultimate goal is the account at a huge money manager, such as Fidelity or Putnam, that trades in huge volumes on a daily basis. Therefore, a salesperson slowly moves up the account chain, yielding B accounts to younger salespeople and taking on bigger and better "A" accounts. Good salespeople make anywhere from $250,000 to beyond $1 million per year in total compensation.

Visit the Vault Finance Job Board — one of the best job boards on the Internet exclusively for finance professionals. Go to www.vault.com.

VAULT   41

Salespeople usually focus by region. For example, an institutional equity salesperson will cover all of the buy-side firms in one small region of the country like New England, San Francisco or Chicago. Many salespeople cover New York, as the sheer number of money managers in the city makes for a tremendous volume of work. Salespeople work on specific desks on the trading floor next to traders. Because so much of their work overlaps, sales and trading truly go hand-in-hand.

Private client cervices

The private client services (PCS) job can be exhilarating, exhausting and frustrating — all at once. As a PCS representative, your job is to bring in individual accounts with at least $2 to $3 million in assets. This involves incessantly pounding the pavement and reading the tape (market news) to find clients, followed by advising them on how to manage their wealth. PCS is a highly entrepreneurial environment. Building the book is all that matters, and managers don't care how a PCS representative spends his or her time, whether this be on the road, in the office or at parties — the goal is to bring in the cash. Culture-wise, therefore, one typically finds a spirited entrepreneurial group of people, working their own hours and talking on the phone for the better part of the day. It is not uncommon for PCS pros to leave the office early on Fridays with a golf bag slung over one shoulder for a game with existing clients or with a few bigshots with money to invest (read: potential clients).

The growth in PCS

Just a few years ago, PCS was considered a small, unimportant aspect of investment banking. PCS guys were essentially brokers, always bothering other departments for leads and not as sophisticated as their counterparts in corporate finance or institutional sales and trading. Times have changed, however. Today, spurred by the tremendous stock market wealth that has been created over the past few years, PCS is a rapidly growing part of virtually every investment bank. While in the past, many banks essentially had no PCS division, or simply hired a few star retail brokers to be PCS representatives, Wall Street is recruiting heavily on MBA campuses today, scouring to find good talent for PCS.

Section 3: Research

If you have a brokerage account, you have likely been given research on stocks that you asked about. The intermediaries between companies and the buy side, corporate finance and sales and trading, research analysts form the hub of investment banks.

To the outsider, it seems that research analysts spend their time in a quiet room poring over numbers, calling companies and writing research reports. The truth is an entirely different story, involving quite a bit of selling on the phone and on the road. Analysts produce research ideas, hand them to associates and assistants and then man the phone talking to buy-side stock/bond pickers, company managers and internal salespeople. They become the managers of research reports and the experts on their industries to the outside world. Thus, while the lifestyle of the research analyst would initially appear to resemble that of a statistician, it often comes closer to that of a diplomat or salesperson.

The players

Research assistants: The bottom-level number crunchers in research, research assistants generally begin with no industry or market expertise. They come from solid undergraduate schools and performed well in school, but initially perform mundane research tasks, such as digging up information and editing/formatting reports. Research assistants also take over the spreadsheet modeling functions required by the analyst. Travel is limited for the budding research assistant, as it usually does not make sense financially to send more than the research analyst to meetings with company officials or money managers.

Research associates: Burdened with numbers and deadlines, the research associate often feels like a cross between a statistician and a corporate finance analyst. Long hours, weekends in the office and number-crunching sum up the routine of the associate. However, compared to analyst and associate analogues in corporate finance, the research associate works fewer hours, often makes it home at a reasonable time and works less on the weekend. Unfortunately, the associate is required to be present and accounted for at 7:30 a.m., when most morning meetings take place.

Mirroring the corporate finance analyst and associate positions, research associates can be bright, motivated kids directly out of top undergraduate universities; at firms dedicated to hiring MBAs in research, the research associate role is the entry-level position once the MBA has been earned.

A talented research associate can earn much in the way of responsibility. For example, the research associate may field phone calls from smaller "B" accounts (i.e., smaller money managers) and companies less important to the analyst. (The analyst handles the relationships with the biggest buy siders, best clients and top salespeople.) When it comes to writing reports, some analysts give free reign to associates. Also, research associates focus on one industry and typically work for only one full-fledged research analyst. This structure helps research associates delve deeper into the aspects of one industry group and enables them to work closely with a senior-level research analyst.

To start, research assistants/associates out of undergrad typically get paid similarly to the corporate finance analyst right out of college. After one or two years, the compensation varies dramatically, depending on performance and the success of the analysts in the industry group, as well as the associate's contribution. For the first-year MBA research associate, the compensation is similar to I-banking associates: $80,000 salaries with $30,000 signing bonuses, plus a $30,000 year-end bonus, are typical.

Section 4: Syndicate

What does the syndicate department at an investment bank do? Syndicate usually sits on the trading floor, but syndicate employees don't trade securities or sell them to clients. Neither do they bring in clients for corporate finance. What syndicate does is provide a vital role in placing stock or bond offerings with buy siders, and truly aim to find the right offering price that satisfies both the company, the salespeople, the investors and the corporate finance bankers working the deal.

Syndicate and public offerings

In any public offering, syndicate gets involved once the prospectus is filed with the SEC. At that point, syndicate associates begin to contact other investment banks interested in being underwriters in the deal. Before we continue with our discussion of the syndicate's role, we should first understand the difference between managers and underwriters and how fees earned through security offerings are allocated.

Managers

The managers of an IPO get involved from the beginning. These are the I-banks attending all the meetings and generally slaving away to complete the deal. Managers get paid a substantial portion of the total fee — called underwriting discounts and commissions on the cover of a prospectus, and known as the spread in the industry. In an IPO, the spread is usually 7 percent, unless the deal is huge, which often means that the offering company can negotiate a slightly lower rate. For a follow-on offering, typical fees start at 5 percent and again decrease as the deal-size increases.

Deals typically have between two and five managers. To further complicate matters, these managers are also often called managing underwriters, as all managers are underwriters, but not all underwriters are managers. Confused? Keep reading.

Underwriters

The underwriters on the deal are so called because they are the ones assuming liability, though they usually have no shares of stock to sell in the deal. They are not necessarily the I-banks that work intimately on the deal; most

Visit the Vault Finance Job Board — one of the best job boards on the Internet exclusively for finance professionals. Go to www.vault.com.

VAULT   45

underwriters do nothing other than accept any potential liability for lawsuits against the underwriting group.

Underwriters are selected by the lead manager in conjunction with the company. This role is often called participating in the syndicate. In a prospectus, you can always find a section entitled "Underwriting" that lists the underwriting group. Anywhere from 10 to 30 investment banks typically make up the underwriting group in any securities offering.

In the underwriting section, listed next to each participant is a number of shares. While underwriting sections list quite a few investment banks and shares next to each bank, it is important to realize that these banks do not sell shares. Neither do they have anything to do with how the shares in the deal are allocated to investors. They merely assume the percentage of liability indicated by the percentage of deal shares listed in the prospectus. To take on such liability, underwriters are paid a small fee, depending on their level of underwriting involvement (i.e., the number of shares next to their name). The managers in the deal will account for the liability of approximately 50 to 70 percent of the shares, while the underwriters account for the rest.

Maintaining the book

So what's syndicate's role in all of this? In short, they act as the go between for their own bank and outside entities. Syndicate professionals put together the underwriting group for deals their bank manage, make sure their bank is included in the underwriting process of deals it is not managing, allocate stock to buy-side firms indicating interest in a deal and determine the price for an offering.

The bank lead managing a deal is responsible for maintaining the book, which is a listing of all investors who have indicated an interest in the deal. Potential investors place orders either for a specified number of shares at any price or for a specified number of shares up to a specific price. The orders start to come together during the roadshow, but a significant number of orders don't come in until a day or two before the pricing of a deal. Thus, a manager often doesn't know until the last minute if they can sell a deal.

Syndicate also attempts to gauge a potential investor's true interest in a deal. The day before an offering is priced, syndicate at a lead manager makes last-minute calls to potential buyers to feel out their interest in the deal. It's important to the manager that investors are interested in holding the stocks/bonds for the long term. Those money managers that don't have long term interest are called flippers; they hope to sell the security shortly after opening for a quick profit. Institutional money managers who buy into a deal just to sell their shares on the first day only cause the stock to immediately trade down.

Pricing and allocation

How does syndicate price a stock? Simple — by supply and demand. There are a fixed number of shares or bonds in a public deal available, and buyers indicate exactly how many shares and at what price they are willing to purchase the securities. The problem is that virtually every deal is oversubscribed, i.e., there are more shares demanded than available for sale. Therefore, syndicate must determine how many shares to allocate to each buyer. To add to the headache, because investors know that every successful deal is oversubscribed, they inflate their actual share indications. So, a 10 percent order may in fact mean that the money manager actually wants something like 2 or 3 percent of the deal. The irony, then, is that any money manager who actually got as many shares as she asked for would immediately cancel her order, realizing that the deal was a "dog."

In the end, the combination of syndicate's experience with investors and instincts about buyers tells them how many shares to give to each buy sider. Syndicate tries to avoid flippers, but can never entirely do so.

After the book is set, syndicate calls the offering company to report the details. This pricing call, as it is known, occurs immediately after the roadshow ends and the day before the stock begins trading in the market. Pricing calls sometimes results in yelling, cursing and swearing from the management teams of companies going public. Remember that in IPOs, the call is telling founders of companies what their firm is worth — reactions sometimes border on the extreme. If a deal is not hot (and many are not), then the given price may be disappointing to the company. "How can my company not be the greatest thing since sliced bread?" CEOs often think.

Because of this tension over the offering price, senior syndicate professionals must be able to handle difficult and delicate situations. But it's not just company management that must be handled with care. During a deal, syndicate must also deal with the salesforce, other underwriters and buy-siders. Similar to the research analyst, the syndicate professional often finds

Visit the Vault Finance Job Board — one of the best job boards on the Internet exclusively for finance professionals. Go to www.vault.com.

VAULT   47

that diplomacy is one of the most critical elements to success. Successful syndicate pros can read between the lines and figure out the real intentions of buy siders (are they flippers or are they committed to the offering, do they really want 10 percent of the offering, etc.). Also, good syndicate associates are proficient at schmoozing with other investment banks and garnering underwriting business (when the syndicate department is not representing the manager).

Who works in syndicate?

As for the players in syndicate, some have MBAs and some don't. Some worked their way up, and some were hired directly into an associate syndicate position. The payoffs in syndicate can be excellent for top dogs, however, as the most advanced syndicate pros often deal directly with clients (management teams doing an offering), handle pricing calls and talk to the biggest investors. They essentially become salespeople themselves, touting the firm, their expertise in placing stock or bonds and their track record. Occasionally, syndicate MDs will attend an important deal pitch to potential clients, especially if he or she is a good talker. At the same time, some syndicate professionals move into sales or other areas, often in order to get away from the endless politicking involved with working in the syndicate department.

Beginners in the syndicate department help put together the book, schedule roadshow meetings and work their way up to dealing with investors, other I-banks and internal sales. Because syndicate requires far fewer people than other areas in the bank, fewer job openings are to be found. Rarely does a firm recruit on college campuses for syndicate jobs — instead, firms generally hire from within the industry or from within the firm.

Investment Management

Section 1: Overview

Investment management aspirants must have keen analytical and math skills — and a passion for the news. Specifically, you'd better love to read *The Wall Street Journal* and business publications like *Barron's* and *Forbes*. The field has typically been a hard one to break into. Once you're in, however, opportunities for advancement and financial gain abound. Some firms will rarely consider someone for the career track from outside the top MBA programs, while at other firms, insiders say having an MBA "is not a huge advantage." One potential job-getting credential: Investment management professionals are increasingly sitting for the "intensive" three-part exam called the Chartered Financial Analyst (CFA) Program, a globally recognized standard for measuring the competence and integrity of financial analysts.

The field is still male dominated. For example, 77 percent of the more than 53,000 candidates who sat for CFA exams in 2000 were male. Why the imbalance? "I don't think it's so much that we chose men, men chose this field," says one female vice president at a large New York firm.

Sane salaries, saner hours

"This is not an industry that jumps up and wows people fresh out of school with some outrageous salary," says Michael Weinstock, who specializes in recruiting for investment management firms. "They're very conservative. They tend to start people at an okay salary — nothing to really go out and buy beers for the world."

Salaries range between $35,000 to $40,000 for someone right out of a bachelor's degree program. Some top firms pay $50,000 base and a small bonus, others report. Someone out of an MBA program can expect to make a base salary in the "high five figures," insiders say. However, if a firm values you, your salary could double or triple in a few years time.

Although entry-level employees start at lower salaries than their counterparts in investment banking, insiders say it's a worthwhile trade-off. Typically, they don't work as many long and tortured hours as their I-banking brethren.

Visit the Vault Finance Job Board — one of the best job boards on the Internet exclusively for finance professionals. Go to www.vault.com.

VAULT   49

For experienced investment managers, the financial picture becomes rosier. Senior asset managers are generally paid based upon the amount of money they manage. The average salary for professionals with 10 or more years of experience is $200,000, according to the Association for Investment Management and Research, a non-profit association based in Charlottesville, Va., composed of 45,000 financial analysts, portfolio managers and other investment professionals worldwide. The AIMR based its findings on 1999 compensation data from more than 8,500 members in the United States and Canada.

Top performers, including the highest-level portfolio managers, analysts and marketers, pull in salaries between $1 million and $3 million. The rewards can also be exceptional for high-risk managers of hedge funds, which are private pools of capital usually limited to wealthy investors.

In this chapter we will provide an overview of the roles and lifestyles of the positions in investment management and paths to upper management positions.

How to break in

As the bull market fueled the popularity of mutual funds over the last few years, freshly minted MBAs were able to score high-paying investment analyst and portfolio management positions. This is a relatively new trend, as investment management is an industry that values experience (read: the more gray hair, the better). Another reason new blood is welcomed: More investment banks have been growing their asset management businesses, and need new employees.

Asset management is largely protected against the volatility of the market, unlike investment banking. Many lines of business for investment banks are very sensitive to the economy in general. For example, underwriting of IPOs and other equity issues declines in times of recession. In asset management, firms make money based on a percentage of the entire amount they handle, whether they make or lose money for the client.

Despite the current increase in available investment management positions, it's still relatively hard to break into the business. Traditionally, someone fresh out of college would work for a few years as a financial analyst in big-money corporations, such as a General Electric, to gain experience, says Donald Tuttle, vice president of special projects at the AIMR and a former college business professor. "You learn to evaluate your own corporation, how a corporation should be financed, how to try to keep costs down," Tuttle says. "Then, after acquiring three or four years of experience in a job like that, you go back to school at a top-line MBA program. You will have a lot of opportunities either on the buy side or sell side."

Investment Management and the CFA

If you're interested in asset management, taking the CFA may be a wise career move. Although it's all take-at-home studying, many insiders say it covers "every intricate aspect" of money managing. Nearly 36,000 professionals are CFAs. Approximately 60,000 people sit for one part of the six-hour, graduate-level exam worldwide every June. The exams get progressively harder from level one to level three — and only about 50 percent of people pass level 1 each year.

"It's typically the benchmark most money management firms use to separate the men from the boys and the ladies from the girls," says one investment manager. "You're telling your firm that you're destined to do bigger, better things. And you're, in a very nice and nonchalant way, telling the firm 'I'm hoping that you're going to come across for me, upgrade me and promote me, or otherwise I'm going to take my CFA designation and shop it to a competitor.'"

The exams, which are taken at least over three years, test ethical and professional standards, securities analysis and investment valuation, financial accounting, quantitative analysis, economics, asset allocation and portfolio management, among other subjects. The exams use problems, cases, essays, multiple-choice and "item-set" questions. It costs $250 to register to enter the CFA and $250 or $300 to take exams, depending on the level.

Besides working in the field for at least three years and passing all three exams, professionals must commit to abide by the AIMR code of ethics and standards of professional conduct to gain their title.

Visit the Vault Finance Job Board — one of the best job boards on the Internet exclusively for finance professionals. Go to www.vault.com.

VAULT   51

Section 2: Career path

New hires with bachelor's degrees come into the business as analysts, though they can also start as assistant portfolio managers or trading assistants. MBAs start on the associate level. One can continue in the same position, as an analyst or other number-crunching roles, while advancing to higher levels and bigger salaries within the company. Others become traders or portfolio managers, a position considered plum because of the "sane" hours and great compensation.

As you advance in the field, titles to aspire to include vice president, senior vice president, executive vice president or managing director — though the meaning of these titles vary by firm. "Being a vice president simply means you're a senior person," explains a portfolio manager who is a vice president at the Bank of New York.

Still, be warned: "It's becoming progressively harder to become a portfolio manager" because "there are only so many portfolios to manage [and] the money can be phenomenal," says one insider. Luckily, "some shops have wised up and made it so that good research analysts can make as much as, if not more than, good portfolio managers." As one source explains, "It is, after all, the good research analysts who generate the ideas that give portfolio managers their out-performance."

The pinnacle of the asset management career path is to become the chief investment officer of a firm.

Undergraduate degrees

At some high-end firms, the typical path is to spend two years in entry-level jobs before moving on to get the MBA. Still, many companies are looking for recent college graduates who haven't yet developed "bad habits," and whom they think are good candidates to be molded in the firm's image.

At one firm, new analysts "go through a sort of management training program where, at the beginning of the day and the end of the day, they're working at the reception desk or the mailroom," says one insider. "But during the six hours of the day between 10 a.m. to 4 p.m., they rotate a week or two weeks at a time in trading or portfolio management to the marketing area to sales and research. The president of the firm started this way."

MBA or not?

Many firms recruit out of MBA programs, but not to the degree that I-banking firms do, says one portfolio manager.

His firm, he says, brings in a class of four or five MBA graduates each year. Under something of a training program, they are brought in first as researchers. After about a year, they start easing into work as portfolio managers. Generally, they are given fewer clients and fewer assets to manage while they learn the business, he says.

Other programs do not seek out MBAs, seeking to groom "smart people just out of college." "When we bring people in we give them a one month-long training program," he says. "Besides, your job is your training." There are no real set milestones — "If we are happy with people, we encourage them to stay and grow with the firm. There's no set time period or career path."

Portfolio management, portfolio administration and analytics

Many asset managers choose a career in portfolio management, focused on managing the portfolios of wealthy clients. As a member of the client services team, you will help put together information and presentations to help clients understand how their money is growing. "You have to know a little bit about everything," says a vice president who started out in marketing. A more senior person in client services can become an account manager, responsible for keeping clients content and informed or drumming up new business.

Portfolio administration positions are the accounting or "back office" part of the team. These analysts aren't involved with transactions at all. They calculate the portfolio's performance on a regular basis and make sure the holdings on record match the bank statements.

On the portfolio analytics team, you will start as a generalist in a supporting role. It's a "nitty gritty" job in which your number-crunching revolves around making sure the portfolios are set up properly and that data from external sources come together. You will be helping to compile daily risk reports and learn about the different sectors, such as technology, biomedical, large cap, etc. These jobs often require the longest hours, often 14-hour days. Second-

Visit the Vault Finance Job Board — one of the best job boards on the
Internet exclusively for finance professionals. Go to www.vault.com.

VAULT   53

and third-year analysts who are working directly with the portfolio managers on analyzing risk in specific sectors will mentor you.

After the first year, analysts typically develop a specialty or jump to equity research. Equity researchers dig for the inside scoop about companies that portfolio managers may be thinking of buying. They may do this by scrutinizing a company's annual reports, press releases, meeting with the company's CFO and seeing what the sell-side analysts say about the company.

Some professionals will stay in portfolio analytics, continuing to work on the portfolio support side while moving up the corporate ranks. Some have become managing directors by staying put. "There is definitely not a requirement to move out of that position," says one portfolio manager.

The entry-level path can also lead to a position on the trading floor. Once the portfolio management team has determined what to buy, the trader comes into play by negotiating the best deals possible. It's not necessarily a job that requires strong analytical skills, but traders do need to understand the market. It's more a "high-energy, relationship-oriented job," says one manager.

The Portfolio Manager Path

There really isn't a clear-cut track to becoming a portfolio manager, insiders say. In most cases, it's more like an apprentice situation. After some years in research, administration or some sort of portfolio support job, one is given a portion of a fund to manage. The amount of assets you manage grows as you gain experience.

The Bank of New York portfolio manager, for example, was a liberal arts major in college who took no business courses outside of economics. He started working on the client side at a firm in 1991, mostly because jobs were scarce in Boston at that time. "I didn't like the job itself, but I liked the industry," he admits. His next job was as a portfolio assistant at a major commercial bank in New York. His role was to review trust accounts to make sure investments complied with the strict rules of the Prudent Investor Act, which governs how trusts are to be managed. He gradually started managing small books of business using the firm's guidelines and advice from more experienced managers to learn the trade. At the same time, he started studying for the three-part CFA exam.

Today, he is managing a book of business (industry jargon for a stable of clients) worth about $600 million for about 80 high-wealth clients. In his job, he knows his clients personally. He likes this kind of money managing better than his previous experiences with mutual fund investment, which were more about "meeting numbers." "This tends to be very relationship oriented," he says. "If you had to compare what we do to another profession, it's the family doctor. We develop the same kind of rapport and relationship."

Knowing clients personally in some ways makes the job more stressful, he says. "You really are the one on the line, the one deciding 'I want to buy this stock and not that stock.'" Strong ethics and a sense of responsibility are necessary, he says, because the ramifications are great. "This is people's retirement money. That's a tremendous responsibility."

Another advantage, he says, are the hours. He says he works an average of 65 or 70 hours a week, but some slow weeks end after 45 hours. "Decembers tend to be bad because you are figuring out taxes," he says. Then again, "there have been times when I've gone home at 4 p.m., which is something I distinctly value." He usually arrives at the work early and can leave when the markets close, but some portfolio managers come in just before the 8:30 a.m. meeting and leave around 7 p.m.

There's flexibility, he says, because he gets to set up client meetings around his life. Client relationships take up about 35 to 40 percent of the time. He crosses the country to visit clients about 10 percent of the time, and sometimes they meet him in Manhattan. Otherwise, he's doing investment research, which sometimes entails attending conferences held by sell-side research firms where he might learn, for example, how "a company plans to use the proceeds of a second public offering to acquire another firm."

Sometimes, he says, clients are surprised when they meet him because they realize how young he is. Age discrimination goes both ways, he says. Some people seek him out because they think a younger manager is going to have a better understanding of technology. Others don't want someone without 30 years of experience touching their money. "I get comments all the time like, 'Hmmm, how long have you been doing this?'" he says. "They're trying to benchmark me in some way without necessarily asking about my age. I find I can address it by simply doing my job well."

Visit the Vault Finance Job Board — one of the best job boards on the
Internet exclusively for finance professionals. Go to www.vault.com.

V/\ULT   55

Commercial Banking

Commercial bankers make their living lending money to companies — some prosperous, some flailing and sliding down a bloody path to bankruptcy and loan default. That's why the largest commercial banks have erected towering, multi-tiered bureaucracies in which someone rates the credit-worthiness of prospective borrowers, someone else sells loans to customers and then monitors the continued financial health of these borrowers and yet someone else makes sure everybody follows bank regulations and banking laws.

Fortunately for these banks, young commercial bankers recruited into this bottom tier learn skills that can ramp them up to a job at much higher levels. As commercial bankers rise through the strata, they come to supervise those who take over positions they left behind.

Section 1: Credit Analyst

Credit analysts examine the credit-worthiness of potential borrowers by studying business models, industry characteristics and sources of cash flow drivers. They also study a firm's profitability, capital structure, leverage, liquidity and management of existing capital. Finally, they consider the financial risk of a loan. Once they've done that, credit analysts will write credit reports that the bank uses in its internal credit approval process and will continue as contacts between their departments, their clients, other banks and other departments within the bank.

"You're at a disadvantage when you're an analyst because you very rarely get to meet the client, and it makes it much more difficult to do your job because you have to go by the numbers and the numbers don't always tell the whole story," says one commercial banker who started her career as a credit analyst with Bank of America.

But at the same time, credit analysts say that they're receiving the training they need to progress in commercial banking or other aspects of finance. Young credit analysts typically must undergo bank-sponsored training programs that last anywhere from a year to 18 months. Part of the time, beginning commercial bankers spend time in the classroom, reading case studies and learning about commercial credit, accounting and corporate finance. Trainees may also be required to perform basic research on

Visit the Vault Finance Job Board — one of the best job boards on the Internet exclusively for finance professionals. Go to www.vault.com.

VAULT 57

prospective borrowers. After the training, these bankers may rotate through different areas of the bank, such as a branch office or private banking operation. Their training ends when they are chosen to fill a full-time opening.

"With the experience and skills I've gained as a credit analyst, I believe that I have many options," says one young analyst. "Credit training allows you to understand businesses and companies, rather than just financial products. In the long term I may enter one of the following fields: corporate finance (company side), venture capital, investment banking, money management or equity research."

Credit analysts say, "The money's pretty decent when compared to other people" in their age group (credit analysts are typically in their early 20s), though they complain the "lifestyle sucks."

Day in the Life of a Credit Analyst

8:30 a.m. — 9:00 a.m.: Arrive at work and check mail and messages. (There's constant phone contact with clients and co-workers from 9:00 a.m. until 5:00 p.m., says one analyst.)

9:00 a.m. — 9:30 a.m.: Speak to vice presidents about new loan deal. (One analyst calls this one of the "fun parts" of the job. "It's great exposure, and you get a great sense of business — as opposed to just finance.")

9:30 a.m. — 10:00 a.m.: Gather information on new deal — financial statements and SEC filings and news releases.

10:00 a.m. — 1:00 p.m.: Perform "brain work" on gathered information. This includes: 1) understanding the company's business model, industry characteristics and main cash flow drivers; 2) analyzing the company's profitability, capital structure, leverage, liquidity and working capital management and 3) assess operating risk, financial risk and other credit risks.

1:00 p.m. — 2:00 p.m.: Lunch or gym…preferably gym.

2:00 p.m. — 5:00 p.m.: Work on financial projections.

5:00 p.m. — 7:00 p.m.: Work on credit memo report.

7:00 p.m. — 8:00 p.m.: Dinner at the cafeteria while complaining to co-workers about all the work that was just dumped on me.

8:00 p.m. — 10:45 p.m.: Resume working on credit memo report.

10:45 p.m. — 11:00 p.m.: Check basketball or baseball scores and take a car home.

Section 2: Loan officer

Loan officers are the workhorses of the commercial banking industry. They structure loans, watch over them for the continued health of the borrower, bring in new customers and new depositors. Working with the credit reports prepared by analysts or based on their own research, loan officers draft the terms of a loan, balancing the need to keep borrowers happy against the bank's need to remain profitable and solvent.

To rustle up new business, commercial loan officers might call up businesses and ask them about their business goals and capital needs. Tax attorneys, accountants and other professional service providers can refer new business, as can existing borrowers. Similarly, mortgage loan officers build relationships with commercial developers and real estate agencies, who might then turn to the loan officer for financing.

Alyssa Lange is vice president and senior relationship manager at City National Bank, a $9 billion (in terms of assets) regional bank headquartered in Beverly Hills, Calif. Lange manages a $90 million portfolio spread out over 12 commercial borrowers, which include a fuel broker, a consumer goods importer and a barbecue manufacturer. To encourage new business, Lange is also responsible for meeting the consumer credit needs that the executives of these 12 borrowers might come up with, whether that's mortgages, personal credit cards or auto loans. To accomplish that goal, Lange works with her colleagues in the private banking and investment departments of her bank.

"I do what it takes to make everybody happy on the business side, as well as for the executives, to make their lives less burdensome," Lange said. "I just let them know what they've got, and if there's ever a time when they need anything, they know they can call me."

Lange structures her own loans, but she typically secures the sign-off from the senior loan officer for the region and one other bank official. The bank's senior loan committee may also review larger loans, those more than $7.5 million. Her biggest deals usually require the sign-off of the chief credit officer of the bank.

"During the process, if you're proposing on a new borrower, you always have credit administrators, if it's in their authority, look over the deal as it's proceeding, so no one's caught off guard," Lange said.

Visit the Vault Finance Job Board — one of the best job boards on the Internet exclusively for finance professionals. Go to www.vault.com.

VAULT 59

Lange spent three years with Bank of America as a credit analyst, but says she's much happier now that she gets to meet the executives to whom she loans money. Those meetings make credit evaluations much easier, Lange said.

"You just become much more familiar with the operation when you've gone out and met them and talked to them," Lange said. "You're much more apt and able if you're talking about their business to ask questions. Something might come up and you'll say, 'I had no idea this was part of your business strategy.'"

Loan officers are also responsible for building up their portfolio with new clients.

"Sometimes I see things in the newspaper, a developer's name or an organization, and think they might be worthwhile calling on," said one assistant vice president at a small regional bank in New Jersey. "We do something here called blitzes. We go out and canvas areas where we have our branches. I may meet prospective clients that way."

Section 3: Loan review officer/loan work-out officer

Loan review and loan workout officers ensure that terms set by loan officers meet both the banks' policies and banking regulations and work with troubled creditors to resolve outstanding loan payments.

Loan review officers scrutinize loans structured by more junior loan officers for the proper authorization, repayment schedules and procedures. For example, a bank might require loans to real estate developers to contain terms on how much rent the developers must charge. Loan review officers must make sure this policy is followed and included in the terms of a specific loan.

Ronald Yancis, now a vice president for quality control at Central Progressive Bank in Hammond, La., a regional bank located about 40 miles east of Baton Rouge, has spent the past 30 years as a loan review officer and loan workout officer, working with everyone from oilmen to shopkeepers.

After graduating from the University of Mississippi, Yancis earned an MBA in 1969. He began teaching finance at a junior college in northern Mississippi, working in the summers with the Comptroller of the Currency in Memphis. That turned into a full-time job as "an unofficial bank examiner," until 1980, when he joined the First National Bank of Jefferson Parish in Louisiana.

Part of Yancis' job today involves loan administration and compliance. "I make sure loans were done by the proper officers, that those people had the authority to prepare those loans," Yancis said. "Now with banking, there's a lot more turnover than you used to see. They're beginning to compress managerial experience. These guys have finance experience, but it's all from college. They'll bring in these deals and try and put them together and not put them together right."

Yancis emphasized that loan officers and loan review officers must maintain a close watch on their borrowers over the life of the loan.

"After 5 years, we'll look over the financial statement," Yancis said. "If it's a fixed-rate loan, then we might raise rates. If a borrower is struggling, we'll raise the rate. It never goes away. If you get a financial statement this year, you'll want a financial statement next year, to make sure the company is doing well."

For companies that can't make their payments or might even default on a loan, Yancis' experience as a work-out officer comes to the fore. Working

Visit the Vault Finance Job Board — one of the best job boards on the Internet exclusively for finance professionals. Go to www.vault.com.

VAULT 61

with a struggling company, Yancis will try to "work out" a way for the borrower to make his payments. In the early 1980s, when the oil business began drying up in Texas, Yancis was placed in charge of an effort to recoup a multi-million dollar loan from a wildcat oil driller whose wells had run dry. With an additional $250,000 from the bank, Yancis assembled a syndicate of oil speculators and begged a Dallas oilman to move his rig to some undrilled wells the borrower still owned.

"Here's what I'll do," Yancis told the Dallas oilman, "I ain't got the money to pay you, but I've asked a handful of investors come together. If you put your rig in and hit oil, you'll be one of the first investors to get paid. He said okay. It cost $600,000 just to move the rig, but he did it on a handshake. We hit, and we did that eight more times. With what was coming out, in the long run, the bank wound up getting its money."

Day in the life of an assistant vice president in commercial lending

9 a.m.: I arrive at work and start typing a commitment letter between the bank and a new borrower that outlines the terms of the loan. This is a new loan for an existing client, a heating and air conditioning contractor, who is expanding his business. This takes most of the morning, since the letter must conform exactly to the proposal I worked up earlier.

Noon: I begin working on a term sheet, or letter of intent, between the bank and a potential client. The term sheet outlines terms for lending money. I'm reviewing some things and I'm looking to see if this is something that meets our lending criteria.

1 p.m.: Lunch at the bank's lunchroom, where I catch up on the news. I read the local paper and try to glance through *The Wall Street Journal*. I get a copy from my boss.

2 p.m.: Finish letter of intent.

3 p.m.: Prepare a memo on loan closing and review a second loan package.

6 p.m.: Drive home. Sometimes, I'll take work home, review loan packages at night or write proposals. If I'm out of the office during the day, I can't do this stuff during normal hours, and I don't want to be in the office at all hours during the night, so I'll just bring it home.

THE VAULT
TOP 25 FIRMS

Goldman Sachs

85 Broad Street
New York, NY 10004
Phone: (212) 902-1000
Fax: (212) 902-3000
www.gs.com

DEPARTMENTS

Equities
Fixed Income, Currency and
   Commodities
Global Investment Research
Investment Banking
Investment Management
Merchant Banking
Operations, Finance and Resources
Technology

THE STATS

Chairman and CEO: Henry Paulson
Employer Type: Public Company
Ticker Symbol: GS (NYSE)
2000 Revenues: $33 billion
2000 Net Income: $3.1 billion
No. of Employees: 20,350
No. of Offices: 42

KEY COMPETITORS

Credit Suisse First Boston
J.P. Morgan Chase
Merrill Lynch
Morgan Stanley
Salomon Smith Barney

UPPERS

- Excellent support staff
- Talented co-workers
- Top-quality name brand

DOWNERS

- Grueling hours
- More bureaucracy since IPO
- Overbearing culture

EMPLOYMENT CONTACT

Investment Banking
Undergraduates:
Robyn Lavender
Goldman, Sachs & Co.
85 Broad Street
18th Floor
New York, NY 10004

Advanced Degrees
Sunshine Singer
Goldman, Sachs & Co.
85 Broad Street
18th Floor
New York, NY 10004

Investment Management
Sarah McNamara
Goldman, Sachs & Co.
32 Old Slip
19th Floor
New York, NY 10005

For more contacts, see
www.gs.com/recruiting

THE SCOOP

Putting the "cult" in culture

Founded in 1869 by Marcus Goldman, a European immigrant, Goldman Sachs is one of the nation's oldest and most prestigious investment banking firms. Goldman has not only distinguished itself from its competitors with its conservative attitude, but has also created a reputation among both employees and outsiders that the firm is the pinnacle of investment banking success. By insisting that the firm come first and individual egos a distant second, Goldman Sachs has achieved unparalleled success among American I-banks in prompting high-flying corporate whiz kids to bow to the overall interests of the firm. Goldman is also legendary for its secrecy. The firm rarely lets the media see what's going on behind the scenes. Even former employees tend not to speak to the press — perhaps as a result of the legal clauses that Goldman reportedly inserts in every employee's contract, requiring that he or she never speak out in public about even the smallest detail of office life.

The IPO trail (and trials)

Contributing to Goldman's mystique for years was its status as a major Wall Street private partnership. In 1998, however, the firm's partners voted to change this status and offer stock to the public. Analysts believe that two major factors drove the decision. One issue was that without stock "currency" Goldman could not acquire other banking businesses and would eventually not be able to keep pace with competitors like Merrill Lynch and Morgan Stanley Dean Witter. Additionally, observers felt that Goldman's partners sensed that the market was at its peak and wanted to cash in their chips.

However, with world financial markets in turmoil in the late summer and fall of 1998, Goldman execs shelved the IPO. The firm's longtime head, Jon Corzine, resigned from his post as co-CEO in January 1999. The firm had absorbed an estimated $500 million to $1 billion in trading losses because of the troubled markets. Some industry observers believe Corzine, who had advocated a public offering, was pushed out of the firm's top spot by other senior execs, including Henry Paulson, John Thornton and John Thain. Paulson had shared the CEO position with Corzine and now is the firm's sole CEO. Thorton and Thain share the roles of president and COO. Firm spokespeople asserted that relieving Corzine of CEO duties would give him the time to concentrate on IPO-related matters.

Visit the Vault Finance Job Board — one of the best job boards on the Internet exclusively for finance professionals. Go to www.vault.com.

VAULT   65

Skeletons in the IPO closet?

In filings for its planned IPO, Goldman revealed details of its finances that had until that time been kept secret. While Goldman's M&A and underwriting businesses were always recognized as impressive, the firm was more dependent on its trading operations (both for clients, when it takes a commission, and on its own account) — far more so than its closest competitors. For example, in 1999, the firm earned 43 percent of its revenue from trading. In comparison, Morgan Stanley earned just 20 percent of its revenue from trading. In every year from 1995 to 1999, Goldman's trading revenues outpaced investment banking revenues. Trading, especially proprietary trading (when a firm trades its own capital rather than that of clients), is a volatile business, heavily dependent on market conditions. Analysts have warned that Goldman's dependence on proprietary trading makes it vulnerable to market downturns. Industry observers interpret the changeover from Corzine to Paulson to be a reflection of the firm's concern over its dependence on trading. Corzine rose through the ranks as a bond trader and is thought to have pushed the firm in that direction; Paulson climbed the corporate ladder as a banker. The firm, of course, denied any internal struggles. In November 2000, Corzine was elected to the U.S. Senate from New Jersey. Paulson, meanwhile, still holds Goldman's reins.

The moment the Street was waiting for

In the spring of 1999, Goldman announced that IPO plans were back on track. In response, investors rushed to secure shares. A week before the company went public, the offering was eight times oversubscribed. Goldman faced so much demand that it was able to choose its investors. On May 4, 1999, Goldman went public. In the second-largest U.S. IPO at that time, the firm raised $3.66 billion and issued 69 million shares. The offering valued Goldman at a hefty $33 billion. The IPO ended 130 years of private partnership and converted the 222 partners into the largest shareholders.

Making markets

In September 2000, Goldman put some of the "currency" from its IPO to use. The firm surprised many Wall Street insiders when it announced it would purchase market maker Spear Leeds & Kellog LP. The move was surprising because Goldman was one of the firms (along with Merrill Lynch and Morgan Stanley Dean Witter) that had lobbied for a central electronic market to take the place of specialists (such as Spear Leeds) on the Nasdaq and New York Stock Exchange.

The acquisition, which was finalized in the fourth quarter of 2000, cost Goldman $6.5 billion in cash and stock. The deal is expected to dramatically increase Goldman's presence in the stock order execution business. It also enhances Goldman's exposure to the retail investor — an area that industry insiders have often cited as a Goldman weak spot. Early reports speculate that Goldman will have difficulty integrating its white shoe culture with the aggressive, secretive culture of Spear Leeds. A number of Wall Street insiders also wondered if perhaps Goldman had paid too high a premium for the company. Such speculation obviously did not bother Goldman. In January 2001, the company announced the purchase of Benjamin Jacobson & Sons, another specialist firm. Goldman reportedly paid $250 million for Jacobson & Sons, whose operations were combined with those of Spear Leads.

After building its market-making capabilities, Goldman sought to improve its retail brokerage operations through acquisition. In June 2001, Goldman acquired online investment bank Epoch Partners for an undisclosed sum. Epoch was a joint venture owned by Ameritrade, Charles Schwab, TD Waterhouse and three venture capital firms. Epoch was originally expected to democratize the IPO process, offering shares to individual investors. In practice, Epoch had difficulty getting in on high-profile IPOs and needed a partner of Goldman's stature to survive.

Can't get too comfortable at the top

While Goldman Sachs may have achieved penthouse status in the Wall Street world, it is not resting on its laurels. The firm is clearly interested in growing its asset management business. Asset management, a fee-based business, is less volatile than trading or banking. Currently, the firm lags behind Morgan Stanley and Merrill in this department. However, Goldman has been pouring personnel and money into building asset management accounts.

Goldman followed an industry trend in May 2001 when it was revealed the firm was cutting 150 jobs in the investment banking sector. The cuts, which numbered approximately 12 percent of the company's investment banking staff, came mostly from senior positions such as managing directors and partners though some vice presidents and senior associates were reportedly affected. According to *The Wall Street Journal*, Goldman was trimming personnel costs while trying to avoid mass layoffs through attrition and transferring employees from weaker units to those performing stronger. Despite the cutbacks, the firm expects to increase headcount by 2 to 3 percent for 2001 by hiring in areas such as asset management.

Visit the Vault Finance Job Board — one of the best job boards on the Internet exclusively for finance professionals. Go to www.vault.com.

VAULT   67

GETTING HIRED

Getting the third degree

Goldman's interviewing process is notorious for its grueling intensity. Candidates undergo at least three rounds of interviews and often many more. The first and second rounds usually consist of two half-hour sessions, during which the applicant interviews with two Goldman professionals, typically one associate and a vice president. The third round is the most rigorous; it consists of five or six two-on-one interviews, each of which is 45 minutes long and involves one or more of the firm's directors. There is no clear delineation of personal and professional questions during the three rounds; candidates must be prepared to answer any question at any time. And the interview process may go beyond the ordinary five-to-six person format. Says one insider: "Goldman is a very, very consensus-driven place. I think in the full-time hiring process, you could literally meet 25 people during that process, which is unheard of at other banks."

One of us

Goldman cares a lot about fit — a lot. This is the unanimous emphasis of firm insiders, who believe that more than any other Wall Street firm, Goldman weeds out those who will not fit with the firm's culture. All candidates are questioned on their willingness and ability to work hard as team players in an intense and demanding work environment. Interviewers say that they look for "people with smart personalities who aren't afraid to work hard. We especially don't want big egos around the place, so we try and find out how you will be able to work with someone you don't like too much personally."

"They stress over and over again that anybody graduating from a top MBA program can do what they want them to do," says one source. "But they can't change his personality or make him pleasant to work with. They really put a lot of effort into the personality part." In fact, one recent hire reports that he received "rapid-fire personal questions: 'Why did you go to that school?' 'How were your grades?' 'How were you perceived by your peers?' 'Your professors?'"

When screening potential summer associates, Goldman generally conducts two on-campus rounds and a third round at the firm's headquarters, which is described as "sort of a super day, but a miniature version," with about four 30-minute interviews.

For summer associates "trying out" for full-time positions, contacts say, "there's very strong attention paid to how well people work together." Play nice!

OUR SURVEY SAYS

Putting big egos in their place

Goldman Sachs' workplace is legendary for an "intense, goal-driven" ethic, where "success is taken for granted." While the rest of the world may exalt Goldman employees as the "Masters of the Universe," insiders themselves note that the firm "cuts their egos down to size." Goldman Sachs makes it clear from the beginning that "individual personalities are insignificant" and that "the firm comes first, second and last." Says one recent hire: "I've seen some people from top schools who came across as a bit arrogant, and they were very unwelcome [at Goldman]."

New hires take some time to get used to the careful scrutiny to which they are subjected, and employees sometimes feel that they "are under constant surveillance." At the same time, analysts and associates praise their fellow employees for being "intelligent and perceptive," yet also "prepared to make the sacrifices that have to be made for the team to succeed." Reports one associate: "Teamwork is a word that's clichéd and overused, and I sort of cringe when I hear it elsewhere, but in some sense that's really what the firm prides itself on." How does teamwork play out in everyday office life? "If you need to talk to someone, they're not going to stop everything they're doing to talk to you, but they'll say come back at the end of the day. Even senior people are very accessible," reports one contact. "Things are very genteel," echoes another.

However, working as part of a team of Goldman Sachs employees "can also be challenging because you have to hold up your end, and there's always pressure to measure up to your co-workers' high standards." Some insiders also feel that Goldman's emphasis on teamwork comes at a cost — "Individuality and creativity usually are considered much less important than being a good team player," says one contact. Even the most enthusiastic confess that "occasionally the stress of work can get to be too much, and you come close to cracking." Another contact says that the culture cannot only cramp individual style but might be limiting the firm as a whole. Explains that source, "Because of the corporate culture and the goody two-shoes image, [the firm is] less inclined to take risks."

Hand your life to Goldman

Goldman Sachs employees work "extremely long hours," but that comes as no surprise. At one of the top investment banks, employees are guaranteed a hefty workload. After all, one of the most commonly asked questions in a Goldman interview is, "How will you cope with working 90-hour weeks, or longer, for three years?" One associate complains that the hours are "long" and "unnecessary." He goes on to say, "While it is somewhat due to the nature of the business, my biggest complaint is they don't hire enough junior people."

This paucity of junior people can increase the workload, depending on how far down the chain you happen to be. "For the first few years, analysts usually work between 80 and 110 hours a week" and generally come in to the office "at least six days a week, though you're usually there every day of the week." Working until 10 at night is virtually a daily affair, and "all-nighters are pretty frequent" as project deadlines draw near. Even those employees who say that they love working for Goldman concede that the hours "just get a bit too much at times." New hires, however, should take heart from the fact that "the hours loosen up as you get promoted." Vice presidents rarely work all day on weekends; they reportedly usually "just drop in for a couple of hours on Saturday mornings, tell the analysts and associates what to do, and then leave."

Things are no better in equity research, insiders report. "I come in the office at 4:30 to 5 a.m.," says one analyst on the West Coast. "I generally leave at 4:30 to 6 p.m., except when a company reports or something unexpected happens (like a preannouncement). Then it could be 9 p.m. or [later]."

Full support

Goldman's support staff wins high marks from employees for being "thoroughly efficient and professional." According to insiders, Goldman bankers enjoy support services that are as good as they get on The Street. Analysts have secretaries to answer their calls, although they have to share — usually one secretary is assigned to four or five analysts or associates. Goldman's support staff infrastructure ensures that back-up secretaries are always available to fill in any gaps caused by illness or absence among the regular support staff. The highly paid support staff (like other Goldman employees, support staff receive year-end bonuses) not only perform standard administrative and clerical duties such as faxing and filing, but also help associates and analysts with making graphs, setting up databases, and creating charts and tables. Every floor at Goldman's New York headquarters has a word processing room staffed with "friendly, knowledgeable" people. Goldman's data resources and library staff members are also "superb," but tend to "grumble about last-minute requests." Overall, Goldman employees remark that the top-notch support staff plays an "integral" role in ensuring the smooth execution of pitchbooks and presentations.

Some feel the firm is lacking in training. "What training?" asks one source. "We were all thrown into our jobs pretty much immediately, and the one-week training program was mostly boring lectures. They did schedule an accounting series later on, but I'm sure I'm not the only one who couldn't attend most of the sessions because of work."

Posh offices

Goldman Sachs' New York headquarters is split into two main locations; 85 Broad Street, Goldman's headquarters, houses the investment banking business and Goldman's administrative functions, while the sales and trading business is located across the street at One New York Plaza. (The firm also has a few smaller offices in New York.) Goldman's offices are "modern" and "beautiful," and the lobbies and hallways are bedecked with "expensive artwork by renowned artists such as Jasper Johns." All analysts and associates are assigned their own cubicles. Our sources complain that working in cubicles eventually "gets tiresome," because they afford very little privacy; one analyst notes that "everyone can listen in on all of your personal phone calls."

Junior employees are particularly irked that "senior people can tell whether you are working or slacking off." One associate complains that "it's obvious whether you've gone home early," and says he took to leaving his suit jacket on his chair if he left the office before 9 p.m. Another former associate recalls, "You can't even read the paper at your desk without the whole floor knowing, so a lot of people take papers to the bathroom and read them in the stalls." However, as employees ascend the corporate hierarchy, the amount of privacy increases considerably. Vice presidents get their own "nice but small" offices, and managing directors have the luxury of large corner offices.

IPO uncertainty resolved

Many industry observers wondered if Goldman's IPO would disturb the mystique and hush-hush culture of the private partnership. Insiders say that post-IPO, the mystique is safe and sound. Explains one associate, "The people who were partners [now managing directors] still control the majority of the firm. The power structure remains the same." One source says the IPO has changed compensation: "Before people would be paid in all cash — now a good portion of your comp will be in stock." That source also notes that the firm has "become more bureaucratic since going public."

"I've seen some people from top schools who came across as a bit arrogant, and they were very unwelcome [at Goldman]."

— *Goldman Sachs insider*

Visit the Vault Finance Job Board — one of the best job boards on the Internet exclusively for finance professionals. Go to www.vault.com.

VAULT   73

2 Morgan Stanley

1585 Broadway
New York, NY 10036
Phone: (212) 761-4000
Fax: (212) 762-9242
www.morganstanley.com

DEPARTMENTS

Asset Management (Individual,
   Institutional)
Credit Services
Institutional Securities (Institutional
   Sales and Trading, Investment
   Banking, Research)

THE STATS

Chairman and CEO: Philip Purcell
Employer Type: Public Company
Ticker Symbol: MWD (NYSE)
2000 Revenues: $45.4 billion
2000 Net Income: $5.5 billion
No. of Employees: 62,700
No. of Offices: 582

KEY COMPETITORS

Credit Suisse First Boston
Goldman Sachs
Merrill Lynch
Salomon Smith Barney

UPPERS

- Bulge-bracket prestige
- Rotation system encourages
  professional development
- Stellar clients, co-workers

DOWNERS

- Brutal hours
- Bureaucratic structure
- Red-faced after recent scandals

EMPLOYMENT CONTACT

Firm-wide Recruiting
Michael Marich, Director
1221 Avenue of the Americas
44th Floor
New York, NY 10020
Attn: Division of Interest

THE SCOOP

Silver only to Goldman?

Morgan Stanley Dean Witter (which operates under the brand name Morgan Stanley) is unquestionably one of the premier bulge-bracket investment banking firms. The firm reported more than $4.5 billion in I-banking revenues in 1999 and is ranked in the top 10 of every significant league table. The firm's retail operations are even more lucrative. Morgan Stanley took in almost $6 billion from its brokerage in 1999. In addition to its securities businesses, MS also has departments devoted to asset management and research. Additionally, the bank owns Discover Card, the third-largest credit card company. While the firm's reputation within the I-banking world is fairly spectacular, it might suffer from a second-fiddle complex in its recent competition with fellow bulge-bracket firm Goldman Sachs. The firm has generally trailed just behind industry leader Goldman in most league tables, including lucrative businesses such as equity underwriting and M&A advisory.

Dodging Glass-Steagall

Morgan Stanley Dean Witter was created in 1997 through the merger of Morgan Stanley and Dean Witter, Discover & Co. Dean Witter was founded in 1924 in San Francisco. Dean Witter milestones include the firm's IPO in 1972, its 1978 merger with New York-based securities firm Reynolds & Co. (at the time, the largest securities industry merger), its purchase by Sears Roebuck in 1981, the 1986 launch of Discover Card and the 1992 spin-off of the Dean Witter, Discover Group.

Morgan Stanley traces its roots to the former securities operations of J.P. Morgan. In 1933, after the passage of the Glass-Steagall Act, which prohibited firms from operating both commercial and investment banking businesses, two J.P. Morgan partners (Howard Stanley and Harry Morgan, son of J.P. Morgan) and several other employees split from the bank and formed Morgan Stanley. The new firm was created to concentrate on the securities business, while J.P. Morgan remained a commercial bank. Great moments in Morgan Stanley history include its admission to the New York Stock Exchange in 1941 and its 1986 IPO.

Accolades

While many feared the merger with retail-oriented Dean Witter would damage the powerful, white shoe operations of Morgan Stanley, the combined firm's results have

Visit the Vault Finance Job Board — one of the best job boards on the
Internet exclusively for finance professionals. Go to www.vault.com.

VAULT   75

hushed the critics. MSDW posted a bevy of achievements during 1999. The firm was named "Best Investment Bank" by *Euromoney* and received four out of a possible 16 "Deal of the Year Awards" by *Investment Dealers' Digest* in both 1999 and 2000. The new millennium saw more success for the firm as it finished in the top 10 in numerous league tables, including M&A advisory (No. 2), IPO underwriting (No. 3), high-yield debt (No. 4) and U.S. investment-grade debt (No. 4).

While continuing to break I-banking records, the firm has also been expanding its retail business. In November 1999, Morgan Stanley jumped headfirst into online trading. Previously, the firm's online clients traded on Discover Brokerage Direct. The bank opened Morgan Stanley Dean Witter Online, its new online trading option, in November after months of asserting that its clients weren't interested in online alternatives. MS charged $29.95 for trades, gradually moving all Discover Brokerage clients who had been paying $14.95 per trade up to the new scale. While many price-sensitive Discover clients moved their accounts to other online banks, analysts felt the firm made the right move, stating that existing Morgan Stanley clients were clamoring for a high-quality alternative. The company is also reportedly investigating "cross-selling" opportunities with Discover Card. The firm hopes to develop brokerage relationships with vendors that currently accept the Discover Card, according to a June 2000 report in *Financial NetNews*.

Hit the road, Mack

While Morgan Stanley was continuing to grow through early 2001, some say an internal power struggle was brewing between Morgan Stanley and Dean Witter executives. The competition came to a conclusion in January 2001 when John Mack, president and COO of the combined company and former CEO at the old Morgan Stanley, announced his departure. Though the firm insisted Mack's departure was amicable, insiders pointed to a clash with Phillip Purcell, the former Dean Witter head who was named CEO of the combined company in 1997. According to *The Wall Street Journal*, Purcell was installed as CEO because Dean Witter officials felt that since the brokerage was technically the acquirer, the first head should be a Dean Witter executive. The companies hammered out a compromise where Mack would eventually succeed Purcell, though there's some dispute as to whether the two sides agreed to a five-year timetable or merely agreed Mack would be Purcell's eventual successor. Whatever the timetable, the *Journal*, citing unnamed company executives, reported that Mack grew impatient with the succession plan. Additionally, Mack's position in the company declined as Purcell won more allies on the board of directors and as senior officials from the old Morgan Stanley left the firm. Mack landed on his feet; he was named CEO at Credit Suisse First Boston in July 2001.

Morgan Stanley people did win a moral victory in April 2001. The firm announced they were dropping the Dean Witter name for marketing purposes, though Morgan Stanley Dean Witter remains the firm's legal moniker. The announcement was hardly a surprise, as the company announced at the time of the merger it would likely drop the Dean Witter name at some point.

Big-time clients

Morgan Stanley remains an unquestioned leader of the investment banking world and has the deals to back it up. The firm led the $1.2 billion IPO of French telecom firm Alcatel in October 2000. In February 2001, Morgan Stanley led KPMG Consulting's $2 billion IPO. One month later, the firm led a $3.6 billion offering for Agere Systems. Additionally, the firm was tapped by consulting firm Accenture to co-lead (along with rival Goldman Sachs) its IPO, tentatively slated for late spring 2001.

The M&A department cleaned up at *Investment Dealers' Digest*'s Deal of the Year awards. The firm was presented with the coveted Breakthrough Deal of the Year award for representing Time Warner in its $165 billion merger with America Online. Morgan Stanley also won Energy Deal of the Year for representing Texaco in its merger with Chevron, Media/Telecom Deal of the Year for advising Seagram in its three-way union with Vivendi and Canal Plus and Technology Deal of the Year for advising Seagate on a three-way transaction with Veritas Software and an investor group organized by Silver Lake Partners and Texas Pacific Group.

PR blunders big and small

While every bank has skeletons in its closet, some bones spilled from Morgan Stanley's metaphorical wardrobe that the firm probably wishes had remained hidden. In April 2000, *The San Francisco Examiner* revealed that San Francisco Mayor Willie Brown had been granted access to several hot IPOs underwritten by Morgan Stanley, making tens of thousands of dollars in profits. It's not unusual for banks to give influential individuals access to high-profile IPOs — in fact, it's almost a standard practice. However, the situation yielded some embarrassment when *The Examiner* reported that a Morgan Stanley spokesperson initially said the firm did not have any bond business with the city; in fact the firm had underwritten numerous bond offerings for San Francisco. The Morgan Stanley spokesman later explained that he did not mention the bonds because "all those bonds were competitive,

Visit the Vault Finance Job Board — one of the best job boards on the Internet exclusively for finance professionals. Go to www.vault.com.

VAULT   77

meaning they were done on a sealed-bid basis where the [bank offering] the low true interest cost to the city wins. There is no opportunity for influence." According to the report, an unidentified "young broker" sold the shares to the mayor, independent of the bank's relationship with the city, in an attempt to develop a relationship with him.

The firm encountered trouble with another regulatory agency in June 2000 when the Equal Opportunity Employment Commission (EEOC) ruled the bank had discriminated against a high-level female broker. Allison Schieffelin, an employee in the firm's institutional equity division, alleged in 1998 that she had been subject to discrimination and harassment at Morgan Stanley and that less-qualified male traders were promoted to managing director while she remained a principal.

The case took another turn in October 2000 when Morgan Stanley fired Schieffelin. *The New York Times* reported that the firm had broken off negotiations that would have prevented a lawsuit in late October and Schieffelin was dismissed soon after. "She was terminated for insubordination and inappropriate behavior," a company spokesman told *The New York Times*. But in March 2001, the EEOC determined that Schieffelin was fired in retaliation for her complaint. The agency is contemplating suing the firm. Schieffelin's attorney has said she will file a suit regardless of whether the EEOC decides to do so.

Morgan Stanley shut the door on another embarrassing incident in September 2000, settling a legal battle with a former employee. Christian Curry was fired in April 1998, after appearing nude in a gay men's magazine; he sued, saying he was the victim of racial and sexual preference discrimination (Curry is African-American). To further his lawsuit, Curry allegedly conspired to plant fake e-mail messages on the firm's computers. Curry was arrested in August 1998, but charges were later dropped after it was discovered that Morgan had paid $10,000 to a friend of Curry's to turn him in. The resulting embarrassment forced two of the bank's top lawyers to resign. In September 2000, Curry and Morgan Stanley dropped lawsuits against each other; Morgan Stanley agreed to pay $1 million to the National Urban League.

Still, the firm has been dogged by criticism. Since dropping the lawsuit, Curry has spent large amounts of money, including a $2 million investment in a publishing venture. That led to speculation that the firm had paid off Curry. In a scathing editorial published in February 2001, *The Wall Street Journal* accused the firm of lying about the payoff and fabricating a false statement on Curry's behalf for the press release announcing the settlement. "In a statement crafted with Mr. Curry's lawyer, Morgan Stanley called the settlement 'complete vindication' while carefully putting the lie in Mr. Curry's mouth — While I receive no payment, I am pleased with the result,'" the *Journal* wrote. The firm refuted the paper's assertions and continues to deny making a payment to Curry.

MS also got off to a rough start in 2001 when former President Bill Clinton spoke at one of the firm's conferences shortly after vacating the White House. Irate clients began calling Morgan Stanley, threatening to take their accounts elsewhere. Many considered the invitation to the former Commander-in-Chief an egregious error because of his personal conduct while in office and his pardoning of fugitive financier Marc Rich, not to mention the hefty paycheck — rumored to be around $100,000 — that Morgan gave Clinton. MS quickly issued an apology to its clients, describing the Clinton speech as "a mistake."

Where do we go from here?

Like many I-banks, Morgan Stanley Dean Witter is the constant subject of merger rumors. With the 1999 repeal of the Glass-Steagall Act (the very act that led to the founding of Morgan Stanley in 1933), some industry analysts believe an increasing number of bulge-bracket firms will merge with commercial banks to form full-service financial "supermarkets." Morgan Stanley has been linked to several commercial banks (including Chase Manhattan, which later merged with J.P. Morgan) as well as other investment banks.

Finally, in response to an industry-wide slump in revenues, Morgan Stanley announced in April 2001 that it was cutting 1,500 jobs in its investment banking and investment management industries. Rumors swirled in early 2001 that the firm considered laying off 1,000 brokers, or 7 percent of its sales force, but the brokerage force was untouched by the layoffs.

GETTING HIRED

Wide variety of interviews

Morgan Stanley Dean Witter's interviews are, according to some current employees, "quite formal, even for the investment banking industry." Technical questions are reportedly common; one business school student interviewing for a trading job reports that for his final round he was asked to sit in a chair while a senior director peppered him with macroeconomic questions. "All he did was pace around and throw questions at me — if I was wrong he'd correct me, and then just go to the next one. I remember thinking, 'God, I'm glad I know some of this stuff.' It was a lot of macroeconomics: inflation, interest rates, currencies." Says that contact: "They had me interview with pretty senior people, the head of all treasury trading, and the second in charge of all fixed income." Some recent associate-level hires report undergoing more than one callback round during the business school recruiting process. "I had three more rounds, all in New York [after the on-campus round]," reports one contact.

MBA recruits for investment banking tell a different story. One associate reports a far less grueling interview process. "It's all in who you meet here," that source explains. "Since it's such a large place, you are going to meet people with very different interviewing styles — I also think that if they have confidence in your technical skills and coursework, then you won't hit many technical questions at all." Another investment banking contact reports that at his business school, Morgan Stanley holds only two rounds (one on-campus and one at an office) for both summer and full-time associate hires. "They make very quick decisions," reports that contact. "That's the difference between Goldman and Morgan Stanley." That insider reports that there was one two-on-one interview ("good cop, bad cop"), though "other people had one-on-ones." The second round was all one-on-ones for this contact.

OUR SURVEY SAYS

Talk the talk and walk the walk

As one of Wall Street's preeminent "white shoe" firms, Morgan Stanley cultivates an "extremely professional environment" geared toward the "bright, motivated individuals who fill the halls." Insiders say that "everyone seems to have an MBA from a top business school" and state that "no other firm matches Morgan Stanley in terms of education and attitude." One former banker says the firm was "a great place to learn how to work in an intense environment with smart people." Not everyone appreciates this atmosphere, however. One former analyst calls "the people at Morgan Stanley" his "biggest disappointment." He explains: "They are boorish, aggressive and elitist — even more so than the rest of Wall Street."

Sources say the firm cultivates a conformist culture. "If you don't fit in, you stand out a lot," observes one banker. "You kind of have to walk the walk and talk the talk." Another insider complains of Morgan Stanley's "extremely rigid organization" and "heavy-handed culture." That insider says the firm takes pride in "the Morgan Stanley way. The firm has this attitude of 'this is how we've always done things and this is how we'll continue to do things.'" However, that insider does concede that the bank puts "a lot of time and effort into developing people."

Investment banking associates at MS are offered a generalist program with three rotations through industry or product groups. These rotations last four months each. Comparing Morgan Stanley to its chief competitor, Goldman Sachs, one insider comments, "There's an incredible amount of mobility when compared to Goldman. You spend your first year as a total generalist and then after two years, if you want, you can switch groups." Another insider brags, "I have a wide latitude to choose my own projects and thus have very interesting projects to do."

Free fruit and shop at J. Crew

The firm, like its Wall Street counterparts, has embraced a full-time business casual dress policy. The firm also issued a brochure highlighting the major do's and don'ts for dressing appropriately at work. Some don'ts: shirts without collars or open-toed shoes. Some do's: khakis and polo shirts in the summer. "Lots of people really push the casual dress envelope," reports one insider. "The pendulum has swung so far that people give you (good-humored) flack if you wear a suit for a borderline reason (e.g., interviewing MBA candidates)."

Morgan Stanley provides a slew of other perks, including tuition reimbursement, subsidized health club memberships, laptops, car service, meal allowances on nights and weekends and other standard investment banking perks. In addition, insiders say the firm sponsors "lavish" company outings and parties: "I feel like this firm really cares about making people feel like they are working for a top-notch organization." For the health-conscious, the firm reportedly offers free fruit on every investment banking floor.

Beep!

One of the famed aspects of Morgan Stanley's culture is that bankers are required to wear beepers, which some other banks enjoy pointing out as a MS shortcoming during MBA recruiting season. "Depending on how you think about that, [omnipresent beepers are] a good thing or a bad thing," reveals one associate. "The bad thing is, everyone's got access to your number. But the good side is that if you

Visit the Vault Finance Job Board — one of the best job boards on the Internet exclusively for finance professionals. Go to www.vault.com.

VAULT   81

ever want to take a two-hour lunch, you can, because they can page you. If anyone ever complains that you weren't in the office, you can just say 'Why didn't you page me?'"

360-degree evaluations

Morgan Stanley is also famed for its innovative evaluation system. The 360-degree review evaluation process takes place once a year, but most analysts are reviewed mid-year as well. "So everyone you work with, you put on your list, and that list goes to the HR department," explains one insider. "The HR department sends an evaluation form to everyone you work with. [Morgan Stanley] takes this very seriously. Everyone you work with will give you a formal evaluation. All the evaluations are collected, and a VP or managing director who's in your group is assigned to collate all the information and pull together what the overall evaluation should be."

"You not only get feedback from people above you, but you give them evaluations. The downward evaluations are named, upward are anonymous," says one former analyst. "So if your associate is being a total pain in the ass, you slam [him or her] in the reviews. They take very seriously the opinions of the junior people when evaluating for bonuses, so associates go out of the way to be helpful." "I'd say that is a very unique thing about Morgan," says one banker, who points out that the Morgan Stanley evaluation model was actually a case study at his business school.

Everything's coming up bulge bracket

Since Morgan Stanley is an unquestioned industry leader, all of the positives and negatives of working in I-banking are exaggerated. The hours required can be brutal — analysts can expect nightmare 100-hour workweeks. Some insiders complain the firm is not near the top of the pay scale. "While I am happy with my salary, Morgan Stanley is notorious for paying below other firms. The attitude seems to be that you should work at Morgan Stanley because of the firm's prestige and reputation for excellence, not necessarily for the money."

"No other firm matches Morgan Stanley in terms of education and attitude."

— *Morgan Stanley insider*

Visit the Vault Finance Job Board — one of the best job boards on the
Internet exclusively for finance professionals. Go to www.vault.com.

VAULT   83

Credit Suisse First Boston

11 Madison Avenue
New York, NY 10010
Phone: (212) 325-2000
Fax: (212) 325-8249
www.csfb.com

DEPARTMENTS

Equity
Fixed Income
Investment Banking
Private Client Services

THE STATS

Chairman: Joe Roby
CEO: John Mack
Employer Type: Subsidiary of
Credit Suisse Group
2000 Revenues: $12.2 billion
2000 Net Income: $1.4 billion
No. of Employees: 28,000
No. of Offices: 97

KEY COMPETITORS

Goldman Sachs
Merrill Lynch
Morgan Stanley

UPPERS

- "Fast track" promotions
- Friendly co-workers

DOWNERS

- High burnout rate
- Uncertain culture after DLJ merger

EMPLOYMENT CONTACT

Investment Banking
Rachel Graves, MBA Recruiting (US)
Pauline Ma, BA Recruiting (US)
Anne Hitchcock, MBA Recruiting (Europe)

Fixed Income
Cynthia Marrone, MBA Recruiting (US)
Lindsay Hobbs, BA Recruiting (US)
Hallie Silver, MBA and BA Dedicated
Programs (US)
Faye Woodhead, MBA Recruiting (Europe)
Sarah Russell, BA Recruiting (Europe)

Equity
Courtney Kirkland, MBA Sales &
Trading Recruiting (US)
Jennifer Murphy, BA Sales & Trading
Recruiting (US)
Beth Kramer, MBA and BA Equity
Research Recruiting (US)
Rachel Denny, MBA and BA (Europe)

Private Client Services
Eileen Duff (US)

For Asia opportunities
Michelle Desena

*For mailing addresses go to
careeropportunities.csfb.com.*

THE SCOOP

A bulging bracket

Credit Suisse First Boston is one of New York's most renowned investment banks and a member of Wall Street's prestigious bulge bracket of top securities firms. Credit Suisse First Boston is the wholly owned investment banking unit of the Credit Suisse Group of Switzerland. Credit Suisse Group (formerly known as CS Holdings) initially invested in First Boston in 1988, renaming the investment bank CS First Boston. Since that infusion of Swiss cash, the firm itself has changed significantly. Credit Suisse First Boston now has a much larger capital base than First Boston ever had.

That base got even bigger in August 2000 when Credit Suisse announced the acquisition of Donaldson, Lufkin & Jenrette in a deal worth approximately $12.4 billion. The companies said they would eliminate approximately 2,500 jobs, with most of them coming from back-office functions that overlap. By the end of 2000, CSFB said it had eliminated nearly 2,000 jobs and expected to finish its cuts by mid-2001. Lauren Smith, banking analyst at Keefe, Bruyette & Woods, told *The New York Times* that she had "mixed feelings" about the deal and predicted the usual culture clashes. "DLJ is more conservative and has a partnership-type feel," said Smith. The deal closed in November 2000. (A minor controversy flared up in the spring of 2001 regarding CSFBDirect (formerly DLJDirect), the company's online brokerage. CSFB made a $4 per share offer for the 17 percent of the online unit not covered in the DLJ acquisition. Some DLJDirect shareholders filed a class-action lawsuit, saying the CSFB offer was too low. The suit is pending.)

Shortly after announcing the merger, the firm disclosed who would hold the top positions in the investment banking division. According to *The Daily Deal*, Ken Moelis, DLJ's head of corporate finance and Charles Stonehill, head of investment banking at CSFB, were named co-heads of investment banking in the U.S. (Moelis didn't last long in his new role. Shortly after the merger was finalized in November 2000, he jumped ship to UBS Warburg, where he became co-head of I-banking.) In April 2001, *The Wall Street Journal* announced the resignations of three senior members of the equities division after they found themselves with "fewer responsibilities and less authority than they had hoped for" following the merger. All three managers had come over from DLJ. Additionally, *The Wall Street Journal* reported in September 2000 that DLJ's president and CEO, Joe Roby, was guaranteed a compensation package more commonly associated with a baseball star. The *Journal* said Roby would receive $82.4 million over six years to act as chairman of

CSFB. The deal includes a retention award, guaranteed bonuses and $5 million per year for three years to serve as a consultant starting in 2004.

With high-profile bankers exiting and reports of Joe Roby's enormous compensation package circulating, morale has been low for the remaining former DLJ employees. At an unofficial gathering of DLJ employees in October 2000, it featured a video that included the DLJ logo getting crushed and a picture of Roby with flashing dollar signs in his eyes.

From New York to Zurich

The mega-bank has a history that spans nearly 70 years. First Boston began as the investment banking arm of First National Bank of Boston. When the Glass-Steagall Act and other legal reforms imposed barriers among commercial banks, investment banks and insurance companies, the investment banking arm became the independent First Boston. In 1988 Credit Suisse, the Zurich-based bank, renamed itself CS Holdings and became a parent company/shareholder of a newly renamed CS First Boston. The alliance became more formalized in 1997, when CS Holdings swallowed the whole investment banking unit and both parent and child emerged with new names: Credit Suisse Group (a global bank headquartered in Zurich) and investment banking arm Credit Suisse First Boston (headquartered in New York).

Boldly growing the business

Since its absorption by the Credit Suisse Group, Credit Suisse First Boston has aggressively built its I-banking business, making several high-profile moves. In a deal announced in December 1997, the firm acquired several divisions of Barclays Bank's investment bank BZW. First, CSFB bought the British and European mergers and acquisitions, corporate finance advisory and equity capital markets businesses. A couple of months later, the firm completed the acquisition BZW's British and European equity sales, trading and research groups, and purchased BZW's Asian businesses. And in June 1998, it announced the purchase of Garantia S.A., Brazil's top investment bank, for $675 million in cash and stock. (This price didn't seem like such a bargain when Brazil's market began collapsing shortly after the deal was made.) The firm also made substantial waves with its acquisition of individual talent. Most notably, the firm hired about 150 technology bankers and analysts, led by superstar investment banker Frank Quattrone, from rival Deutsche Bank in the summer of 1998.

Too much tech?

Quattrone's advent made headlines and most industry insiders attribute CSFB's subsequent success in technology-related businesses largely to Quattrone's presence. Of course, the unprecedented boom in tech and Internet-related banking coincided nicely with Quattrone's arrival in 1998. Over the next two years, the firm quickly became a major player in equity underwriting. In 1999 the firm ranked fourth among lead managers of common stock issues (right behind the big three: Goldman Sachs, Morgan Stanley and Merrill Lynch), climbing up from the eighth spot on the list in 1998 according to Thomson Financial Securities Data. Much of this equity success was attributed to the firm's strong technology banking group. The momentum carried over into 2000 as CSFB was No. 4 globally in equities underwriting and No. 3 in IPOs.

Despite CSFB's rise to the top of the league tables, Quattrone's tenure at the firm has been less than smooth. Though the exact details of his compensation agreement have never been made public, it's assumed throughout the industry that Quattrone has a profit-sharing agreement that eats into a good portion of the deals his group lands. Additionally, in early 2000 rumors began to float that Quattrone was looking to jump ship. Those rumors were quashed in June 2000 when the firm announced he signed a contract extending his stay at CSFB until at least 2005.

Quattrone's group lost some stature when the tech market dried up in late 2000 and some tech bankers were let go amid firm-wide layoffs in early 2001. The group took another blow when several brokers were terminated pending an investigation into ethical questions regarding the allocation of IPO shares. (Quattrone himself has not been accused of any wrongdoing.) Despite the questions, Quattrone remains a force at CSFB. In May 2001, Quattrone was reportedly considering the option of running a $1 billion private equity fund within the firm. According to *The Wall Street Journal*, the move wouldn't take place until the end of 2001 and Quattrone might win the title of chairman of the technology group along with his new role.

The trouble with IPOs

CSFB and its parent haven't been immune to negative publicity. Its latest problems stem from a probe conducted by the National Association of Securities Dealers regarding possible regulatory breaches during the sale of IPO shares. Although the regulatory agency's investigation is looking at a number of Wall Street firms, it appears that CSFB and its treasured technology group are being more closely scrutinized than the others. Since mid-2000, the NASD has been looking into

Visit the Vault Finance Job Board — one of the best job boards on the Internet exclusively for finance professionals. Go to www.vault.com.

VAULT   87

whether brokers coerced clients to pay higher commissions and buy aftermarket shares in exchange for larger allocations of future IPOs. In May 2001, NASD determined that six CSFB employees be charged with violating NASD rules; about a week later, the firm concluded in an internal investigation that two brokers had violated firm policy; the two were later dismissed by CSFB.

Wheat cut down

Wall Street observers were surprised in July 2001 when CSFB replaced CEO Allen Wheat with John Mack, who had resigned as president at Morgan Stanley in January 2001. Published accounts of Wheat's departure indicated that there was no single reason for Wheat's sudden departure, though *The Wall Street Journal* suggested Credit Suisse Group had grown impatient waiting for CSFB to compete against industry leaders Morgan Stanley and Goldman Sachs. In a conference call announcing the move, CSFB denied the IPO probe was a factor in the decision; Lukas Muhlemann, Credit Suisse Group's chairman and CEO, told the Journal that Mack would "bring the kind of leadership that allows Credit Suisse First Boston to make very successful developments going forward."

GETTING HIRED

This is how they do it

Credit Suisse First Boston posts a list of entry-level job openings on its web site, www.csfb.com. The firm's on-campus recruiting program is managed on a firm-wide basis and organized by each of the bank's target schools. Each school is assigned an "ambassador" (a member of the firm's operating committee), a "team captain" (a director or managing director) and a "team leader."

At all of the bank's target schools, there is a campus presentation, which provides an overview of the firm, a Q&A session and in some cases, a dinner. The firm also participates in other get-to-know-you events such as golf tournaments and various student-organized functions. Those who make it past the initial campus interview are then interviewed by several bankers at one of CSFB's offices. Applicants with bachelor's degrees are hired as analysts. MBAs are hired as associates. At the associate level, the firm also hires JDs into its investment banking division and PhDs into its fixed income division (because of the math-heavy derivatives and risk management products).

CSFB conducts a summer analyst program for college students. Students are placed in the investment banking, fixed income or equity divisions. CSFB also offers a summer associate program that gives students finishing their first year of business school a chance to learn about the investment banking industry; the program runs for a minimum of 10 weeks. Summer associates participate in new business presentations and financial advisory assignments and complete transactions. The firm has a flexible sales and trading summer associate program which allows summer associates to focus on fixed income or equity or pursue a rotational program that offers exposure to both. CSFB also has an equity research summer associate program, where summer associates are assigned to work with a research analyst for the summer. According to the firm, all summer associates are assigned mentors and reviewed periodically.

OUR SURVEY SAYS

Friendly folks

The level of aggressiveness and tension "varies from place to place within CSFB," according to employees. One trader comments that "the culture in trading is very macho because it's immediate and you can make or lose a lot of money. It's certainly very physical. I'm walking around and yelling at people. Trading is definitely a lot more fast-paced than investment banking." The work environment at all divisions of Credit Suisse First Boston is "well balanced" between "entrepreneurial drive" and "collegial amiability." The company expects its employees to "grunt hard and work," but also "knows how to let them relax when appropriate." As for the influence of parent Credit Suisse Group, says one insider, "there's been more Swiss influence since the beginning of 1997. It's somewhat more conservative, [with] a little more regulation."

Credit Suisse First Boston fosters a "collegial" environment in which new employees enjoy a large degree of "interaction with senior management." One former associate reports: "We would go out at least once a week. Anytime there was someone new in our group visiting from one of the other CSFB offices, it was basically their duty to take you to a bar." One former analyst notes that the best aspect of working for the firm was "definitely the people. I've made some great friends at the firm, both in my analyst class and in my group. I still keep in touch with many of them — I was also struck by how genuinely nice people were compared with what I had expected when I went into investment banking."

Insiders also rate the firm favorably in terms of diversity. Says one source: "CSFB is one of the most diverse banks on Wall Street." That source mentions a downside to diversity, though: "I think the diversity does hurt [CSFB] in one respect because the firm lacks a strong sense of firm culture. I don't think [the people] here take as much pride in the firm as counterparts at other firms." However, some contacts say the firm could do more regarding diversity. An associate in one of the international offices, for instance, says he considers the number of women there to be below the industry average.

CSFB employees "regularly" receive free tickets to sporting and cultural events, as well as opportunities "to go out for nice dinners in restaurants." The only impediment to enjoying those fancy meals is the amount of time CSFB people spend in the office. CSFB emphasizes "teamwork" and says its employees must possess "quantitative and modeling skills."

Nice work and you get it

Insiders describe the deal flow as "incredible" and "excellent, particularly in the technology group." One analyst says simply, "You work on lots of live deals here." Junior insiders also praise the opportunity to interact with a "wide range of bankers." One source notes, "We tend to get some of the best deals in the technology sector, and associates get a tremendous amount of responsibility with the smaller companies."

Support services, such as word processing and graphic design, receive low marks and are described by one insider as "one of the weakest points at the firm." Administrative assistants are rated in similarly poor fashion. Says one contact, "Secretaries are terrible." That grumbler goes on to complain, "My phone never got answered — [my secretary] was technically supposed to be able to do word processing as well, but I wouldn't for a second trust him to do any of it."

Insiders say the firm has made lifestyle improvements to retain talent. To help with the long hours, CSFB has improved the meal policy. "We used to have one of the stingiest meal allowances on The Street," reports one insider, "and they have relaxed that considerably." Despite having to work in a cubicle, one associate in London considers the company's accommodations pretty sweet because they have "the largest corporate gym in Europe and a fantastic cafeteria. They're also building a 'fun room', whatever that is," he adds. Along with a business casual dress policy, salary increases are being implemented and employees are also offered honeymoon and paternity leave in addition to standard vacation packages. For associates, the firm is offering a "wealth creation" plan in which associates can take advantage of private equity opportunities. Analysts who are promoted to associate are given a one-month paid leave and the firm has introduced sabbaticals for employees who have been with the organization for a minimum of five years.

Healthy options

Working at CSFB offers other, more basic benefits. "[The firm offers] lots of health care options, including one in which you can save money for health care expenses tax-free," says one insider. "So say you know that later in the year you'll have $2,000 in medical expenses that won't be covered by insurance. You can save for that in a pre-tax account. So if you didn't have that account, you might have to earn $2,800 to pay for the $2,000 in expenses." For those looking to re-energize, there's the firm's health club. The monthly fee for the club depends on one's position — "for people below VP it's $30 a month." Perhaps the biggest perk, say New York employees, is that "you get to live in Manhattan — and earn enough money to enjoy it."

Don't see anyone over 30

Like most on Wall Street, CSFB's employees contend with "long," "intense" workdays and "excruciatingly tight deadlines." According to one analyst, "The hours vary. I pulled almost no all-nighters, but I worked a lot of days until four or five in the morning." Another analyst says, "You burn out by the time you're 30. Most people only last until they're about 35, then go off and do something else." Many employees comment that their jobs "require a high level of energy and dedication."

4 Merrill Lynch

World Financial Center, North Tower
250 Vesey Street
New York, NY 10281-1332
Phone: (212) 449-1000
Fax: (212) 236-4384
www.ml.com

DEPARTMENTS

Asset Management
Corporate and Institutional Client
  Group
Private Client Group

THE STATS

Chairman and CEO:
David H. Komansky
Employer Type: Public Company
Ticker Symbol: MER (NYSE)
2000 Revenue: $44.9 billion
2000 Net Income: $3.8 billion
No. of Employees: 72,000
No. of Offices: 900

KEY COMPETITORS

Credit Suisse First Boston
Goldman Sachs
Morgan Stanley
Salomon Smith Barney

UPPERS

- Bulge-bracket prestige
- Commitment to diversity

DOWNERS

- Maddening bureaucracy
- Won't match competitors' pay

EMPLOYMENT CONTACT

Investment Banking

Carrie Higginbotham
Assistant Vice President, BA Recruiting

Denise Patton
Vice President, MBA Recruiting

Sales and Trading

Claudine Rippa
Vice President

Merrill Lynch
World Financial Center
250 Vesey Street, 2nd Floor
New York, NY 10281-1302
Fax: (212) 449-3130

THE SCOOP

Strong as a bull

In 1914 Charles Merrill formed an underwriting firm, Charles E. Merrill & Co. Merrill took on Edmund Lynch as his partner, and the firm was renamed Merrill, Lynch & Co. in 1915. Following the market crash in 1929, Merrill decided to focus on investment banking and sold off its retail operations to E.A. Pierce, a brokerage firm. A decade later, Merrill recaptured the retail business when Merrill, Lynch & Co. merged with E.A. Pierce. Charles Merrill (who ran Merrill Lynch until his death in 1956) was a true renaissance man. In addition to his activities in the financial world, he founded *Family Circle* magazine (you've likely seen it at the grocery store checkout line) and even played semi-pro baseball as a young man. He quickly decided his fortune lay not in the hit-and-run, but in sales and trading. In 1971 Merrill Lynch became the second Big Board member to have its shares listed on the New York Stock Exchange (the first was Donaldson, Lufkin & Jenrette, now a part of Credit Suisse First Boston). Later in 1971, the company unleashed its "Merrill Lynch is bullish on America" ad campaign. For better or worse, the firm has been linked to its bull mascot since then.

Ranking high

Part of the investment banking bulge bracket, Merrill Lynch is a global powerhouse. The firm has a top-notch research staff and private equity group, and employs 1,600 investment banking professionals in 22 countries. Almost all of Merrill's departments are at the top of their respective league tables or, at the very least, hover somewhere in the top five. According to Thomson Financial Securities Data, Merrill finished No. 1 in total equity and debt both in the U.S. and internationally in 2000. The firm was No. 5 in IPOs, No. 3 in investment grade debt, tops in convertible securities and No. 4 in common stock underwriting.

Merrill couldn't compile those numbers without being in on some big deals. In August 2000, the firm co-led a $4.3 billion IPO for Petroleo Brasileiro. Merrill co-led a $476 million IPO for Asia Global Crossing in October 2000. In other international dealings, Merrill was the co-lead manager on Telekom Austria's November 2000, $993 million IPO. Don't let the proliferation of co-leads fool you; the firm can fly solo. For example, Merrill led oil giant Cnooc's $1.2 billion IPO in February 2001.

Visit the Vault Finance Job Board — one of the best job boards on the Internet exclusively for finance professionals. Go to www.vault.com.

VAULT   93

The numbers would indicate the firm has slipped a little in M&A advisory. After consistently coming in second to competitor Goldman Sachs in this high-profile, high-fee business, Merrill placed a respectable No. 5 in worldwide M&A in 2000. However, Merrill won Investment Bank of the Year honors for 2000 from *Mergers & Acquisitions* for its role in the Pfizer/Warner-Lambert (for Pfizer), AT&T/MediaOne (for AT&T) and Tribune/Times Mirror (for Tribune) deals.

All of Merrill's underwriting prowess would mean little if not for its distribution capabilities. The firm employs more than 19,000 financial consultants and account executives. Brokers' commissions consistently contribute the largest chunk to Merrill's annual net revenues (commissions represented 29 percent of the firm's revenues in 1999 and 26 percent in 2000).

Power lust

The last half of 2001 should be interesting at Merrill Lynch. Chairman and CEO David Komansky, who is scheduled to retire in 2004, is expected to announce his nomination for successor at the end of the year, a choice Merrill's board will take very seriously. The race to succeed Komasky already claimed at least one victim. Herb Allison, president and COO, resigned from Merrill Lynch in July 1999 after 28 years. Though the reasons behind Allison's departure aren't clear — the firm chalked it up to retirement at the time — some published reports indicated he left after it was made clear he was not being considered for the top spot.

Allison's departure left the question of succession wide open. Komansky himself has muddied the waters, telling CNBC in May 2001 that there are "at least three" potential successors under consideration. One of the main contenders to fill Komansky's shoes is E. Stanley O'Neal, the company's former CFO who was named head of the brokerage division in February 2000. O'Neal's promotion was viewed as a sure sign he was in line snag the top spot. (If selected, O'Neal would be the first African-American to head a major U.S. investment bank.) According to *BusinessWeek*, however, O'Neal has his competition. Jeffrey Peek, who is credited with resurrecting the company's asset-management division, is a strong candidate, as is Thomas Davis, head of investment banking, and Winthrop Smith, Jr., head of global private client services (and son of the firm's former chairman).

Getting commercial

Merrill caused a stir in February 2000 by announcing plans to compete with commercial banks for customer deposits. For years, Merrill had provided customers with cash management accounts (CMA), a combination of brokerage accounts and interest-bearing checking accounts. Under the company's proposed plans, any customer funds in a brokerage account that are not invested in securities will be swept into accounts insured by the Federal Deposit Insurance Corporation (FDIC). Previously, these funds were funneled into a money-market fund that was not FDIC-insured. Merrill owns two banks that will hold the accounts and lend the money out. (This is the standard practice with deposits at commercial banks.) Merrill also plans to offer higher rates on deposits than other commercial banks. This move, made possible by the Financial Services Modernization Act, took some of the risk out of investing, but was met with skepticism by the FDIC. The government agency was worried that if other banks followed suit, it would overtax the system by creating too much insured money. In the worst-case scenario (a complete market collapse similar to the one in 1929), the FDIC would have insufficient funds to pay off all insured accounts.

The firm further embraced commercial banking activities in April 2000, when it announced a billion-dollar partnership with London-based HSBC Holdings to form an online financial services company for individuals outside the U.S. The alliance will offer investors integrated banking and brokerage services.

Cutting back

With approximately 72,000 employees (as of the end of 2000), Merrill is the largest of the bulge-bracket investment banks. While size has its advantages, Merrill is also a prime target for cutbacks when the industry struggles. In 1998, when the industry struggled after the near-collapse of hedge fund Long Term Capital Management and the Russian financial crisis, Merrill laid off 3,400 employees, or approximately 6 percent of its staff. The firm was later criticized for the wide-scale cutbacks as the industry quickly rebounded and some said Merrill wasn't equipped to handle the upturn. Merrill was slightly more cautious, then, in early 2001. Responding to reduced profits, Merrill announced it was cutting 1,000 jobs in April, including 200 investment bankers.

GETTING HIRED

Resumes submitted to Merrill through college career centers and direct mail are sorted by Merrill's recruiting personnel; all qualified applicants are invited for interviews. The first round of interviews is held on the applicant's campus, and those

Visit the Vault Finance Job Board — one of the best job boards on the Internet exclusively for finance professionals. Go to www.vault.com.

VAULT   95

candidates who make the cut are invited to further rounds at the New York office. Merrill Lynch often gives preference to applicants who have worked as summer associates or analysts at the firm. Who you know is important. "Merrill Lynch Investment Banking has a target roster of schools numbering in the dozens," reports one insider. If you're not from one of these schools, and don't happen to know a big wig, getting attention from recruiting is tough." But big wigs aren't the only ones with influence, continues that contact. "Resume books with hundreds of resumes (i.e., Penn has over 400) are handed out to analysts to comb through. Our selections (mostly people we know with a few others we're in some other way impressed by) are then given first-round interviews. From there it's all about who you meet and how you do." Insiders also report that Merrill's interviews (even the initial on-campus screening interviews) "can last a lot longer than the typical half-hour interviews that other firms conduct." Summer hires who receive offers are generally required to respond within 30 days.

OUR SURVEY SAYS

No more elephants

Gigantic Merrill is known for having many subcultures, as insiders say that Merrill's culture varies "from department to department." According to one analyst, the investment-banking division "is more laid-back than at most bulge-bracket investment banks, primarily because investment banking at Merrill is relatively new." Says that contact, "Historically, you must remember, Merrill was a 'huge lumbering elephant' because that was the culture in the dominant retail side of business. However, things are changing as Merrill becomes one of the top three investment banks, and we're becoming more like Goldman or Morgan Stanley day by day." One contact adds, "We're different from other places. The people are nicer than at other banks." Another source says Merrill has a "Midwestern corporate culture — bland, collegial, inoffensive; nobody swears in public." One insider notes, "As with any big company, there will be people who are nasty for no particular reason. But there are fewer at Merrill." Merrill Lynch is "probably the leading firm on Wall Street that is attempting to improve its diversity," according to Tony Chappelle, publisher of *Securities Pro*, a New York newsletter for African-Americans in the financial industry. Most recent hires say that they "are truly impressed by Merrill's efforts to diversify." However, one analyst says, "Although the company may be making a real effort to get non-whites, you don't see too many of them around — yet."

Do you read Kafka?

The major drawback of working for Merrill, most agree, is the "horrendous" bureaucracy, which "can sometimes combine with office politics to make life miserable and incomprehensible." An insider repines, "Sometimes, for no apparent reason, you get blamed for things you didn't do and get assignments you're not supposed to have, and there's no one to complain to — life becomes like a page from a Kafka novel." Another source agrees, "While I'm in the world outside, I'm proud to be working for Merrill. But on the inside, I know that bureaucracy and politics can make life pretty miserable."

Merrill Lynch's headquarter offices are "impressive and large." While "they're not furnished in a particularly lavish fashion, they're always tastefully decorated." Employees at the New York office state that "the most impressive feature of Merrill's offices is that they're located in the World Financial Center — Merrill has an entire building to itself." A source remarks, "The views from that office are spectacular! The analysts are actually housed in a bullpen and you have a corner view of the Statue of Liberty." A different contact describes the office's surroundings: "The World Financial Center neighborhood has great bars and shops, though everything is priced exorbitantly." While the view might be nice, insiders say the firm spends most of its decorating cash on impressing clients. One source notes, "The conference rooms and other areas visited by clients are very nice, but some of the analyst bullpens are kind of dumpy."

How low can they go?

One area where Merrill lags is pay. While the firm is around the industry average, insiders complain ML is slow to match competitors' increases. Gripes one banker, "[The firm] doesn't ask, 'How much do we have to pay to get people to stay?' but 'How little do we have to pay people to get them to stay?' They look at Morgan Stanley and Goldman Sachs and then price at the lowest."

Perks at Merrill, according to employees, are "the same as those you get at other banks. If you stay past a certain hour, you get dinner and transportation home." Officially, you have to stay past 8 p.m. to get a car, and past 7 p.m. to get dinner. The firm's dinner plan utilizes restaurants with which Merrill has negotiated

Visit the Vault Finance Job Board — one of the best job boards on the Internet exclusively for finance professionals. Go to www.vault.com.

VAULT   97

discounts. Some insiders say they get sick of the food, "but a lot of the associates love it." Those who work on Saturday or Sundays get three meals covered.

Other perks include "free travel and accommodations when you travel with clients." "When you travel," one analyst notes, "you have it pretty good because you use airlines and hotels that must be up to the standard of your clients." The dress code, as at most bulge-bracket firms, is now all business casual.

Living large

The lifestyle at Merrill certainly doesn't help employees stay in shape. One New York analyst complains: "I worked so many hours at the office that I gained a substantial amount of weight. I got fat, to avoid euphemisms. The problem is, you spend so much time sitting at your desk, with no time to exercise, and you're always eating a lot at meetings at night or ordering food from different restaurants. There's no company gym for easy, during-the-day access to weights or jogging." There is an "executive gym" in the building for those high up on the ladder; as for the hardworking junior employees, "some associates go to the nearby Marriott, some go to another club."

"We're different from
other places. The
people are nicer than at
other banks."

— *Merrill Lynch insider*

Visit the Vault Finance Job Board — one of the best job boards on the
Internet exclusively for finance professionals. Go to www.vault.com.

VAULT   99

J.P. Morgan Chase

270 Park Avenue
New York, NY 10017
Phone: (212) 270-6000
Fax: (212) 270-2613
www.jpmorganchase.com

DEPARTMENTS

Asset Management
Commercial Banking
Consumer Banking
Credit Cards
Diversified Consumer Lending
Global Markets
Investment Banking
Private Banking
Private Equity
Treasury and Securities Services

THE STATS

President and CEO: William Harrison
Employer Type: Public Company
Stock Symbol: JPM (NYSE)
2000 Revenues: $32 billion
2000 Net Income: $5.7 billion
No. of Employees: 95,000
No. of Offices: 66

KEY COMPETITORS

Bank of America
Citigroup
Credit Suisse First Boston
Deutsche Bank

UPPERS

- Flexible work environment
- Great diversity
- Increased global reach after merger

DOWNERS

- Reputation not established
- Uncertain culture after merger

EMPLOYMENT CONTACT

Human Resources
J.P. Morgan Chase & Co.
270 Park Avenue
New York, NY 10017

THE SCOOP

Coming together

J.P. Morgan Chase & Co. (known informally as Morgan Chase) is the product of a merger between two diversified financial institutions, J.P. Morgan and Chase Manhattan. Morgan Chase provides the full slate of investment banking services, as well as commercial banking services such as accepting deposits and issuing loans to consumers and businesses.

The merger, which was announced in September 2000 and completed on the first day of 2001, was valued at approximately $38.6 billion. The combined firm instantly became the third-largest financial institution (in terms of assets) in the U.S. (behind Citigroup and Bank of America). The combination resulted in approximately 5,000 layoffs. William Harrison, formerly chairman at Chase Manhattan, was named Morgan Chase's president and CEO; J.P. Morgan's CEO Douglas Warner was appointed chairman. The two are co-chairing the company's executive committee.

Pistols at dawn

Chase Manhattan's history can be traced back to 1799, when The Manhattan Company was chartered to supply water to New York City. Included in the company charter was a provision that capital not needed for the water-supply business could be diverted toward the founding of a bank. Thus, the Bank of The Manhattan Company was formed. Historians are unclear whether Aaron Burr, one of the backers of The Manhattan Company's water business, intentionally inserted the clause so a bank rivaling Alexander Hamilton's could be formed. The two Founding Fathers had a long-running dispute, which came to an abrupt end in 1804 when Burr killed Hamilton in a duel. (The pistols, by the way, have been preserved as part of Chase's historical collection.)

The bank continued to grow, surviving the Great Depression (with a little assistance from the Rockefeller family) and two World Wars. In 1955 the Bank of The Manhattan Company merged with Chase National, a bank founded in 1877 by currency expert John Thompson and named after former Secretary of the Treasury Salmon Chase. The Chase Manhattan Bank, as it became known, went seeking another commercial merger partner in the mid-1990s, settling on Chemical Bank, then the third-largest bank in the U.S. following its 1992 merger with Manufacturers

Hanover. The 1996 coupling made Chase Manhattan one of the largest banks in the United States

Chase continued its acquisition strategy in late 1999 and early 2000, starting with its purchase of Hambrecht & Quist, a San Francisco-based boutique specializing in the tech sector. The December 1999 purchase cost Chase $1.35 billion. The bank's next target was Robert Flemings Holdings, a London-based bank Chase purchased in April 2000 for $7.9 billion, a price many considered too high. However, the purchase added some needed underwriting muscle, especially in Asia. In August 2000, the firm finalized its purchase of The Beacon Group, a New York boutique founded by former Goldman Sachs partner Geoffrey Boisi, who joined the firm as its lead investment banker.

The venerable house of Morgan

J.P. Morgan traces its roots back to 1838, when American George Peabody opened a London merchant bank. Junius S. Morgan became Peabody's partner in 1854, and eventually the firm became known as J.S. Morgan & Company. Seven years later, Junius' son, J. Pierpont, established J.P. Morgan & Company, a New York sales office for securities that were underwritten by his father. Working on both sides of the Atlantic, the Morgans brought capital from Europe that was crucial to U.S. growth. In 1895, five years after Junius' death, J. Pierpont consolidated the family businesses under the J.P. Morgan name.

The firm's growth continued unimpeded until the enactment of the Glass-Steagall Act in 1933. Because of the newly formed barriers between commercial and investment banking, the firm experienced many changes. Several partners, including Harry Morgan (grandson of J. Pierpont) left the firm to form an investment banking firm, Morgan Stanley. Following a merger with Guaranty Trust Company, J.P. Morgan moved into the commercial and personal loan business.

In the 1960s, J.P. Morgan began underwriting securities in Europe, where there were fewer banking regulations. The company craved such business in the United States, especially once corporations began looking to bonds as a cheaper alternative to bank loans. In 1989 J.P. Morgan received permission from the Federal Reserve to enter debt underwriting; one year later, the door to equity underwriting was opened.

Unholy alliance?

Management, shareholders and industry pundits have hailed the merger as beneficial to both companies. They say Chase will have access to an established I-banking business and expand its reach in Europe, while J.P. Morgan gains a foothold in the consumer market and greater exposure in Asia. But many employees are not sharing their joy. Since the announcement, there have been rumblings of culture clashes between the two companies. Some question how Morgan's traditionally blue-blooded, independent environment will fare now that it's part of a more laid-back company comprised of workers from a hodgepodge of prior mergers.

The most potentially threatening problem may be the perception among some Morgan people that Chase is a third-rate institution whose employees lack both intelligence and ambition. This stems mostly from the fact that Chase is not considered to be in the top echelon of global financial services management companies. During an address to students at Columbia University, president and CEO William Harrison, acknowledged some anxiety about the differing cultures. "I'm a little bit concerned about that because Morgan is an insular company," he said. "But competence overcomes a lot of cultural differences, if there are any."

Then there is the fear that accompanies any merger about who will stay and whose jobs will be eliminated. Harrison and Warner attempted to ease some of the tension and speculation by immediately announcing 50 senior executive positions when the merger was announced. The slots for 200 more executive positions were announced shortly thereafter. Increased merger costs and a less than spectacular fourth quarter in 2000 for both companies may have contributed to the employee insecurities and definitely had a negative impact on both stocks. The companies announced in December 2000 that the cost of the merger had increased by $4 million, bringing the total cost to $3.2 billion. Another sore point: Chase, as the acquiring company, has control in terms of board seats (eight from Chase's former board to five from Morgan), but some Chase employees seem mystified about Morgan preceding Chase in the new corporate name. Morgan employees point to the name as yet another sign that Chase couldn't go it alone and bought Morgan to enhance its prestige.

The upside

With so many previous acquisitions under its belt, the merger game is obviously old hat for Chase. If Chase can face head on — and find some positive way of embracing — the cultural differences between it and J.P. Morgan, the transition may be less painful than many anticipate. Peter Eavis, a senior columnist for TheStreet.com, notes that

Visit the Vault Finance Job Board — one of the best job boards on the Internet exclusively for finance professionals. Go to www.vault.com.

VAULT   103

by combining five of Morgan's business units with Chase's investment banking unit, the merged company is likely to see an immediate increase in the contribution to overall profits and revenues from investment banking. One good sign for the merger: GE tapped Chase's lead investment banker, Geoffrey Boisi, to advise its planned acquisition of Honeywell. Although the completion of the deal is in question due to regulatory roadblocks, the selection of Chase still has given pause to many who speculated that Chase didn't have the chops to be a major player in M&A, even with Morgan on board.

GETTING HIRED

The process

At least for the time being, hiring of new associates and analysts is being conducted separately by Chase and Morgan staffers in much the same way as prior to the merger. Each company recruits at a number of the top-tier schools such as Harvard, Wharton, Columbia and UCLA, but candidates from other schools are considered. Be prepared to discuss a range of business-related topics and display your knowledge of accounting or finance. For both companies, at least two rounds of interviews are required. The final round is typically conducted in a Super Saturday format, with candidates spending the day at the firm and interviewing with a number of managers — at least four to six people. As daunting as the day sounds, it is the final hurdle to landing an offer. While some interviewers will ask complex questions intended to measure an individual's quantitative skills, others may simply engage in a few minutes of small talk for the sake of gathering how well an individual will fit into the organization. After offers are extended, candidates are often invited to a sell day, during which they meet more managers and learn more about the firm before deciding to accept the offer.

Undergrads applying to Chase need at least a 3.0 cumulative GPA and, according to the firm, "strong quantitative, analytical, and computer skills and excellent oral and written communication skills." The same basic requirements go for MBAs, but there's no minimum GPA requirement. The first step is an on-campus interview. If you pass muster there, it's on to Super Saturday. Undergrads have a dinner with analysts the night before, and on Saturday meet with four bankers/managers. The MBA process is pretty much the same, excluding the dinner. "For final rounds [for MBAs] there are five two-on-one interviews and all must agree to hire a particular candidate," reports one source. Analyst candidates can expect a Super Saturday with four one-on-one interviews.

In general, Chase bankers note that interviewers are trying to "get a feel for who you are." Says one source, "It is really about your personality and vision, which should be clear." Typically, offers are extended the Monday or Tuesday following Super Saturday.

Morgan's global markets, investment banking, asset management services and consulting divisions recruit at about 50 undergraduate and business schools. The firm typically makes a presentation giving a company-wide overview of Morgan's business, and later makes division-specific presentations in association with school clubs. Some of these are social events such as cocktail parties or lunches, and lucky schools like UCLA get beer blasts. Morgan also hosts dinners at the major business schools. "The goal is to get to know you," explains one recruiter.

First interviews tend to be lengthy and require speaking with several Morgan employees, including VPs, MDs and associates. These are generally conducted on campus unless the candidate applied online and isn't a student at one of the schools where Morgan recruits. These interviews are conducted by phone. Second-round interviews often follow the familiar Super Saturday format. A candidate may interview with anywhere from five to eight people during the second round. A research analyst who did not attend one of the firm's target schools says he interviewed with managers from three different industry groups. This source says the questions he was asked ranged from the standard accounting and finance questions to "'Why J.P. Morgan?' 'Why research?'" Depending on the position, offers are extended anywhere from a few days to a month after the second interview.

OUR SURVEY SAYS

What you see, and what you get

Blending the cultures of Chase Manhattan and J.P. Morgan is proving to be quite a challenge. While the popular public image of Morgan was that of a starched-shirt, mahogany-paneled firm cloistered in 19th century beliefs and manners, the company was known on Wall Street as being rather progressive. Chase was in a state of flux, even before the Morgan merger. Although the bank had a reputation among its consumer banking customers as being focused on customer service, it had been in search of a corporate identity as it sought to combine previous mergers into a cohesive unit. Rumors persist that loyalists from both firms are eyeing each other with suspicion, and defections on all levels since the merger was announced have only fueled the talk.

But this is not the picture that some insiders paint, especially among those in the lower ranks. "I would say that the job is not perfect, but management is committed to making the analyst experience worthwhile. People are always willing to help their coworkers, the lifestyle is great and the pay is quite good," an analyst tells us. A co-worker agrees that "working here is fulfilling," and even though dealing with "the bureaucracy isn't, things are improving." Furthermore, little time is "spent on internal or dead-end projects," freeing analysts and associates up to learn more about developing deals. One analyst says he's lucky to work with someone who "has delegated responsibility downward, so I can get my hands on as much as I feel comfortable with — and sometimes more." Others caution that not all the bosses at Morgan Chase will hand over the reins of responsibility so freely. One insider moans, "Analysts are first and foremost data retrievers." However, this contact deems it a necessary function because "it forces the analyst to understand the business."

A (mostly) happy step-family

As for interaction with senior bankers, associates and analysts say they feel respected by managers and receive good feedback from them. According to one contact, "Senior bankers typically show concern for the development of junior resources." Another says he enjoys working at Morgan Chase because "analysts are praised for doing good work." Proclaims one confident insider: "I take my job seriously, and as a result, the senior guys pay attention — and don't give me trouble when I argue with them."

Employees give the firm high marks for diversity, especially regarding women. Reports one source: "There are quite a few women, including senior MDs." Another insider shares that "the head of investment management, Ron Dewhurst, is always having group sessions or coffee talks that invite minority groups to voice their opinions." Even prior to the merger, the parent companies had records of being diversity-friendly. Before combining, each firm made several appearances on the "50 Best Companies in America for Minorities" list, as compiled by *Fortune*. J.P. Morgan had also instituted a Diversity Steering Committee (DSC), composed of managing directors from each business group to oversee the issues affecting the firm on a global basis. Additionally, J.P. Morgan was the first firm on Wall Street to grant benefits for partners in same-sex relationships.

Dressed for success?

Both firms also had casual dress codes. Unfortunately, say some Morgan Chase employees, the firm is becoming a little too casual for their tastes. While officially, "no jeans [or exposed] toes, navels or tattoos" are allowed in the office, reports are that it "has slipped to the point where some people are coming in [wearing] jeans." One insider finds the attire violations disturbing. "I think it hasn't improved the overall attitude. Wearing a tie on the trading floor didn't slow me down before." A bemused analyst describes his co-workers' style of dress as "J. Crew and Banana Republic at war."

Fidelity Investments

82 Devonshire Street
Boston, MA 02109-3614
Phone: (800) 544-6666
Fax: (617) 476-6150
www.fidelity.com

DEPARTMENTS

Brokerage
Corporate Systems and Processing
Employer Services
Financial Intermediary Services
Management and Research
Strategic Investments

THE STATS

Chairman and CEO:
Edward C. "Ned" Johnson III
Employer Type: Private Company
No. of Employees: 33,000

KEY COMPETITORS

Charles Schwab
Janus Capital
T. Rowe Price
Vanguard Group

UPPERS

- Numerous and flexible maternity leave options
- Profit sharing
- Tuition reimbursement

DOWNERS

- Lack of teamwork in equity division
- Little at-work (or after-work) socialization

EMPLOYMENT CONTACT

Fidelity Investments — Resume Central
82 Devonshire Street, Z1F
Boston, MA 02109

THE SCOOP

From one fund to many

Edward Crosby Johnson II founded Fidelity Management and Research (FMR Corp.) in 1946 to act as investment advisor to the Fidelity Fund, which was started in 1930. During the 1970s, Fidelity began to make funds directly accessible to individual investors and set an industry standard by eliminating mutual fund sales charges. An early leader in discount brokerage, Fidelity was the first to see that the future of financial services depended on empowering individual investors to take advantage of investment opportunities. Fidelity also provides insurance both through its own life insurance unit and through affiliations with insurance.com and John Hancock Financial Services.

Fidelity Investments is the housemark for FMR Corp., the holding company through which CEO Edward "Ned" Johnson III controls the empire of financial institutions that his father established. The Johnson family (including Abigail Johnson, who was named president of FMR Corp. in May 2001) controls 49 percent of the company; the remaining 51 percent is owned by Fidelity senior managers. Ned has received some kudos on his own. He was No. 2 on *SmartMoney*'s list of the 30 most influential people in the world of investing, behind only Federal Reserve Chairman Alan Greenspan. The company itself has won a number of awards: Research firm J.D. Power and Associates ranked Fidelity No. 1 in customer satisfaction and the firm's online trading division has been similarly honored by Gomez.com, *Forbes* and *Money Magazine*.

Mutual fund behemoth

To describe Fidelity is to make use of superlatives. With $907.2 billion in mutual fund assets under management and approximately 17 million customers as of April 2001, the company is the largest privately held financial services company in the nation, the second-largest discount brokerage firm in the nation, the leading provider of company-sponsored 401(k) retirement plans to Fortune 500 companies and the largest mutual fund company in the U.S. Notable funds include Contrafund, Growth & Income and Magellan, the largest actively managed mutual fund on the market with $87.2 billion in assets as of April 2001.

Size, though, does have its disadvantages, especially when it comes to mutual funds. *Forbes* pointed out in August 2000 that because of Magellan's size (at the time, it had

$109.8 billion in assets and held positions in 370 stocks) it's almost impossible for the fund to beat the market by a significant margin. In fact, many of the company's mutual funds have the same problem. According to *Forbes*, this represents a shift in Fidelity's strength. Whereas the company's funds were once known for stellar performance — for example, during superstar manager's Peter Lynch's 13-year tenure as Magellan's manager the fund averaged 29 percent returns — Fidelity has now shifted to a service-oriented business.

The company seems to be in an expansion phase. Robert Reynolds, Fidelity's chief operating officer, told *BusinessWeek* that the company plans to increase its technology budget by 20 percent over the course of 2001 to $2.3 billion. Internet spending will rise 30 percent to $350 million, and the company will spend the same amount on telephone support staff. The increased spending will lead to more jobs; the company expects to employ 36,000 people by the end of 2001.

Don't bet on it

Fidelity employees would be wise to avoid office pools. The firm fired nine employees and disciplined 16 others in November 1997 for using company e-mail to participate in betting pools. According to *The Wall Street Journal*, the company's senior vice president of administration, David Weinstein, sent a company-wide e-mail after the incident reminding employees of the company's policy on e-mail and Internet usage. The firm said that no customer accounts or funds were affected.

GETTING HIRED

While Fidelity does not specify educational requirements, it does look for entrepreneurial candidates who can succeed in a fast-paced environment. Most new hires have some financial or business background, but there are also opportunities for those with technology and computer expertise. Fidelity's employment web page, jobs.fidelity.com, discusses the different departments within the company and the skills that they require. The web page also allows applicants to search a job database, build their resumes online and submit resumes via e-mail.

Fidelity prefers MBAs for positions such as quantitative equity analysts, regional service representatives, product/service consultants, investment managers, quantitative analysts and performance analysts. For MBAs applying for analyst positions, having a love for the stock market seems to be the most important qualification. If you are sending in your resume, insiders recommend attaching a stock report. "They love that," says one insider. "It will definitely increase your chances of getting an interview."

OUR SURVEY SAYS

Flexible culture

Fidelity's corporate culture wins high marks from employees for being "enlightened" because of its "high degree of tolerance in dealing with its people." According to one recent summer associate, "Fidelity understands that workers can't always be perfect. They don't have a problem with people being grouchy." Unlike many other companies in the industry, Fidelity "assigns a great deal of autonomy, both personally and professionally" to its employees.

You like stocks or bonds?

Recent hires say that one of the "striking" characteristics of working for Fidelity is that "Fidelity's workplace has a major dichotomy between the fixed income and equity divisions. The culture at fixed income is completely different from the culture in the equity division." Employees in the fixed income division praise their "team-oriented work place" and feel that "the best part of working for this company is your coworkers, the best in the game." However, an associate in the equity division laments his department's "individualistic, even 'dog-eat-dog' environment." "Equity," he notes, "is not very social at all." He goes on to add: "It's not for someone who really likes a team effort environment. Not that it's not friendly, but although you interact with other people, you work a lot on your own. It's also stressful, so if you can't handle up and down stressful times, you should look elsewhere." Another equity employee says that "Fidelity and its culture are more solitary than at other companies. In general, your job's going to be solitary if you work in the buy-side mutual environment. But Fidelity's even more solitary than usual — absolutely no after-work social life. It's stressful during the day, but then people go their separate ways after work. It's not a place for someone who wants work to be the center of their lives."

Visit the Vault Finance Job Board — one of the best job boards on the Internet exclusively for finance professionals. Go to www.vault.com.

VAULT   111

A one-man show

It's "impossible to talk of Fidelity without mentioning Ned Johnson somewhere," insiders assert. "Ultimately, this place is an autocracy, and one man is ruler — Ned Johnson," one longtime employee comments, adding ruefully, "Ned Johnson has the power to make decisions with no checks on that power. He's a smart guy, but occasionally he makes a very non-optimal decision. And we have to bear the consequences of his occasional wackiness." Another agrees: "This is Ned's candy store. He was given this firm by his father. He'll come up with the quirkiest, strangest idea in the middle of the night, and everyone has to deal with it. It's very frustrating."

Good firm for women

A recent female summer intern in the fixed-income division states that "Fidelity is very anxious for women to work for it. My immediate superior was a woman and was very candid with me when soliciting my assistance in identifying good female candidates." One contact notes: "One of the most powerful people around the company is a woman — Abigail Johnson." (Johnson became president of FMR Corp. in May 2001.) Another, when asked about the effect of Abigail Johnson on the workplace, replies: "I don't think it matters. There were a few other women where I worked. I felt like we were treated fine. They don't treat women any different, there are just fewer of them. In a lot of ways that can be an advantage — there are more opportunities."

Employees are particularly appreciative of Fidelity's many family-friendly programs, which according to one female employee, ensure that "Fidelity's a good place for working women and families." Another contact agrees, noting that "there are a ton of people here on maternity leave." Fidelity's family programs include adoption assistance, child care assistance, vacation programs for school-age children, college planning and scholarship information, elder care resource and referral, an employee assistance program and mortgage assistance. Other perks that draw praise include Fidelity's comprehensive training opportunities and an "excellent" retirement benefits plan consisting of a 401(k) package with a matching contribution by Fidelity.

"Fidelity understands that workers can't always be perfect. They don't have a problem with people being grouchy."

— *Fidelity Investments insider*

Visit the Vault Finance Job Board — one of the best job boards on the
Internet exclusively for finance professionals. Go to www.vault.com.

VAULT   113

Salomon Smith Barney

388 Greenwich Street
New York, NY 10013
Phone: (212) 816-6000
Fax: (212) 793-9086
www.salomonsmithbarney.com

DEPARTMENTS

Asset Management
Equities
Fixed Income
Global Relationship Bank/Foreign
 Exchange
Investment Banking
Public Finance
Research
Sales and Trading

THE STATS

Chairman and CEO:
Michael Carpenter
Employer Type:
Subsidiary of Citigroup
2000 Revenues: $23.4 billion
2000 Net Income: $2.8 billion
No. of Employees: 35,000
No. of Offices: 500+

KEY COMPETITORS

Credit Suisse First Boston
Goldman Sachs
J.P. Morgan Chase
Merrill Lynch
Morgan Stanley

UPPERS

• Exposure to big deals
• Top training program

DOWNERS

• Bureaucracy
• Long hours

EMPLOYMENT CONTACT

Investment Banking Recruiting

Caitlin McLaughlin
Director, MBA Recruiting

Kate Schwab
Assistant Vice President,
Undergraduate Recruiting

Sales and Trading Recruiting

Susan Glendon
Director, MBA, Undergraduate
Recruiting

Equity Research Recruiting

Debbie Bertan
Vice President, Recruiting

Salomon Smith Barney
388 Greenwich Street
New York, NY 10013

THE SCOOP

Merger mania

Salomon Smith Barney, now the investment-banking arm of Citigroup, has a long history of mergers. The firm traces its roots back to 1873, when trader Charles Barney founded a securities firm in Philadelphia. In 1892 Edward Smith started his brokerage business in the City of Brotherly Love. The two firms eventually combined to form Smith Barney. Smith Barney was acquired by Primerica, a financial services firm run by Sanford "Sandy" Weill, in 1987. Primerica was sold to Hartford-based insurance giant Travelers Group in 1993. In December 1997, Travelers bought Salomon Brothers for more than $9 billion, and merged Salomon Brothers with Smith Barney to create Salomon Smith Barney. Travelers then merged with Citicorp, the New York-based commercial bank, creating the merged entity Citigroup in October 1998.

As a full-service investment bank, SSB offers sales, research and trading for individuals and institutions; underwriting, advisory and specialty financing for corporations and government entities; mutual fund services; and futures and asset management. SSB is also the second-largest retail brokerage firm in the U.S. The firm employs an army of nearly 11,000 brokers who manage more than 6.2 million client accounts, representing over $816 billion in client assets.

Propelled into the big leagues

Though the coupling with Travelers went smoothly, it took the 1998 merger with Citicorp to thrust Salomon Smith Barney into the big leagues of investment banking. According to *Crain's New York Business*, Weill (by then CEO at Travelers) initiated contact with Citibank CEO John Reed in 1998 with the intention of forming a financial services powerhouse. The two CEOs began discussions in February 1998 and by April had secured board approval for the merger, valued at $70 billion.

Go to the source

The merger faced another hurdle after board approval. The Glass-Steagall Act, the Depression-era law prohibiting a mix of financial services businesses, threatened to cancel the deal. The companies were able to buy some time under the Bank Holding Company Act of 1956, a rule that allowed financial services partnerships for five years, but Weill and Reed knew that if the merger was to survive, they had to act to

Visit the Vault Finance Job Board — one of the best job boards on the Internet exclusively for finance professionals. Go to www.vault.com.

VAULT   115

repeal the Glass-Steagall Act. (Such a move had been discussed in both political and business circles, but no significant progress had been made.) Weill and Reed took the initiative in affecting change, phoning President Bill Clinton the night before the merger announcement to enlist his help in repealing Glass-Steagall. Eventually, their efforts proved successful — the Financial Services Modernization Act of 1999 has removed the obstacles to full-service financial institutions. (According to *Crain's New York Business*, Weill has the pen used by President Clinton to sign the Financial Services Modernization Act into law displayed in his office.) The cooperation between Weill and Reed didn't last long. Reed retired in February 2000, reportedly after a power struggle with Weill.

Initial results of the Citicorp/Travelers merger were excellent and analysts raved about the company's future. *Euromoney* named Salomon Smith Barney "Most Improved Investment Bank" in July 1999. In October 1999, SSB was able to lure former Treasury Secretary Robert Rubin to the firm, making him chair of the executive committee and part of the chairman's office. After his appointment, rumors surfaced that Rubin was under consideration for the CEO post at Citigroup and chairman of the Federal Reserve. Those rumors have been extinguished as Rubin has denied interest in becoming the company's CEO and Alan Greenspan was re-appointed Fed chairman.

Inroads in Europe

After SSB secured its place in the U.S. bulge bracket, the firm turned its attention to expansion in Europe. In February 2000, SSB announced it would acquire the investment banking operations of Schroders plc, a London-based firm that was 50 percent family-owned. Weill told *The New York Times* that the acquisition, valued at $2.2 billion, would put his firm "two or three years ahead of where we would have been" in investment banking in Europe. In Europe, the firm is known as Schroder Salomon Smith Barney. Schroders' U.S. operation, known as Schroder & Co., was folded into Salomon Smith Barney, and the firm laid off Schroders employees who overlapped with existing I-banking personnel. The Schroders family retained the asset management and private banking units.

The merger seems to have provided an immediate boost to SSB's European profile. *Investment Dealers' Digest* named the firm Bank of the Year for 2000, partly because of the Schroders acquisition. Part of the successful integration of Schroders may be due to the fact that there was very little bloodletting on the other side of the Atlantic. "We retained all of the senior management team," SSB CEO Michael Carpenter told *IDD*. *IDD* also honored co-head of global investment banking Michael Klein as

Banker of the Year for 2000. *International Financing Review* rounded out SSB's trophy case, naming it Bank of the Year and Loan House of the Year for 2000.

Mergers for others

In addition to its own merger activity, Salomon Smith Barney has been busy advising its clients on mergers and acquisitions. The firm was ranked fifth among advisors of announced U.S. M&A transactions in 2000, according to Thomson Financial Securities Data. The company advised on 198 domestic announced deals worth $423.4 billion. Salomon Smith Barney was also fifth in worldwide announced M&A, advising on 435 deals worth $666.8 billion.

Despite the firm's status, some industry observers were surprised when Salomon Smith Barney was chosen as lead adviser to America Online in its blockbuster merger with Time Warner. The bank was an unexpected choice because others in the industry perceived SSB's technology and Internet teams as weak. "I don't even know the names of anyone over there," one competitor told *The Industry Standard* after the deal was announced. That competitor should take note of the name Eduardo Mestre. Not only did Mestre lead the AOL deal team, but also led the team that advised WorldCom on its acquisition of MCI in 1998. That transaction helped him capture the Banker of the Year award from *Investment Dealers' Digest* in 1998.

Debt expertise

Salomon Smith Barney is a perennial leader in underwriting fixed income offerings and providing liquidity in those markets. According to TFSD, the firm was tops in U.S. investment-grade debt underwriting, managing 432 deals worth $68.1 billion. SSB was second in high-yield offerings in 2000, underwriting 51 deals worth $6.9 billion. Solly also finished first in U.S. asset-backed debt, raising $51.2 billion in 231 deals. One client of note is Rite Aid; along with J.P. Morgan, Salomon Smith Barney helped Rite Aid restructure $550 million in notes so the drug chain could avoid bankruptcy. The firm's fixed-income division scored a coup similar in stature to the AOL deal when they managed the sale of $500 million in global bonds for Dow Chemical in February 2001. Dow originally hired Solly rivals Goldman Sachs and Deutsche Banc Alex. Brown to do the offering but the firms couldn't sell the notes at the price Dow wanted.

Though Salomon Smith Barney's equity underwriting practice doesn't match its debt figures, the company is still a top-10 underwriter. SSB ranked fifth among underwriters of all common stock in 2000, lead managing 76 issues with total

Visit the Vault Finance Job Board — one of the best job boards on the Internet exclusively for finance professionals. Go to www.vault.com.

VAULT   117

proceeds of $19.1 billion. In the lucrative IPO underwriting business, SSB ranked fourth among domestic lead managers, up from ninth the year before. The firm underwrote 32 deals in 2000 worth $8.9 billion. Recent deals of note include, John Hancock Financial Services' $2.0 billion January 2000 IPO, the massive $10.6 billion April 2000 AT&T Wireless IPO and Mosanto's $700 million IPO in October 2000.

New blood

The firm also made some key personnel moves in 2000. In September, the firm snagged a director from Donaldson, Lufkin Jenrette and another from J.P. Morgan for its energy group. This was quickly followed by the addition of four executives to the equity research team in London and two executives to the technology M&A group. The biggest coup came in November when the firm grabbed another eight DLJ bankers (right after its merger with Credit Suisse First Boston), including Hal Ritch, who joined SSB as global co-head of M&A. That wasn't the only November surprise DLJ received from Solly: Six people left Donaldson's Dallas branch to run Salomon's newly established I-banking office.

A little trouble

Large corporations are vulnerable to public relations disasters, and Salomon Smith Barney is certainly no exception. In December 1999, the treasurer's office of San Bernardino County, California accused the firm of yield burning. (Yield burning is the practice of overcharging for U.S. Treasury securities.) Dick Larsen, the current San Bernardino County treasurer, claimed Salomon Smith Barney bilked his predecessor, Tom O'Donnell, out of $308,000 in the county's 1997-1998 fiscal year.

A few months after the San Bernardino accusations became public, Salomon Smith Barney became embroiled in a conflict-of-interest brouhaha. In March 2000, Dime, a New York-based savings and loan, sued Salomon Smith Barney to prevent the investment bank from representing North Fork, another New York savings and loan, in an attempted hostile takeover of Dime. According to the suit, Salomon Smith Barney had signed a confidentiality agreement with Dime when it represented the commercial bank in a 1997 transaction. A federal judge agreed with Dime in April 2000, barring Salomon from further participation in the deal. Salomon Smith Barney said it would appeal the decision, which will cost the firm $8.4 million in fees.

The bank that dare not speak its name

Though rich in history, the Salomon Smith Barney name is not long for this world. Parent Citigroup plans to combine Salomon Smith Barney's operations with Citibank's corporate bank, renaming the group Citigroup Corporate and Investment Bank. In a company-wide e-mail in May 2001, Chairman Weill told employees they wished to exploit the strength of the Citigroup brand name, as well as strengthen the "common culture we are developing as Citigroup." The change is scheduled to take place in early 2002.

GETTING HIRED

Looking for bankers in all the right places

Like most bulge-bracket firms, Salomon Smith Barney focuses its recruiting efforts on top-20 schools. However, like many banks, SSB has been forced by recent market pressures to look elsewhere for talent. Top regional schools (contacts give examples like Berkeley, Vanderbilt, Washington University and Emory) are becoming increasingly important in the bank's recruiting strategy. This expanded recruiting strategy receives mixed reviews. "Salomon always was selective in choosing candidates that fit the culture of intelligent and hard-working people," says one source. "Yet I feel the current batch of both analysts and associates has definitely moved downstream in terms of quality — mainly of intelligence and work ethic," that source gripes. Another insider disagrees, saying: "Some of our best recruits come from the lesser-known schools."

Recruits — no matter what school they're from — can expect two or three rounds of interviews with up to 10 Salomon Smith Barney bankers. In most cases, expect one or two preliminary rounds followed by a Super Saturday, "with an average of four one-on-one interviews." According to one source, "Interviewers are mostly interested in gauging a candidate's understanding of the job responsibilities and the candidate's eagerness to embrace these responsibilities." The specific questions will vary. "Questions are usually not ridiculously difficult or abstract and will definitely be appropriate for your background," offers one New York banker. A recruit with a finance background had better be prepared. One insider warns, "If you are a CPA, you had better know your accounting." Don't sweat too much, though. "[The] company usually stays away from trick questions," reports another source.

OUR SURVEY SAYS

Happy campers

Overall, employees at Solly agree that the firm has a good reputation and that a stint there can do good things for your career. Furthermore, many find the atmosphere refreshing in that it's free of the office politics typically associated with the industry. "The people are smart, professional and for the most part fun to be with," says one banker. This contact goes on to add, "The junior bankers tend to get along well. There isn't a strong sense of competition among them, but rather a sense of teamwork." Another source says one of the best things about the company is "working with smart people who want to get things done and who constantly push you to do better."

Training is another area where SSB gets high marks. One worker describes the firm's training program as the "longest program on The Street; very comprehensive." Says another: "The 10-week training program for associates is known to be the best on Wall Street." However, this same contact says once the official training ends, the variety of skills learned on the job depend largely on whose group you end up in. In addition to the 10-week program, seminars and training sessions are conducted on a fairly regular basis.

Out of flux?

Much of the sense of instability created by the Travelers/Citibank merger and Schroders acquisition seems to have dissipated. In fact, one respondent notes that now that Citi has integrated its major acquisitions, it's fun "watching our competitors try to merge to get what we have." Another insider says, "Over the past four years, our firm has integrated no less than six major acquisitions." Although this employee acknowledges that the continuous merger activity has caused its share of turnover, he believes "we are now reaping the benefits of the integration process — meaning the dust has long since settled and I expect to be working with my current colleagues for many years to come."

Fine tuning compensation

In the past, insiders have complained that Salomon Smith Barney was reactionary in setting compensation, waiting until competitors had announced salary and bonus increases before matching. That perception is now changing. "I think SSB has done a very good job of responding to professionals' concerns about salary and total compensation," says one source. "Furthermore, senior management has been very forthright in their discussions about the issues and the process." "SSB pays for performance," echoes another insider. "Those employees that are highly ranked are consistently paid well above other comparable firms." Additionally, insiders report that if you help bag prize recruits there's a little something extra in your paycheck. "There is a portion of our bonus that is rumored to be based on our involvement with recruiting," says one contact.

And now for the downside...

Predictably, long hours topped the list of drawbacks to working at SSB. Eighty-five-hour weeks are the norm, although working 130 hours a week is not unheard of. New grads should expect to work for at least a few hours most weekends. Bureaucracy was also a common complaint. One employee describes feeling frustrated by "bankers who can't seem to get past the old way of doing things and are afraid to shake things up." According to another, "The size of the firm or 'the factory system,' prevents opportunities on the junior level to move up ahead of schedule." One recent hire puts it succinctly, "The organization is so big, there can be lots of hoops to jump through."

Experiences with senior bankers seem to vary depending on the group you end up in. One insider gripes about "not feeling like senior bankers value you as part of the team" and a "general lack of interaction" with top bankers. "I do not have the kind of relationship with the senior bankers that I did in my previous job," another source says, "but the firm does provide a challenging environment that keeps me motivated each day." But another confides, "When working with decent officers and intelligent associates, this is a terrific job. Unfortunately, all officers are not decent and some associates are lacking." However, there is a strong consensus that Solly tends to provide young bankers with a lot of responsibility. As one associate puts it, "The quality of work falls on broad spectrum. For the most part, if you prove yourself capable, assignments will follow."

Putnam Investments

One Post Office Square
Boston, MA 02109
Phone: (617) 760-8900
Fax: (617) 348-8925
www.putnaminv.com

DEPARTMENTS

Corporate Development
Corporate Support
Investment Management
Investor Services
Mutual Funds

THE STATS

President and CEO: Lawrence J.
Lasser
Employer Type:
Subsidiary of Marsh & McLennan
2000 Revenues: $3.2 billion
2000 Operating Income: $1 billion
No. of Employees: 6,000 +
No. of Offices: 5

KEY COMPETITORS

Alliance Capital
Fidelity Investments
Franklin Resources

UPPERS

- Autonomous work environment
- Long-standing reputation

DOWNERS

- Decline in firm assets
- Stuffy, political

EMPLOYMENT CONTACT

Putnam Investments
Resume Processing Center
7 Shattuck Road, (C-36-H)
Andover, MA 01810
Fax: (617) 760-0613
Recruiter1@putnaminv.com

THE SCOOP

We've got the money

Putnam Investments is a global asset management firm that specializes in mutual funds and retirement plans. With $345 billion in assets under management (as of May 31, 2001), primarily in mutual funds, Boston-based Putnam is the fifth-largest mutual fund manager in the U.S. Putnam also has offices in Japan, Italy and Canada. The firm is a wholly owned subsidiary of professional services firm Marsh & McLennan, which acquired Putnam in 1970. In past years, Putnam has accounted for about half of Marsh & McLennan's profits.

Illustrious beginnings

Putnam began managing money in the 19th century when clipper ship captains hired trustees to handle their financial affairs while they were away at sea. One of those trustees, Justice Samuel Putnam, wrote the following credo for professional investment management: "Those with the responsibility to invest money for others should act with prudence, discretion, intelligence and regard for the safety of capital as well as for income." Known as the "prudent man rule," this ideology has since become the industry standard for responsible money management, giving Putnam Investments bragging rights for its creation. In 1937 Justice Putnam's great-great grandson founded Putnam with The George Putnam Fund of Boston. This balanced mutual fund, a flexible mix of stocks and bonds, marked the beginning of Putnam's strength in both those key areas of the investment business.

In 2000 Putnam racked up new sales of $14.6 billion through August, second only to Janus Capital over that time frame. Putnam's head, Larry Lasser, attributes some of the firm's success to the strength of its individual funds. "Most of our competitors have one fund that's doing almost all their business, 50 or 60 percent," he told *The Boston Globe*. Comparatively, Lasser said, 11 of Putnam's funds had brought in at least $1 billion each in new business in 2000.

That surge in performance did not hold up throughout the year, however. According to *Barron's*, the firm, which had $422 billion in assets in March 2000, saw that figure tumble to $343 billion by February 2001. As a result, the company laid off 256 employees, including five fund managers, in April 2001. The April reduction of approximately 4 percent of Putnam's staff came sharply on the heels of an earlier round in March 2001; that layoff affected 21 employees. On the upside, *The Boston*

Visit the Vault Finance Job Board — one of the best job boards on the
Internet exclusively for finance professionals. Go to www.vault.com.

V/\ULT   123

Globe reported that Putnam has not changed its plans to hire about 20 MBAs sometime in 2001. Despite the huge losses, the company elected to give Lasser a $33 million bonus for 2000.

The new home office

One of Putnam's most interesting endeavors in 2000 involved its expansion outside Massachusetts. The company started operations in Vermont and Maine with teleworkers to augment its client service staff in the Boston area. The firm also has approximately 450 employees in Massachusetts who work from home. The rising cost of office space and low unemployment rate forced the company to look elsewhere for employees. Employees who work at home are supplied with a high-speed phone line, computer and fax machine. The company intends to hire 400 teleworkers, but hasn't made plans so far to expand the program beyond support staff.

GETTING HIRED

Minimum qualifications

Putnam looks for people with strong academic backgrounds and utilizes a rigorous screening process. Industry experience in the form of prior jobs or internships is preferred. To find out about open positions, visit the firm's web site, www.putnaminv.com, which allows job seekers to search for positions by location (in Massachusetts) and function. Candidates can send resumes via fax, e-mail or regular mail to the firm. Putnam does not accept resumes e-mailed as attachments (they should be sent in text form).

Don't expect an easy jaunt into employment at Putnam. Says one insider, "It is very competitive, but if you make it through our screening process it can be a very rewarding place to work." Applicants are gained "mainly through referrals within the company" but are also recruited from "six or seven carefully selected schools."

"This doesn't mean that you can't get a job if you don't attend one of them, but it certainly becomes harder" explains one contact. An applicant can expect at least two interviews before being hired.

OUR SURVEY SAYS

Inside info

Putnam strives to provide employees with an autonomous, yet "team-based environment" in which to work. Contacts describe the approach as one that fosters collaboration, but affords analysts and managers the opportunity to make their own decisions. According to one investment analyst, "[Managers] let you do your job and they listen — if not agree" with your opinions. Additionally, insiders say the firm's breadth of financial instruments gives investment managers a wide assortment of products through which they can hone their investment skills. Like on Wall Street, analysts can expect to work long hours — 10-12 hours a day is not unusual. Although the firm has been described as "a bit political" and "stuffy," as an investment management firm, Putnam lacks the frenetic pace of investment banking.

Janus Capital

100 Filmore Street
#300
Denver, CO 80206
Phone: (303) 333-3863
Fax: (303) 321-2125
www.janus.com

DEPARTMENTS

Asset Management
Marketing
Research
Sales

THE STATS

Chairman, President and CEO:
Thomas Bailey
Employer Type:
Subsidiary of Stilwell Financial
No. of Employees: 2,470
No. of Offices: 6

KEY COMPETITORS

Fidelity Investments
Franklin Resources
Putnam Investments

UPPERS

- Comfortable offices
- Relaxed culture

DOWNERS

- History of scandal
- Layoffs due to poor market

EMPLOYMENT CONTACT

Human Resources
100 Filmore Street
#300
Denver, CO 80206

THE SCOOP

New beginnings

Janus Capital was founded in 1969 by Tom Bailey in Denver. The company started out in a one-room office in the Mile High City but has grown into one of the largest mutual funds in the world with $265 billion under assets and 2,470 employees in early 2001. Janus is a unit of Stilwell Financial, a Kansas City, Mo.-based holding company that controls several money managers.

Bailey named his firm after Janus, the two-faced Roman god of new beginnings. His choice is interesting in that the company represented a new beginning of sorts for him. After getting his MBA from the University of Western Ontario in the late 1960s, Bailey worked odd jobs near Aspen, Colo., to support his skiing habit. Bailey quickly realized his MBA was going to waste on the slopes and took a job in sales in a Denver-area finance firm. After a short stint there, Bailey founded Janus. Richard Goldstein, one of Bailey's early partners, fondly recalled the early days to *Fortune*: "Bailey had a pair of Gucci loafers, a Porsche and $2,000 to his name. Janus was basically bankrupt." The business took off in the early 1970s when the original Janus Fund converted to a no-load fund (i.e., no sales charge).

Here comes trouble

Janus began rocketing to a success that the firm — and Bailey — had trouble handling. In November 1976, the Securities and Exchange Commission claimed Janus' partners were getting more favorable prices on trades both for their personal accounts and for the firm, then giving false statements to the SEC on the matter. Bailey claimed innocence but settled, agreeing to a two-week suspension from the securities business. His partner, Goldstein, received a two-month suspension because he had benefited from the arrangement more. Goldstein left Janus as a result of the scandal.

That wasn't Janus' last brush with the law. In the early 1980s, soaring returns made the Janus Fund a popular spot for investors — too popular, as it turned out. The fund was oversubscribed, with more orders than legally authorized shares. Janus was forced to give refunds to thousands of investors and the company eventually settled a class-action lawsuit filed as a result of the confusion.

Visit the Vault Finance Job Board — one of the best job boards on the Internet exclusively for finance professionals. Go to www.vault.com.

V/\ULT   127

Cashing out

By 1984 Janus had grown so large that Bailey was looking to sell — both to cash out and to relieve the pressure of managing such a large and growing company. Janus sold 80 percent of the company for $18 million to Kansas City Southern Industries (KCSI), a railroad company that had some financial services holdings. Bailey retained approximately 17 percent of the company.

Though KCSI might seem like a strange fit for Janus, the pairing was favorable to the company. Janus management retained a great deal of autonomy, making the deal agreeable to Bailey and his partners.

Some insiders felt that Bailey enjoyed his newfound freedom too much. According to an article published by *Fortune* in January 2001, Bailey began handing off many of his management duties to underlings and spending more time away from the office. Furthermore, *Fortune* charged that Bailey stepped up a drug habit that he'd maintained for years. "He was into marijuana and cocaine," ex-partner Goldstein not-so-fondly recalled to *Fortune*. When Bailey did work, he was often out of bounds. Bailey allegedly asked a female job applicant inappropriate questions about her personal status and made an insensitive remark about Adolph Hitler during an employee orientation. (Bailey later apologized.) Janus declined to comment on the magazine's coverage of Bailey's nightlife.

The firm continued to grow in the early 1990s, mostly under the management of fund managers Jim Craig and Tom Marsico and chief operating officer Jack Thompson. According to *Fortune*, some executives, including Marsico, continued to feel that Bailey's leadership was lacking. Marsico reportedly urged Bailey in 1995 to instill a better work ethic at Janus, especially among younger managers. Bailey complied by arranging for monthly meetings of company shareholders. The briefings usually ended in bickering and became known as "viper meetings" at Janus. When Thompson, the long-time COO, resigned later in 1995, Bailey handed more control to the young managers, which only served to make the meetings worse. Marsico, after a 1997 attempt to take over as CEO was rejected, left the firm to strike out on his own.

Marsico's departure may have been a blessing of sorts. His call for discipline among the company's management was, by most accounts, at odds with a culture the company likes to call collegial. An unnamed industry source told *Mutual Funds* magazine that Marsico was "overbearing" and that his treatment of junior fund managers was stifling. The source further opined to *Mutual Funds* that Marsico leaving "freed these people up to think more freely; they became emboldened."

Company insiders (fund managers especially) now speak of daily roundtables where ideas are more easily expressed than under the viper-room format.

Spin room

In 1999 Janus' managers began actively seeking separation from the company's railroad parent. KCSI obliged by spinning Janus off along with KCSI's other financial units. Janus management lobbied hard against the plan and managed to delay it for several months. KSCI eventually prevailed and the company became part of Stilwell Financial in July 2000. (The company was named after Arthur Stilwell, Kansas City Southern's founder.)

The company has had its post-spinoff struggles. Janus funds boomed in 1998 and 1999 as the company aggressively snapped up technology stocks. When those stocks flopped in 2000, the company's funds slumped as well, and investors fled the firm. A month later Jim Craig, who had been elevated to chief investment officer, left Janus. His departure sparked speculation that the firm would start hemorrhaging managers. That speculation accelerated in early 2001 when Bailey and other top employees were allowed to sell their shares of Janus stock to Stilwell. Bailey sold half his stake in Janus for $600 million in January while several portfolio managers filed to sell shares in February 2001. Though the firm insisted the employees were merely trying to cash out some of their holdings, some investors were nervous. "I'm not sure you want to invest your money with a fund organization that is displaying such uncertainty," Ric Edelman, a financial adviser based in Fairfax, Va., told *The Wall Street Journal* in February 2001.

Stilwell has also been beset by rumors of an impending takeover. When the company's stock slid in December 2000 (shares were down 40 percent from the September high), some speculated that a large financial institution such as American International Group might buy Stilwell and, with it, Janus. In order to boost the flagging shares Janus cut 468 workers in February 2001, then added 45 more layoffs in April 2001. The cuts, approximately 16 percent of the company's workforce, were mainly in the operations division. The company said that a boon in new accounts opened over the Internet rather than over the phone made the positions expendable.

GETTING HIRED

Janus maintains an employment page on its web site (www.janus.com) where potential employees can search for positions and apply online. The firm "only recruits from the top schools," according to one insider. Expect "four interviews," including a meeting with human resources and "managers and supervisors" from your prospective department.

OUR SURVEY SAYS

Insiders at Janus describe a "casual" culture where they "do not feel intimidated talking to the heads of the company." The surroundings are comfortable as the firm provides "nothing but the best for office location and equipment." Despite the luxury, insiders say turnover is high. "But they do attempt to maintain the best talent," reports one source.

"They do attempt to maintain the best talent."

— *Janus Capital insider*

Visit the Vault Finance Job Board — one of the best job boards on the Internet exclusively for finance professionals. Go to www.vault.com.

VAULT   131

Lazard

30 Rockefeller Plaza
New York, NY 10020
Phone: (212) 632-2000
Fax: (212) 632-6060
www.lazard.com

DEPARTMENTS

Asset Management
Capital Markets
Corporate Advisory Services
Principal Investing

THE STATS

Chairman: Michel David-Weill
CEO: William Loomis
Employer Type: Private Company
No. of Offices: 22

KEY COMPETITORS

Allen & Company
Dresdner Kleinwort Wasserstein
Goldman Sachs
Morgan Stanley

UPPERS

- International prestige
- Top-notch pay

DOWNERS

- Killer hours
- Little support staff

EMPLOYMENT CONTACT

Corporate Advisory Services
Basil Bliss
Lazard
30 Rockefeller Plaza
New York, NY 10020

Capital Markets
L. Gregory Rice
Managing Director — Equities

F. Harlan Batrus
Managing Director — Bonds

John Rohs
Managing Director — Research

Michael Weinstock
Managing Director — High Yield

Lazard
30 Rockefeller Plaza
New York, NY 10020

Asset Management
Amy DeAngelo
Lazard Asset Management
30 Rockefeller Plaza
New York, NY 10020

THE SCOOP

A classic

Lazard might be called the classic advisory boutique, specializing primarily in providing mergers and acquisitions advice. The firm also has a small underwriting and trading practice and a respectable asset management arm with approximately $70 billion under management. Despite the firm's specialization, Lazard's profits and influence are hardly limited. Quite the opposite, in fact: Lazard is known for a superstar culture. Its elite, well-connected bankers are known as the trusted advisers to the princes of business. The firm touts itself as "the only private partnership in global investment banking."

French bred

The Lazard family's U.S. business ventures can be traced back to 1848, when the clan immigrated to the United States from France and opened a dry goods enterprise in New Orleans. In 1849 the family moved to San Francisco after a fire destroyed the New Orleans operation. The Lazards arrived just in time for the gold rush and the resulting economic boom caused by arriving prospectors. The company began banking operations in Paris in 1852, adding offices in London in 1877 and New York in 1880.

Much of the firm's growth is attributed to Alexandre Weill, a cousin of the Lazards who opened the New York office. The company has remained in the hands of the Weill family for more than 120 years. Michel David-Weill (the family hyphenated the family name to David-Weill in the 1920s to add aristocratic luster) took the helm of the company in 1977.

Mr. Congeniality

Michel David-Weill is rumored to be a tyrant. *Forbes* reported in September 2000 that he's been nicknamed the Sun King after Louis XIV, a French king whose rule lasted 72 years. *Forbes* went further, charging that David-Weill is disliked among Lazard's partners and minority shareholders. Lazard's monarch allegedly angered colleagues in a 1998 meeting by pointing at selected partners and declaring, "I don't need you. I don't need you. I don't need you — and I don't need you." David-Weill made more friends among minority shareholders in a meeting when he dismissed their claims and literally blew smoke in their faces. "He was unhelpful and incredibly arrogant," an institutional shareholder told *Forbes*. "He lit up a humongous cigar and puffed it in our faces for a half an hour. He really dismissed us as totally unimportant ... and we had been large shareholders in his companies for years." David-Weill concluded his goodwill tour at a firm event by failing to thank influential partners Felix Rohatyn and Antoine Bernheim for helping build Lazard.

M&A powerhouse

Lazard's most notable strength is in mergers and acquisitions advisory, and the firm's prominence is evident in the league tables. In 2000 the bank ranked ninth among advisors of completed worldwide M&A, according to Thomson Financial Securities Data, advising on 173 transactions worth $367.3 billion. Lazard's M&A engagements include Abott's $6.9 billion acquisition of BASF's pharmaceutical business, Enel SpA's $6.5 billion of Infostrada, Thames Water's $9.9 billion purchase by RWE and Halifax Group's $40 billion merger with Bank of Scotland. The firm counts Daewoo, Armstrong World Industries, Fruit of the Loom, Owens Corning and Vlasic as restructuring clients.

While M&A advisory is the firm's primary expertise, it isn't Lazard's only business. The firm has a relatively small equity underwriting practice, mainly because the firm does not have equity distribution channels like those of competitors such as Morgan Stanley or Goldman Sachs. The equity business is helped by a joint venture in France with French securities firm Credit Agricole Indosuez. The Lazard/Credit Agricole partnership was the top bookrunner for equity offerings in France for 2000. The firm co-led a $190 million IPO for Orient-Express Hotels in August 2000 and a $224 million IPO for W.P. Stewart in December 2000.

Coming together

The firm, traditionally known for its avoidance of publicity, has been increasingly in the news in recent years. In the late 1990s, Lazard garnered negative press that eventually resulted in changes at the firm. Michel David-Weill's son-in-law and expected successor, Edouard Stern, left the firm in mid-1997 after the two clashed repeatedly over issues such as Stern's role in the company and the company's direction. Felix Rohatyn, who gained fame by orchestrating New York City's recovery from bankruptcy in the 1970s, also left Lazard in 1997 to become the U.S. ambassador to France. (Rohatyn has since returned to Lazard as a senior advisor.) As a result, David-Weill was forced to reevaluate Lazard's management structure.

David-Weill's solution was to consolidate the firm's London, Paris and New York offices. Post-merger, the firm changed its name from Lazard Frères to Lazard. The firm is now managed by a seven-person committee headed by David-Weill and CEO William Loomis. The merger, announced in June 1999 and finalized in March 2000, met with some resistance from partners before its completion. *Investment Dealers' Digest* reported that two partners in the Paris office, Antoine Bernheim and David-Weill's son-in-law Stern (who retained an ownership stake despite leaving the firm in 1997) balked at the reorganization. Their specific objections were never publicized, but the concerns were a significant issue because under French law a partnership cannot be reorganized without unanimous partner approval. David-Weill acknowledged the need for cooperation, telling *BusinessWeek*, "[The reorganization] has to be done in a spirit of partnership and avoiding the feeling that any part of the firm would dominate any other part." He added, "What is clear is that in some respects the businesses have to be unified." David-Weill quashed speculation that the company would go public after the consolidation, saying a public Lazard would "tend to serve two masters: your [outside] owners and your clients."

Whatever his opinions are about going public, David-Weill's changes to Lazard's structure haven't pleased all the partners. Some who are unhappy with David-Weill's reign — and his reported $100 million annual take of Lazard's profits — want him to reconsider going public or at least make changes to the firm's ownership structure and compensation formula. Those partners were backed by Vincent Bollore, a French industrialist who quietly amassed a large block of shares in Rue Imperiale de Lyon. Incidentally (or perhaps not), Rue Imperiale de Lyon controls more than 17 percent of Lazard. Then, a few days into 2001, it was announced that Bollore sold his interest in Rue Imperiale to the French bank Credit Agricole. David-Weill now has the satisfaction of knowing that Bollore is no longer gunning for him, but the chunk of stock that Bollore controlled has merely shifted to a new owner. While the 17 percent stake isn't enough to wrest control of the firm from the David-Weill family, the battle with Bollore has been enough to force the Sun King to study Lazard's structure and make some changes.

The first changes were announced in November 2000. Eurafrance SA, one of the holding companies that indirectly owns a piece of Lazard, offered to purchase the remaining 43 percent of Azeo SA, another Lazard owner. At the same time, a similar consolidation plan was announced for two Italian finance companies that may eventually sever ties between Lazard and the two firms. Finally, David-Weill named American Bill Loomis as CEO. There was speculation that Loomis would succeed David-Weill when he eventually steps down, and David-Weill told *The Wall Street*

Visit the Vault Finance Job Board — one of the best job boards on the Internet exclusively for finance professionals. Go to www.vault.com.

VΛULT   135

Journal, "[It] would not be abnormal that he becomes my successor when I disappear." Although no date for his retirement was announced, Loomis has embraced the challenge of running the firm. He told the *Journal* that his focus would be getting Lazard involved in large deals. That may be tough considering the plethora of large investment banks recently created through mergers. "It will require us to be more Lazard," Loomis said. "We want to have local relevance with a more global view."

Despite these changes, many observers feel a new structure is needed if Lazard is to compete with bulge-bracket players. "The business model of the Lazard bank no longer seems to be in line with the evolution of the investment banking profession and market," Laurent Marie, an analyst at Credit Lyonnais Securities Europe, told the *Financial Times*. A buyout by an international partner — similar to the $1.4 billion purchase of Wasserstein Perella by Dresdner Bank in late 2000 — has reportedly piqued the interest of some Lazard partners. Deutsche Bank and Merrill Lynch have been named as possible suitors, but Lazard has flatly denied any interest in a deal.

Going places

The merger led some Lazard executives to seek greener pastures. Steven Rattner, David Tanner, Peter Ezersky and Joshua Steiner left to form Quadrangle Group, a private equity firm, in March 2000. Rattner's departure was expected. A well-respected M&A player, whom David-Weill called "a wonderful business getter and a deal guy" in *BusinessWeek*, Rattner stepped down as deputy CEO after the announcement of the combination and took the title of deputy chairman. The other departing bankers, while not as high-profile, still represented significant losses for the firm. *The Daily Deal* reported that Ezersky's client roster included Polygram and America Online and called Steiner, 34, a "young rising star." Thomas Dunn and Ira Handler, the heads of the asset management group's fixed-income department, departed the firm in January 2000 after a poor performance by the fixed-income group.

One of the president's men

The firm did manage to add some muscle to its business — Lazard added 18 managing directors in the U.S. since the June 1999 merger announcement. The firm also poached a 16-member restructuring group, led by managing directors Barry Ridings and Terry Savage, from Deutsche Bank in late June 1999. Pehr Gyllenhammar, chairman of U.K. insurer CGU and former CEO of Volvo, joined Lazard in December 1999. Gyllenhammar was the second-most important addition to Lazard that month; the firm also added Vernon Jordan, formerly a partner at Washington, D.C., law firm Akin, Gump, Strauss, Hauer & Feld. (Jordan stayed on at the law firm as "of counsel," a title usually reserved for senior, non-equity lawyers.) Jordan, a close friend of former President Bill Clinton, was previously scrutinized for his role in finding intern Monica Lewinsky a job after her time in the White House. "Life is about new occasions and new duties, and this is another hill to climb," Jordan told *Black Enterprise* regarding his new position.

In November 2000, Lazard hired John Kornblum, who had been U.S. ambassador to Germany, to improve the firm's standing in the Rhineland. Early in 2001, the company hired Harvey Golub as a senior adviser. Golub recently retired from the CEO post at American Express.

GETTING HIRED

Looking for talent

Lazard's investment banking division recruits at undergraduate colleges and business schools, but other departments, such as asset management, fill their open slots primarily through word of mouth, sources say. A recruiting schedule for investment banking and contact information for other departments are available at the firm's web site, www.lazard.com. Like other Wall Street firms, Lazard aims to hire full-time associates through its summer associate program. However, the firm also tries to find candidates through on-campus recruiting efforts. Lazard also maintains a summer analyst program for college juniors, but you'd better know someone. "Internships (not all, but many) are reserved for clients' kids or friends of the firm," reports one insider. The firm contests that statement, saying that summer hires are culled from on-campus recruiting. No matter how you get in, you'll still have to prove yourself. "Those [internships] that lead to hires are more (but not always) meritocratic." That contact advises candidates to consider divisions other than M&A to start. "Getting hired in a less attractive division can lead to promotions or transfers to better areas."

B-school insiders report mostly two-on-one interviews. One insider reports that "[the] firm recruits heavily from Columbia but also from business schools nationwide," including Wharton, Harvard and the University of Chicago. At some schools, after the initial screening round, "they call you later on that night and have

you come back and do some more interviews, and they will give you the offer then."
Other contacts report, "They fly people to New York."

Hey good lookin'

People with the inside scoop advise showing up for your interview at the firm with a "nice expensive suit." "The people they hire — there's no way to say this, really — but they tend to be attractive people," says one Lazard employee. "They're not looking for the nerdy number-cruncher that you get at some of the banks like Goldman. They want it so when there's a meeting, you can tell Lazard walked in the door."

A source says his interviewer asked "questions on my own experience and quantitative and acquired knowledge skills." Reports one recent hire: "One question they like to ask is, 'What was the hardest thing you did — what was the most complicated deal?' If you brought up an M&A deal, then from talking to you about that deal, they can tell where you are." Says that contact: "I strongly stress to anyone who wants to work there as an associate — you've got to be a banker. They expect you to walk in the first day and be ready. My first day, my phone rang, and they said you're late. I said, 'I'm late? I just walked in the door.' It was a secretary of one of the senior people, and she tells me, 'There's a meeting up on 62 and you've got to get up there.' I get up there and there's the CEO and he's talking about what type of company he wants to acquire. I start taking notes. That evening and the rest of the night I cranked out merger models."

OUR SURVEY SAYS

You have no life

To say Lazard "demands total commitment" is an understatement. "Working hours are just crazy," says one insider, who sometimes wishes for "more time for family, friends and non-professional areas of interest." Says another: "You will definitely work over 100 hours during an average workweek." Another insider puts the figure at "110 to 130" hours weekly. One employee criticizes the "superhuman expectations" at the firm. "You can't work any harder than they work," a former Lazard banker attests. "There were people carried out by ambulance — they had collapsed from exhaustion." The firm says these reports are exaggerated.

How bad it is for Lazard bankers depends almost entirely on where one is on the totem pole, according to sources. Contacts concur that "analysts have no life." Explains one insider: "The attitude is that the analysts are not bankers. It's 'I want to work you for two years and then spit you out, and you're lucky to be here.'" That source continues: "The analysts do not exercise, they do not leave, they are there all the time." "The analysts for the most part are extremely bitter," says one associate. "I think they're going to do better in the future, because they're starting to realize that it's not good," says that contact. Despite Lazard's hard-work reputation, the firm reports that in 2000, 10 out of 24 second- and third-year analysts stayed on at the firm after the completion of the analyst program.

Associates don't have it much better, insiders say, but "they know what they're getting into" and morale is pretty high. "The first three years as an associate — you're throwing those years away," says one banker. "You're just trying to survive." Why do associates put up with the intense work? For the promotion to VP that happens in three or four years. "If you can survive the four years, you're looking at a pretty good lifestyle," explains one insider. "A VP at Lazard is very different from a VP at other places. At other places, the VP gets dragged down to do associate work and still gets dragged into the office on weekends. A VP at Lazard — they really know their shit, and if they want to, which pretty much everyone wants to, they refuse to do associate-level work. They want to be working on getting clients and things like that." During the week, insiders report, VPs are there "until 9:00 — even MDs put in long hours at Lazard"; on the weekends "they'll be at the Hamptons with a fax machine."

On the plus side, some insiders report having meaningful work at least some of the time. "I get to do interesting things which Lazard is comfortable doing, but there tends to be resistance to new ideas," says one source. "I also do more mundane work, being low enough on the totem pole." That source continues, "I personally have gotten a lot of respect and recognition for my intelligence in conversation and to some extent responsibility." The firm was one of the last to go business casual, but some worry that privilege might be pulled. "Now that the dot-coms have crashed and burned we don't expect [business casual] to last, but it's been nice," says one source, who adds "we are waiting for the memo to go back to suits and ties."

I've never seen so much decadence

"Lazard is like Wall Street was in the early 1980s," says one former insider. "Cigar smoke is thick on the floor by 10 in the morning — they're all smoking. They play polo. They've got their polo gear in the office. I've never seen so much decadence in a firm. They all had huge houses in the Hamptons, and they didn't mind talking

Visit the Vault Finance Job Board — one of the best job boards on the Internet exclusively for finance professionals. Go to www.vault.com.

VAULT   139

about it — 'Oh, the roof in my Hamptons house is leaking, and now I can only sell it for $3 million.'"

The amazing luxury that the Lazard lifestyle affords is the reason the firm's bankers endure the almost unconscionable hours. "Bankers at Lazard are usually paid 25 to 50 percent more than the market salary [for] comparable positions at other banks," says an analyst. "They basically tell you that their goal is to be the highest-paying firm, and they're looking to start private equity stuff up in order to expand what they can do as far as compensation," reports another banker. "This is serious stuff."

Insiders also agree that Lazard is at the top of the list when it comes to prestige. "It's an amazing place," says one source. "They really do have great relationships with the CEOs of major companies." Says another: "We're the cutting edge of management and finance theory. The culture is very focused on production, merit and profits." Says a former banker: "They're not spinning their wheels, working their hours. They really put some time and thought into the work they're doing."

Not great diversity

One employee maintains that the firm is "relatively progressive, with active recruitment of women and minorities," but notes that "there are very few women investment bankers at Lazard, not because we do not hire them, but because many of them leave due to the inhumane working environment." Says one contact: "It's a lot more of the old-boy WASPy network rather than the Jewish network at other banks." One employee criticizes Lazard's "limited resources," noting that the firm's lack of consolidated databases forces employees to "fish for information using highly unorthodox methods, sometimes making life miserable. If you were working at a bulge-bracket firm, most of the information would be a telephone call or a click of the mouse away."

"The attitude is that
the analysts are not
bankers. It's 'I want
to work you for two
years and then spit you
out, and you're lucky
to be here.'"

— *Lazard insider*

Visit the Vault Finance Job Board — one of the best job boards on the
Internet exclusively for finance professionals. Go to www.vault.com.

V／\ULT   141

Lehman Brothers

3 World Financial Center
New York, NY 10285
Phone: (212) 526-7000
Fax: (212) 526-3738
www.lehman.com

DEPARTMENTS

Corporate Advisory
Equities
Fixed Income
Global Economics
Investment Banking
Operations and Corporate Services
Private Client Services
Private Equity
Risk Management

THE STATS

Chairman and CEO:
Richard S. Fuld, Jr.
Employer Type: Public Company
Stock Symbol: LEH (NYSE)
2000 Revenue: $26.4 billion
2000 Net Income: $1.8 billion
No. of Employees: 11,300
No. of Offices: 67

KEY COMPETITORS

Goldman Sachs
Merrill Lynch
Morgan Stanley

UPPERS

- High-quality deals
- Meritocratic culture

DOWNERS

- Frat-like atmosphere in some divisions
- Long hours

EMPLOYMENT CONTACT

**Investment Banking —
Analyst Recruiting**
Candace Darling

**Investment Banking —
Associate Recruiting**
Bess Frank

3 World Financial Center
24th Floor
New York, NY 10285

**Sales, Trading & Research —
Analyst Recruiting**
Joycelyn Arencibia

**Sales, Trading & Research —
Associate Recruiting**
Stephanie Amanatides

3 World Financial Center
8th Floor
New York, NY 10285

**Private Client Services —
Associate Recruiting**
Valerie Demartino

1 World Financial Center
28th Floor
New York, NY 10281

THE SCOOP

Southern roots

Lehman Brothers was founded in 1850 in Montgomery, Ala., by brothers Henry, Emmanuel and Mayer Lehman. The enterprise began as a commodities brokerage and trading firm and opened a New York office in 1858. In 1887 Lehman acquired a seat on the New York Stock Exchange and underwrote its first stock offering two years later. Expanding over the last 151 years, the company is currently a full-service global investment bank providing a wide range of services, including fixed-income and equities sales, trading and research, M&A advisory, public finance, and private client services. Lehman's investment banking group serves 11 industry segments: chemicals, communications/media, consumer/retailing, financial institutions, financial sponsors, health care, industrial, natural resources, power, real estate and technology.

An auspicious start

American Express purchased Lehman in 1984 as part of its strategy to become a full-service institution covering all consumer and business financial needs. But Amex changed its tune 10 years later, deciding to refocus on core businesses. Amex's new strategy resulted in a spin-off that once again created an independent Lehman Brothers.

The newly independent Lehman Brothers stumbled out of the starting gate, implementing considerable layoffs and cost cuts to survive. By some estimates, within the first two years after the spin-off Lehman cut both expenses and staff by approximately 20 percent. The firm managed to rebound and made significant strides in high-margin businesses such as equity and high-yield underwriting and M&A advisory.

Lehman Brothers has regained its footing has been one of the most profitable investment banks in recent years. While competitors such as Merrill Lynch were announcing staff cuts in mid-1998, Lehman — which has a reputation for lean staffing — reported no layoffs. Despite posting lower first quarter profits in 2001, Lehman had managed to avoid layoffs even as a wave of workforce reductions spread throughout the investment-banking industry in late 2000 and early 2001. In fact, the firm claims to have added 600 people over the first three months of 2001 after increasing its staff by 27 percent in 2000.

Lehman was able to avoid job cuts by posting big-time profits. The firm's net income for fiscal year 2000 was approximately $1.8 billion, up from $1.1 million in 1999. That steady performance allowed Lehman Brothers to capture the title of "Most

Profitable Banking Company" from *U.S. Banker*. Lehman was also honored by *BusinessWeek*, which rated it No. 11 in its 50 Best Companies in the S&P 500 index.

In Fidelity?

In June 1999, Lehman Brothers announced an alliance with Fidelity Investments, the Boston-based asset management and mutual fund firm, to provide Fidelity customers access to Lehman-led debt and equity offerings as well as Lehman's research products. As a result of the partnership, Lehman could access a larger distribution network for public offerings and presumably attract more deals from companies eager to issue securities.

At the time of its announcement, the partnership yielded speculation that the two firms would merge. The rumors disappeared shortly after the announcement, only to resurface a year later. *The Wall Street Journal*, which first resurrected the rumors in June 2000, conceded that a merger was "a long shot" and said formalization of the Lehman/Fidelity distribution alliance was more likely. A Fidelity spokesman quashed the gossip, telling *The New York Times*, "We have no such plan[s] and there is nothing under discussion."

All around Lehman

In July 2000, Lehman boosted its private client business, acquiring SG Cowen's high-net-worth business. According to *The Wall Street Journal*, the deal was worth $50 million, much of which was money set aside for retention bonuses for the 140 SG Cowen brokers joining the Lehman team. Including the SG Cowen purchase, Lehman's brokerage force grew to approximately 450 brokers during 2000.

Big-league clients

Lehman has a client list befitting its status as a top-tier investment bank. The firm led a $1.5 billion convertible and common stock offering for Cendant, a $2.3 billion convertible securities offering for Tecnost/Telecom Italia and a $617 million IPO for Tele1 Europe Holding. Lead-managed debt offerings included a $5.75 billion offering for Wal-Mart, named "U.S. Dollar Bond Deal of the Year" and "U.S. Investment-Grade Corporate Bond Deal of the Year" by *International Financing Review*. The firm also managed a $2.8 billion offering for Ford Motor, a $2.3 billion offering for Pepsi Bottling Group and a $1.25 billion offering for Liberty Media Group. M&A transactions of note include the MediaOne/AT&T merger. (Lehman represented MediaOne in the $63.1 billion merger, completed in June 2000.) The bank also advised US West on its $48.5 billion pairing with Qwest Communications.

GETTING HIRED

Good impressions count

First impressions are key at Lehman. After meeting students at colleges and business schools, the firm's recruiters will hone in on top candidates. Says one recent MBA hire: "I was targeted and was pursued hard." In fact, the firm prefers to have identified its targets by the time campus interviewing starts. Lehman focuses on 10 graduate business schools (Chicago, Columbia, Wharton, Tuck, Fuqua, Stern, UCLA, Kellogg, Harvard and MIT) for recruiting MBAs. For analysts, Lehman conducts on-campus interviews at top-20 schools but considers candidates from other schools. A Lehman analyst from a top-20 school reports, "We do hire a lot of write-ins."

Playing the game

How does Lehman select its candidates? In part, through on-campus get-to-know-you functions. For example, the firm's sales and trading recruiters host a "Trading Game" on campus, where they simulate three to four "pits" similar to those on the Chicago Futures exchanges. The "game" (read: tryout) lasts four to five hours. The trading game allows Lehman to observe students in action so it can identify strong candidates. Lehman also hosts cocktail parties to identify targets. Despite the ulterior motives, the firm tries to keep the events as informal and social as possible, insiders say: "The focus is on personalities." A banker who was hired to fill a vacant position in the firm's London office had interviews with three managers. Of course, this contact says, the process was much faster than for new graduates.

Like the summer programs at most bulge-bracket firms, Lehman's summer associate programs act as a feeder system for full-time hires. Summer associates receive their offers within two weeks of the end of the program. Most associates report an excellent recruitment process. Says one: "There was no bullshit in the recruiting process. They were honest with us." Interested candidates should visit the firm's web site, www.lehman.com, which is chock full of detailed recruiting information, including a list of contacts for several departments.

Visit the Vault Finance Job Board — one of the best job boards on the Internet exclusively for finance professionals. Go to www.vault.com.

VAULT   145

Analysts and associates begin their careers at Lehman with a five-week training program in New York. Associates then move on to three one-month rotations in various departments. Regional associates may elect to spend a year in New York before being assigned to a permanent group in their home office, while analysts are immediately placed in a group.

OUR SURVEY SAYS

Life at Lehman

Lehman bankers report working long hours. However, the opportunity to work on top-notch deals seems to ease some of the pain. "I work more than my friends at other firms, as do most of the people in my group, but it is because the group is aggressively gaining market share faster than we are adding people," a contact tells us. "We are constantly competing for the best assignments in the industry," boasts one banker. "I am very proud of both the number and the quality of the deals I have had an opportunity to work on." Additionally, sources describe Lehman as being comprised of "highly motivated colleagues" who "feel like partners in the franchise." If there is a downside to life at Lehman, employees say it could be the perception that the firm, which has been climbing the rungs of the league tables in last few years, is still not on par with Goldman Sachs and Morgan Stanley.

Effort rewarded

Perhaps the most attractive aspect of working for Lehman, employees say, is that "the firm rewards effort. This place is as close to a meritocracy as it gets." An associate calls the company's culture "fluid," commenting that "managers tend to move around the firm." "I've been given more responsibility than I'd ever imagined," says one associate in trading. Another associate in Lehman's fixed-income group calls the firm "an aggressive firm that will let you take risk, if you can justify it." According to one capital markets associate, "[Lehman gives] lots of responsibility early. They push employees to progress quickly." Another associate in that area boasts, "The opportunity is fantastic. The firm has focused on a number of growth opportunities and is aggressive about getting people involved." That doesn't mean analysts are free of cumbersome tasks. One I-banking analyst warns, "It's easy to get pigeonholed into doing a lot of pitches."

Insiders generally report a "young culture" that is "very entrepreneurial." Reports one insider, "The firm is very open to people moving around departments where it makes sense; they don't really mess around — if something makes sense, they just do it." One Lehman analyst complains the firm is a little behind the bulge bracket in terms of pay, though the bank did come through with raises in response to recent competitor increases. First-year analysts received 40 percent raises, second-years 45 percent and third-years 54 percent. Lehman also offers a leveraged investment account for all employees.

Scrappy, friendly survivors

Lehman's culture is one of "survivors and fighters — people have been through a lot together, and they are very loyal to each other," according to one recent hire. Employees speak enthusiastically about Lehman's "social" corporate offices, where "most employees are extremely nice and friendly and very down-to-earth, unlike at some other places on the Street." As one new hire says, "[Lehman's] culture is open," largely because of the "affable" upper management who "make an effort to be readily approachable." "Culture very much depends on which business and which desk, but overall, it is not at all stuffy," says one associate in trading. "There are fairly honest professional people."

"Lehman has more of a laid-back collegial environment than other firms that I've worked at. I've seen all the other firms, and also over the summer I visited a bunch of firms," says one associate who summered at Lehman. "It's not laid-back in that people are easygoing, it just doesn't have the pretension that you might have at other places," continues that associate. "People work hard, but people also are welcoming, no one's putting on airs, that's the feeling that I got. I've been all around the firm, and I never had a situation where someone blew me off or wasn't interested in talking." Says one analyst in the firm's research department: "It's warm and less intense than your typical Wall Street firm." Some insiders believe the firm's culture and growth story are selling points to employees at competitor firms. Explains one I-banking analyst, "We're getting more people from top-tier firms like Morgan Stanley and Goldman interested in us."

Frat brothers

Although Lehman may be laid-back in the sense of not being stuffy or aristocratic, that doesn't mean the temperature doesn't rise at the firm. One ex-employee in New York notes, "There's a lot more yelling at Lehman Brothers than at my current firm."

Visit the Vault Finance Job Board — one of the best job boards on the Internet exclusively for finance professionals. Go to www.vault.com.

VAULT 147

Insiders say that Lehman, like most major investment banks, has a "macho culture" and "many arrogant attitudes." According to one: "Antics are somewhat unprofessional. Many employees have something of a locker-room, fraternity culture." Reports another: "It's meritocratic but can be easily abused by overly aggressive people." Another associate says, "This is definitely a culture of a work ethic — they put in the hours." Still, insiders generally note the firm has been receptive to recent changes in the industry. In addition to salary and expense improvements, one insider notes that "management is showing more of an interest in people having well-rounded lives."

"This place is as
close to a meritocracy
as it gets."

— *Lehman Brothers insider*

Visit the Vault Finance Job Board — one of the best job boards on the
Internet exclusively for finance professionals. Go to www.vault.com.

VAULT   149

Vanguard Group

100 Vanguard Boulevard
Malvern, PA 19355
Phone: (610) 669-1000
Fax: (610) 669-6605
www.vanguard.com

DEPARTMENTS

Asset Management
Research
Sales
Trading

THE STATS

Chairman and CEO: John J. Brennan
Employer Type: Private
No. of Offices: 7
No. of Employees: 11,000

KEY COMPETITORS

Charles Schwab
Fidelity Investments
Merrill Lynch

UPPERS

- Onsite store, cleaners, cafeteria
  and health club
- Internal training program

DOWNERS

- Work sometimes not challenging
- Business attire required most days

EMPLOYMENT CONTACT

Kathleen C. Gubanich
Vanguard Group
100 Vanguard Boulevard
Malvern, PA 19355

THE SCOOP

Not like the others

As the manager of the second-largest group of mutual funds in America, Vanguard Group would have made penny-pinching Benjamin Franklin proud. Holding to the maxim that money saved is just as good as money earned, Vanguard religiously sticks to a no-frills business model in which it spends virtually no money on marketing. Instead, the firm chooses to pass along savings to its investors. This is no corporate philosophy mumbo jumbo — Vanguard is unlike any other mutual fund firm. It spends about $8 million annually on advertising, which, as *Forbes* pointed out, is half the amount that General Mills spent on advertising to launch Sunrise cereal in 1999. U.S. mutual funds spend on average 1.24 percent of their assets annually; Vanguard — which manages more than $560 billion in mutual fund assets — spends 0.27 percent.

Vanguard's cost cutting can be attributed in part to a unique ownership structure. Unlike all other mutual fund companies, which — whether public or private — have shareholders who look to earn money that is not distributed to those invested in the funds, Vanguard is run like a mutual insurance company. Under this structure, the funds themselves (and their investors) own the parent company. Investors apparently are sold on Vanguard's model. The firm is the fastest-growing mutual fund company, and analysts are predicting that it will soon surpass industry leader Fidelity Investments. Vanguard has been praised as a top place to work by *Fortune* (the company made its "Best Places to Work" list) and *Computerworld* (Vanguard was No. 6 on its list of 100 Best Places to Work in IT).

Not always on top

Vanguard was founded by John C. Bogle in 1974 after Bogle was fired as CEO of Wellington Management. Bogle had written a senior thesis at Princeton that described his theory that mutual funds should be run with low overhead and no sales commission. Basically, Bogle's thesis described Vanguard, or at least the fundamentals of the firm — an investor-owned family of funds with low expenses. Vanguard is the first (and still the only) investor-owned fund company.

The index funds

In 1976 Vanguard launched the first index fund open to individual investors, a fund designed to mimic the Standard & Poor's 500. The fund was originally known as the

Visit the Vault Finance Job Board — one of the best job boards on the Internet exclusively for finance professionals. Go to www.vault.com.

VAULT   151

First Index Trust but is now known as the Vanguard 500 Index Fund. Unlike other funds that are based on idea and research-heavy management, index funds require no stock-picking prowess from human managers. As with the firm itself, the index funds did not immediately take off. Now, however, these funds are the keys to Vanguard's rapid growth. In 1998 66 percent of the new money invested in Vanguard's stock funds went into index funds — 19 percent went into the 500 fund. The Vanguard 500 Index fund surpassed Fidelity's massive Magellan fund as the single largest fund in 2000.

Not just the funds

Working off the success of its mutual funds, Vanguard is currently expanding into new businesses. In the past couple of years, the firm has gone on a hiring spree of brokers, financial planners, client service representatives and IT personnel, with the goal of bulking up its advisory services, variable annuity business and its online services. And in 1998, the firm quietly launched an online trading service. As one firm official told the *Philadelphia Inquirer*, "We're not thinking of ourselves just as a provider of a lineup of mutual funds, but as a focal point for financial services for our clients." Industry analysts, however, are skeptical of Vanguard's ability to push its way into brokerage and other service businesses, as they require a sales culture anathema to the firm's Spartan sensibility.

In 2000 the firm looked to expand on its offerings by announcing the creation of VIPERs — Vanguard's brand name for its version of exchange-traded index funds (ETFs). Like index mutual funds, ETFs are based on an index, but trade on a stock exchange, therefore causing daily fluctuations in price. Vanguard ran into a snag when it tried to introduce VIPERs. Standard & Poor's, which receives a license fee from Vanguard for the Vanguard 500 fund (because it is based on the S&P 500 Index), claimed that extending a license to Vanguard would infringe on other contracts. Vanguard replied that the VIPER is essentially the same product as the fund, just sold in a different way. S&P disagreed and filed a lawsuit. In December 2000, the SEC held a hearing and sided with Vanguard, clearing the way for the VIPERs. But S&P's parent, The McGraw-Hill Companies, filed suit, and a federal judge granted a permanent injunction against Vanguard in April 2001. Vanguard says it will appeal this ruling, but did manage to introduce a VIPER product in May 2001 and has plans for more starting in late summer 2001.

GETTING HIRED

The basics

Vanguard lists job openings at its web site, www.vanguard.com, for those who wish to become Vanguard crew members. The firm allows applicants to submit resumes through an online form, as well as through the typical means. Vanguard also posts its recruiting schedule at its web site. Insiders say the firm recruits from a variety of schools in the Northeast and South, "including Penn State, the University of Pennsylvania, Temple, UNC-Charlotte, Duke, Georgia Tech, NC State, Vanderbilt and others."

One source says: "We're growing at such an incredible pace, so there are always openings," reports one insider. One contact reports having "one phone interview and one on-site visit that consisted of three or four more in-person interviews." Others report interviewing with an HR representative, a department manager and a principal. Expect "two major categories of questions: behavioral-based and technical."

OUR SURVEY SAYS

Frugal, but respectful

"Upper-level management and crew are always on a first-name basis with other crew members," one source tells us. "Generally," says another insider, "superiors treat you with respect as long as you share your opinions and views." Perks include on-site cafeterias, health clubs and stores with dry cleaning and other services. And the firm's "university" offers training in management and other areas. However, the dress code (the firm is business casual only on Friday) does promote a certain level of formality among employees. In keeping with its philosophy of providing low-cost investment vehicles, insiders say Vanguard's offices are no-frills. They are "comfortable, but not extravagant," according to one source.

Sources say that the company is flexible about work hours (normal office hours are 8:30 to 5:00), enabling some employees to come to work earlier (and thereby leave earlier) or work longer hours and have a four-day workweek. But don't be fooled into believing that Vanguard employees have it easier than those at other investment firms. Says one Vanguard employee: "I am paid for a 37.5-hour week, but routinely

Visit the Vault Finance Job Board — one of the best job boards on the Internet exclusively for finance professionals. Go to www.vault.com.

VAULT 153

work 45 to 50 hours and take work home." The work assignments can also leave something to be desired. One of the above-quoted sources describes his job as "very easy" and "only occasionally requiring deep thought." The firm counters that its retention rate is three times the industry average.

"I am paid for a 37.5-hour work week, but routinely work 45 to 50 hours and take work home."

— *Vanguard Group insider*

Visit the Vault Finance Job Board — one of the best job boards on the Internet exclusively for finance professionals. Go to www.vault.com.

VAULT   155

Pequot Capital Management

500 Nyala Farm Road
Westport, CT 06880
Phone: (203) 429-2200
www.pequotcap.com

DEPARTMENTS

Asset Management
Research
Sales
Trading

THE STATS

Chairman and CEO: Arthur Samberg
Employer Type: Private Company
No. of Employees: 200
No. of Offices: 5

KEY COMPETITORS

Putnam Investments
T. Rowe Price
Vanguard Group

UPPERS

- Potential to shine
- Relaxed culture

DOWNERS

- Killer travel requirements
- Nearly impossible to break in as a junior employee

EMPLOYMENT CONTACT

Human Resources
500 Nyala Farm Road
Westport, CT 06880
HR@pequotcap.com

THE SCOOP

Hedging from the bottom up

Founded in 1986 as a unit of another asset management company, Pequot Capital Management has become one of the largest hedge funds in the world. Pequot follows a rather unusual investment strategy. Most hedge funds — especially the largest — invest in a broad range of vehicles ranging from equities to currency and interest rate hedges. (Indeed, it is currency and interest rate investment that resulted in the downfall of many hedge funds in the late 1990s.) But Pequot (pronounced PEA-kwat) sticks mainly to equity investments ranging from venture capital and private equity to positions in mid- to large-cap public companies. Pequot, based in Westport, Conn., manages approximately $10 billion in assets. The company has 23 funds and over 200 employees.

The original Pequot Fund was a unit of Dawson-Henry Capital Management, a money manager in Southport, Conn. Pequot was the brainchild of Arthur Samberg, a Columbia MBA and current chairman and CEO at Pequot. According to *The Wall Street Journal*, Pequot, which was started with $3.5 million, grew so quickly that the firm was renamed Dawson-Samberg Capital Management in 1989. The renamed firm made a killing in the tech boom of the late 1990s. Pequot funds were early investors in America Online in 1994 and secured a chunk of Yahoo! when the company went public in 1996.

Pequot schism

Samberg and Dawson went their separate ways in January 1999 when Pequot was spun off as a separate company with Samberg as the head. While the company claimed the split was amicable, some say a division over the risks Pequot was taking was a factor. *Alternative Investment News* claimed that Dawson felt the company's investments were spread too thin and that Pequot was too tech-heavy, while Samberg pushed for more risk-taking. Dawson soon split from Samberg altogether, leaving to run Dawson-Giammalva Capital Management.

Rumors of a similar divide within Pequot surfaced in early 2001. This time Samberg was afraid the company was too big while Daniel Benton, Pequot's president, pushed the firm to focus on technology companies both in the public and private marketplace.

Visit the Vault Finance Job Board — one of the best job boards on the Internet exclusively for finance professionals. Go to www.vault.com.

VAULT   157

Despite the reported conflict in investment styles Pequot continues to grow. The firm opened offices in London and Taiwan in March 2001. That same month it closed a $725 venture capital fund dedicated to expansion-stage companies.

GETTING HIRED

With only 200 employees, Pequot is a very selective employer. The firm does accept resumes at its Westport, Conn., Headquarters and maintains an e-mail account for employment questions (HR@pequotcap.com). But you'd better be on top of your game if you want to get in, and fresh graduates are all but excluded from consideration. The firm "rarely takes candidates out of school," according to one source. "[Pequot] prefer[s] to hire from the sell side (banking or research) with one to three years of experience." Have a good story ready. "Candidates generally need to show some compelling case for why they are specifically interested in the buy side — too many are just looking for better pay and an escape from the crappy conditions of the sell side."

OUR SURVEY SAYS

Flat structure

Insiders say the culture at Pequot is "extremely informal. You can dress and act as you please, as long as you are productive." That source continues, "We live well and enjoy many diversions to help with the inevitable stressful days when the market moves against us." Additionally, the firm provides "great ability to make an impact, [the] ability to be paid for performance, intelligent and likeable colleagues, [and] very little annoying bureaucracy or hierarchy. I could not imagine a better work environment."

Insiders boast of the firm's ability to retain its employees. "Extremely competitive compensation means that people seldom leave voluntarily. However, there is somewhat of an up-or-out mentality. Employees either need to show they can scale to the next level or they risk being asked to leave."

Meet your mentor

One area where Pequot lags is training. "We're not really set up for formal training, which is why we generally prefer not to hire straight out of school." However, they hardly throw new hires into the deep end. "We do set up junior employees with mentors who help them learn the process of modeling, talking to companies and doing basic research," says a source. The support staff, such as it is, is generally praised. "Secretaries are well paid and highly professional. We do not have elaborate support structures, however, because we don't tend to produce much in terms of written material."

Another potential Pequot drawback is the travel schedule. "I am on the road about a week a month," says one mid-level employee. "More junior employees travel about twice that much to visit companies in which we are potential investors."

Finally, insiders say diversity is not an issue. "For a small firm, I think we have worked hard to create a welcoming environment. We do mandatory training for all employees on gender and racial bias issues."

Visit the Vault Finance Job Board — one of the best job boards on the
Internet exclusively for finance professionals. Go to www.vault.com.

VAULT   159

T. Rowe Price

100 East Pratt Street
Baltimore, MD 21202
Phone: (410) 345-2000
Fax: (410) 345-2394
www.troweprice.com

DEPARTMENTS

Brokerage
College Funding
Mutual Funds
Private Account Management
Retirement Plans

THE STATS

Chairman and President:
George A. Roche
Employer Type: Public Company
Ticker Symbol: TROW (Nasdaq)
2000 Revenue: $1.2 billion
2000 Net Income: $269 million
No. of Employees: 4,000
No. of Offices: 21

KEY COMPETITORS

Fidelity Investments
Janus Capital
Vanguard Group

EMPLOYMENT CONTACT

staffing@troweprice.com

THE SCOOP

Investing pioneer

Thomas Rowe Price, Jr., began his investment firm in 1937 after a dozen years at Mackubin Goodrich & Co., a Baltimore-based brokerage firm now known as Legg Mason. Price didn't particularly enjoy selling stocks, but discovered he had a knack for picking them. Price had a theory that companies with new products, services or technology could enjoy a sustained growth curve, and that investing in these companies during this growth stage would prove profitable. The goal was to buy stocks in such firms and hold them for the long term — an idea practically unheard of in post-Depression America. Through his company, Price promoted his philosophy by providing advice to investors on picking stocks. In 1950 he introduced his first mutual fund, the T. Rowe Price Growth Stock Fund.

Although Price's reputation as a stock-picker is impeccable, his reputation as a manager is less impressive. Price's own son reportedly called him "a bear to work with" and colleagues, including company co-founder Thomas Kidd, said he was aloof. Yet through his intuitive understanding of the market, along with a grueling work schedule, Price built his company into one of the leading investment management firms. In 1966, perhaps tired from the grind of nearly 30 years, Price sold his stake in the firm for a relatively small sum (published reports say he received less than $800,000) with the condition that control of the company remain with previously agreed upon successors. T. Rowe Price went public in 1986 and now has $148.7 billion in assets under management (as of March 31, 2001).

Higher highs, lower lows

Through the mid-1990s, the firm instituted an investment strategy that many analysts felt was more conservative than even Price's personal philosophy. For example, Price's funds never got swept up in the tech and Internet mania of the late 1990s. Though the firm had a healthy dose of tech stocks in its funds, the company's risk-averse style precluded it from getting on board the New Economy bandwagon. That strategy led to short-term results that were slightly below the market. (The T. Rowe Price Science and Technology fund, for example, grew 101 percent in 1999. While this growth was impressive, it was still lower than the 134.8 percent average for all tech funds in the same time period.) Management maintained that its focus on value was much more prudent and echoed what many investment gurus had been saying for quite some time: that tech and Internet stocks had been highly overvalued. "We've got to stick to our principles, even though those principles may hurt us in the short term," vice chairman James Riepe told *The Wall Street Journal* in March 2000. Those principles have been proven true, as Price's funds haven't experienced a downturn as dramatic as those who were more tech-heavy, such as Janus Capital.

There was a downside for T. Rowe. The firm experienced a net outflow of $2.5 billion from its funds in 2000, one of the largest redemption rates in the industry for 2000. The bulk of the outflow was from two sources. California Savings Plan Plus dropped three of the four T. Rowe Price funds it had in its list of investment choices, while another large Price client completed a merger and consolidated its pension funds to a different provider.

The irony of the market downturn is that while it increased the appeal of T. Rowe's investment strategy, the company's financial results suffered after the correction. When earnings reports came out in January 2001, T. Rowe was among the companies bearing bad news; the firm announced that its net income for the fourth quarter was $55.5 million, down from $70.1 million in the prior-year period. The slump carried over into early 2001 as the company's net income fell from $75 million in first quarter 2000 to $49.3 million for 2001. Despite the profit shortfall, the firm has said officially it doesn't expect to have significant job cuts. However, Chairman George Roche indicated in April 2001 that the company is looking to cut costs, inspiring Merrill Lynch analysts to predict impending layoffs. Again, the firm downplayed the prospect of layoffs, telling the *Baltimore Business Journal* that other costs, including advertising and consulting spending, were being reviewed.

Scrappy, and proud of it

The current trend towards consolidation in the financial services industry has made T. Rowe Price the subject of merger rumors, with insurer American International Group listed as one possible suitor. T. Rowe Price, however, has maintained its desire to remain independent.

The firm isn't letting its troubles in the U.S. put a damper on its international strategy. In April 2000, the company announced that it would purchase U.K.-based Robert Fleming's stake in the companies' joint venture, Rowe Price-Fleming International. (The catalyst for the transaction was the acquisition of Flemings by Chase Manhattan, now part of J.P. Morgan Chase.) The unit has offices in London, Paris, Hong Kong and other cities, but the terms of the joint venture barred T. Rowe from selling advisory services to international clients. As sole owner, T. Rowe is no longer restricted by those terms. After completing the purchase of Fleming's 50 percent stake in August 2000, T. Rowe Price changed the name of the company to T. Rowe Price International.

GETTING HIRED

T. Rowe Price recruits at a number of colleges, mostly on the East Coast, for analysts and associates. The firm also scouts out marketing and IT talent during its campus visits. There is also a summer program for associates, analysts and IT specialists. Check out the company web site at www.troweprice.com for a complete listing of available openings and schedule of campus visits.

Citibank

399 Park Avenue
New York, NY 10043
Phone: (800) 285-3000
Fax: (212) 793-3946
www.citigroup.com

DEPARTMENTS

Emerging Markets
Global Consumer Banking
Global Corporate and Investment
  Bank
Private Banking Group

THE STATS

Chairman and CEO: Sanford I. Weill
Employer Type: Public Company
Stock Symbol: C (NYSE)
2000 Revenues: $118.8 billion
2000 Net Income: $13.5 billion
No. of Employees: 230,000

KEY COMPETITORS

Bank of America
Bank of New York
Credit Suise First Boston
J.P. Morgan Chase

UPPERS

- Company-wide business casual
- High level of diversity

DOWNERS

- Mergers have resulted in undefined culture
- Bureaucracy typical of a large firm

EMPLOYMENT CONTACT

Michael Schlein
Citibank
399 Park Avenue
New York, NY 10043

THE SCOOP

From historic beginnings to financial powerhouse

Founded in 1812 by Samuel Osgood, the first commissioner of the U.S. Treasury, the City Bank of New York began by serving cotton, sugar, metal and coal merchants, and became a pioneer in overseas expansion during the early 20th century. Since then Citibank has gone on to become the first commercial bank to make personal loans, the first to provide high-interest specified-term CDs and the first to introduce ATMs on a large scale.

In April 1998, the company stunned the financial world when it announced its plans to merge with Travelers Group to create Citigroup, Inc. Travelers had purchased investment bank Salomon Brothers in December 1997 and combined it with its own I-banking unit, Smith Barney. The new entity offers one-stop shopping to its customers, whether they be institutional investors in need of derivatives to hedge bets on the market or homeowners looking for a mortgage. The U.S. Federal Reserve, anticipating changes in federal banking law, gave its conditional approval to the merger in September, and trading of the group's stocks began in October 1998. (Both companies lobbied for the Financial Services Modernization Act of 1999, which made the arrangement legal. *Crain's New York Business* claims Citigroup CEO Sanford Weill has the pen used by former President Bill Clinton to sign the act into law on display in his office.)

Citigroup's debut was clouded, however, by reports of huge losses overseas, diminishing the combined entity's net income by more than half the earnings from each company in the same 1997 quarter. Moreover, news reports in September 1998 indicated that 8,000 jobs would be chopped from Citigroup's various operations. These reports followed layoffs announced in August 1998 at Citicorp's corporate bond-trading department, an area in which Traveler's Salomon Smith Barney is much stronger.

The chaos continued. Conflicts over the future of Salomon Smith Barney led to the departure of Wall Street darling Jamie Dimon and Citigroup exec Stephen Black in November 1998, triggering a downgrade of the company by several Wall Street analysts. Dimon received a separation package worth an estimated $30 million. In return, the bank's former president agreed to restrictions of up to three years on his ability to hire any Citigroup staff.

Visit the Vault Finance Job Board — one of the best job boards on the Internet exclusively for finance professionals. Go to www.vault.com.

VAULT 165

Branding strategy

Legendary for its ability to use the latest technology to make life easier for its customers, Citibank has actively developed web-based banking services. Overall, the bank is making good progress toward the mission first articulated by former Citigroup co-CEO John Reed: to transform the Citibank name into an internationally recognized and trusted brand name on par with the likes of Coca-Cola or Xerox. Industry observers predicted that if the Citicorp/Travelers combination proved successful, it would likely spur similar mergers in the future.

Citibank is the world's largest issuer of credit cards, a position cemented by the bank's acquisition of AT&T's Universal Card Services. But the company's interests are not limited to banking and credit: In December 1999, Citigroup announced a 50-50 partnership with Boston-based State Street Corp. to form a joint venture, called Citistreet, to sell 401(k) retirement plan services.

Lonely at the top

In October 1999, former Treasury Secretary Robert Rubin joined the firm as chair of the executive committee, as well as the corporate inner circle known as the chairman's office. Rubin, described by *The Wall Street Journal* as "one of the world's most coveted financiers," repeatedly denied reports that he sought the Citigroup CEO post. (Speculation that he was to succeed Federal Reserve Chairman Alan Greenspan was stamped out when Greenspan was approved for another term as watchdog of the U.S. economy.)

The chairman's office got a little smaller in February 2000. Co-chairman and CEO John Reed announced his retirement, effective April 2000. While observers said that Reed and his co-chairman and CEO, Sanford Weill, had personality and style clashes, Reed said he merely sought the peace and quiet of retirement. However, after Reed's departure some of his disagreements with Weill were made public. For example, the job descriptions for both were more clearly defined in July 1999, reportedly after the two butted heads. Weill assumed day-to-day control and Reed headed Citigroup's Internet and technology initiatives.

A *Wall Street Journal* article, published in April 2000, suggested the split was far more contentious than most had previously realized. The *Journal* suggested that Weill and Reed were consistently at odds with one another over issues varying from the company's Internet strategy to the departure of Jamie Dimon, co-head of Citigroup's global corporate and investment bank and Weill's protégé. Dimon left in the fall of 1998. Additionally, the presence of two CEOs was disruptive to Citigroup senior management, and executives complained on several occasions. The issue finally came to a head in late February 2000, when the board of directors debated for several hours the fate of the company's two CEOs. At one point, said the *Journal*, a compromise was offered: Reed would stay as non-executive chairman and Weill would be CEO. Reed rejected that compromise and the board unanimously voted to ask Reed to retire.

Despite the shake-ups, Citi has turned in an outstanding performance. In 2000, the firm earned a record $13.52 billion, according to *The Wall Street Journal*. Weill has been handsomely rewarded for his work: His 2000 paycheck was a whopping $28.6 million, nearly double what he made in 1999.

Not so fast

Contrary to all the talk of a succession plan, Weill really hasn't shown any interest in retiring, and the board isn't pressuring him to do so. Not only is the board pleased with the company's results, many of its members are among Weill's staunchest supporters. Word has it that Weill wants to hang around until 2004 or longer. Lest anyone get the impression that he's short sighted, Weill did name Charles Prince and Jay Fishman co-chief operating officers in December 2000. Still, insiders say there are at least four additional Citi execs vying for Weill's approval for the top spot. There are also rumors of an outside contender: American Express CEO Kenneth Chenault.

Again, growing through mergers

In January 2000, Citigroup announced it was buying London-based investment bank Schroders PLC for about $2.2 billion. The purchase is being structured as a merger with Salomon Smith Barney, Citigroup's I-banking division. The combined company is known as Schroders Salomon Smith Barney in Europe, while in the U.S., the smaller Schroders & Company unit has been folded into Salomon. The merger resulted in a huge loss of jobs for Schroders employees in the U.S., where there was significant overlap between the two companies.

The dealing continued throughout the year. In August 2000, Citigroup announced plans to acquire AST StockPlan, a New York-based stock plan administrator. AST manages employee stock options and purchase plans for more than 545 corporate clients with a total of 645,000 participants.

In September 2000, the bank announced plans to acquire Associates First Capital, a consumer finance company providing credit cards and sub-prime lending in the U.S.,

Visit the Vault Finance Job Board — one of the best job boards on the Internet exclusively for finance professionals. Go to www.vault.com.

VAULT 167

Europe and Japan. The $31.1 billion acquisition came at a time when other large commercial banks, including Conseco and First Union, were eliminating such businesses because of heavy losses. Citigroup predicted approximately $600 million in savings over two years from the purchase despite the fact that few layoffs were expected. The deal was completed in November 2000.

Industry insiders also speculated that the Associates purchase may have brought a successor to Sandy Weill. *The Daily Deal* reported that Keith Hughes, Associates First's 53-year-old chairman and CEO, would become vice chairman and a director and is a potential leader once Weill retires.

But any Citi executives holding their breath for Weill to retire might as well inhale, as the CEO demonstrated that he still has at least one big deal left in him. In February 2001, the bank announced the acquisition of 100 branches of the European American Bank (EAB) from the Dutch group ABN Amro for $1.6 billion. The deal is significant because it will heighten Citigroup's exposure to wealthy depositors in the densely populated (and high income) Long Island area. The purchase also got a lot of folks in banking circles talking; they speculated that Citi snapped up EAB to keep it out of the hands of FleetBoston.

GETTING HIRED

MAP of the world

Each year, about 150 Citibank hires take full-time jobs at the bank via its Global Management Associate Program. The process begins on campus and is followed by a "Super Saturday"-style affair, where candidates are shuffled from one office to another for (usually) five 30-minute interviews with associates and VPs. One contact characterized her interview as "pleasant" and "not very stressful," but don't expect a chat over coffee — Citibank interviewers will give out brainteasers, which in the words of one contact "sound like they probably got them out of a book."

Outside of the Management Associate Program, such as branch management or personal banking, the job-seeking process is less formal — one of our contacts, for example, reports obtaining an interview simply "by picking up the telephone book and calling someone at Citibank."

For those one year from graduation, Citibank offers summer associate programs in global consumer global corporate, operations and technology, and in the bank's advanced development group. The global consumer bank's summer program rotates its summer hires through different areas, while in global corporate, summers choose one particular area and work there for the duration of their internship. Citibank also offers internships during the semester that may count for credit. Another tip: Salomon Smith Barney and Travelers Insurance recruit independently; check Citi's web site for more details.

Those interested in working at a particular branch should direct their inquiries to the branch manager of that branch. If no opportunities are currently available at that branch, the branch manager will direct the applicant to Citibank's main staffing department, where his or her resume will be kept on file. When a branch manager contacts Search & Staffing to fill an opening, he or she receives a list of appropriate resumes on file. The branch manager then selects the most appealing resumes and arranges for interviews; sometimes, two or three branch managers with openings will interview a pool of applicants jointly and decide which candidates are most appropriate for the different branches.

OUR SURVEY SAYS

Life in the Big Citi

An accurate picture of Citigroup's culture is difficult to nail down, considering its gargantuan size. "Your perspective on the firm's culture will depend on which part of the bank you are in," says one contact, who describes the company as still being "in flux" due to the merger and subsequent acquisitions. Despite the firm's growing pains, associates and analysts say the treatment they receive from senior managers is "very respectful."

Whatever uncertainty there may be regarding the firm's culture, Citigroup employees generally give their company high marks in a number of areas, including work/life issues. In particular, sources say they're pleased that "Citigroup initiated a company-wide business casual policy last year." "I believe that casual dress is great" because it enables "employees to work in a more comfortable environment," says one banker. Another insider notes that "the farther away you are from client contact, the more casual you can be." "I don't think I could find a financial services company where I

Visit the Vault Finance Job Board — one of the best job boards on the
Internet exclusively for finance professionals. Go to www.vault.com.

VAULT   169

would have a better balance between my work and home lives," adds a banker who describes the work environment as "very comfortable." While one contact believes "Citibank is one of the most diverse corporations in the financial industry sector," another says, "There are issues being [addressed] about gays."

Some employees warn that challenging work assignments can be hard to come by during the first couple of years at the company. According to one source, "A number of people who entered the bank with me have left for this very reason." Insiders lay some of the blame on the bank's "lack of focus" and "bureaucracy." One of the previously quoted bankers says, "I am not finding the work itself to be very challenging, which impacts my satisfaction." These opinions contrast those of a banker in the company's Management Associate Program, who praises the program for giving him "opportunities for international exposure and [a] breadth of work experience"

"I don't think I could
find a financial services
company where I would
have a better balance
between my work and
home lives."

— *Citibank insider*

Visit the Vault Finance Job Board — one of the best job boards on the
Internet exclusively for finance professionals. Go to www.vault.com.

VAULT   171

16 Deutsche Bank

31 West 52nd Street
New York, NY 10019
Phone: (212) 469-5000
Fax: (212) 469-3660
www.db.com

DEPARTMENTS

Corporate and Investment Banking
(Global Markets, Global Equities,
Global Credit Products and Global
Corporate Finance)
Private Clients and Asset
Management

THE STATS

Chairman, Management Board:
Rolf Bruer
**Head of Corporate and Investment
Banking:** Josef Ackermann
Employer Type: Public Company
2000 Revenue: $27 billion
2000 Net Income: $4.7 billion
No. of Employees: 98,300
No. of Offices: 2,300

KEY COMPETITORS

Citigroup
Credit Suisse First Boston
Goldman Sachs
J.P. Morgan Chase
UBS Warburg

UPPERS

- Global presence
- Growing in the U.S.

DOWNERS

- Bureaucracy
- Slow on perks for juniors

EMPLOYMENT CONTACT

Corporate Finance
Nebal Fahed
130 Liberty Street
12th Floor
New York, NY 10006
Cfcampus.teamus@db.com

Sales, Trading & Research
Caryn Blumenfeld
130 Liberty Street
12th Floor
New York, NY 10006
Stcampus.teamus@db.com

Global Technology & Operations
Jacqueline Murray
130 Liberty Street
12th Floor
New York, NY 10006
Gtopscampus.teamus@db.com

THE SCOOP

German giant

With approximately $894 billion in assets (as of March 31, 2001), Deutsche Bank AG is one of the largest financial institutions in the world. The company recently initiated a reorganization that established two distinct business groups. The Corporate and Investment Bank Group includes corporate finance, sales and trading, and transaction banking, while the Private Clients and Asset Management Group contains the bank's personal banking, private banking and asset management operations.

Deutsche Bank was founded in 1870 in Berlin. The company expanded first throughout Germany and later through the rest of Europe (its first branch outside Germany was its London outpost, opened in 1873). The company first made its mark in the U.S. in the 1880s when it helped finance the construction of the railroads that linked the East and West Coasts. Deutsche Bank's growth in the late 1800s can largely be attributed to mergers as the company merged with or acquired a number of European banking firms.

Like most German corporations, Deutsche Bank's actions during World War II are a sensitive subject. The company has admitted that it helped finance the construction of the Auschwitz concentration camp and has participated in the $1.25 billion settlement fund offered by Swiss and German companies to Holocaust victims. To its credit, Deutsche Bank hasn't hidden its past and even mentions unseemly events such as the 1933-1934 ouster of Jewish board members in the history section of its corporate web site.

More merging

The company's growth continued after the war but it wasn't until the late 1990s that the firm made the move that placed it among the major international players. In June 1999 Deutsche Bank acquired Bankers Trust for approximately $9 billion. BT had purchased Alex. Brown & Co., a U.S. investment bank with nearly 200 years of history, two years earlier, giving Deutsche Bank significant corporate lending and underwriting prowess. (According to *The Baltimore Sun*, Mayo Shattuck, who had been president and COO at Alex. Brown, battled Deutsche Bank management to keep the Alex. Brown name. The name survives as some of Deutsche Bank's U.S. investment-banking business is conducted under the Deutsche Banc Alex. Brown marketing name.)

Visit the Vault Finance Job Board — one of the best job boards on the
Internet exclusively for finance professionals. Go to www.vault.com.

VAULT **173**

Some analysts were initially skeptical about fate of the Deutsche Bank/BT deal. "I'm not bullish on this deal," Evangelous Kavouriadas, an analyst at Sanford C. Bernstein, told *The Baltimore Sun* when the deal was announced in November 1998. The combined company experienced the typical post-merger departures, including a handful of managing directors from the health care investment banking group in June 1999.

The initial skepticism has worn off as Deutsche Bank has had time to integrate the BT acquisition. Although the deal "was marked by the usual clash of cultures that occurs when a commercial and investment bank come together, Deutsche Bank has done a terrific job now in getting over the hurdles and moving forward with the acquisition," Robert Bostrom, head of the financial institutions practice at New York law firm Winston & Strawn, told *The Wall Street Journal* in November 1999. The best praise, however, came from a competitor: J.P. Morgan research analyst Stuart Graham said in a research report, "We consider there is now no doubt that Deutsche has created a bulge-bracket investment bank."

Not this time

While the company has certainly received praise for pushing itself into the bulge bracket, Deutsche Bank experienced a major setback in an attempt to become even more formidable. In March 2000, Deutsche Bank announced plans to merge with Dresdner Bank AG, the third-largest German bank. The deal, estimated at $31.6 billion dollars, was the second union the banks had planned; the firms had previously discussed combining retail operations in 1999, but the talks went nowhere. The full merger rapidly fell apart amid a dispute over the future of Dresdner's investment-banking division, Dresdner Kleinwort Benson (DKB). According to published reports, Deutsche wanted DKB closed or sold, a move opposed by Dresdner chairman Bernhard Walker, who was slated to become co-CEO at the combined firm. In April 2000, with the dispute over DKB's future raging on, Dresdner called off the deal. Dr. Rolf Breuer, head of Deutsche's board of managing directors, told *The Wall Street Journal* that "no solution acceptable to both sides could be found," and that Deutsche had no other mergers in the pipeline. As a result of the failed merger, Dresdner CEO Bernhard Walter resigned. Some industry observers speculated Breuer would be the next to go, but Deutsche's chairman announced his intention to stay at the helm until 2002, when Josef Ackermann would assume control.

Deutsche continues to make waves about possible merger plans. At Deutsche Bank's annual meeting in May 2001, Breuer told shareholders, "We are … keeping an eye open for possible partners or acquisition targets in Europe and America, and will take advantage of suitable opportunities." The company disclosed it was exploring a possible distribution alliance with insurance giant Axa Financial, but those discussions were terminated shortly after the Deutsche Bank annual meeting.

Tasty offerings

The company's equity underwriting practice has been busy, even as the market for new issues has dried up. Deutsche Bank's tasty foods division co-led a $63 million IPO for Krispy Kreme Doughnuts in April 2000 and a $154 million follow-on offering in January 2001, as well as a $79.5 million IPO for California Pizza Kitchen in August 2000 and a $114 million secondary offering in February 2001. If the bankers needed to work off the weight, they were helped by the firm's participation in Bally's Total Fitness Holding Corp.'s March 2001 secondary offering, worth $108 million. Other equity offerings include a $70 million IPO for Watson Wyatt in October 2000 and a $130 IPO for Align Technologies in January 2001.

Deutsche Bank's M&A team brought home several awards, including Best Foreign M&A House in the U.S. and Best Domestic M&A Advisor in Germany from *Euromoney* and Deal of the Year from *Institutional Investor* for representing NTT Communications. *International Financing Review* honored Deutsche Bank's derivatives practice, naming the company best derivatives house and best credit derivatives house for 2000.

GETTING HIRED

Show some initiative

Deutsche Bank's recruiting process for investment banking generally begins with an on-campus interview. "The on-campus interview usually consists of two interviews that last for a half an hour," says one source. A pared-down group of candidates is then invited to visit the firm's offices in New York or Baltimore, where candidates typically interview in a "Super Saturday" format with several of the firm's bankers. "Usually, there's a get-to-know-you reception the night before," says one insider. In the interview, "questions vary from the typical 'Why do you want to be in banking?' to the finance question." The firm says that it looks for candidates who demonstrate "initiative" and "excellence" and who will work well in a team environment. MBA candidates who are interested in international opportunities generally interview on campus before being invited to offices in Europe or Asia. Current bankers suggest applicants "talk to people with experience in the industry" before interviewing at the firm. Consult either the firm's job hotline or its web site, www.db.com, for a list of current job openings.

Both analysts and associates are recruited by, and hired directly into, specific departments. One financial analyst reports that the firm "looks for smart people and thinks that grades are very important in determining mental horsepower. Also, the company looks for a strong work ethic, and an outgoing and engaging personality, because you have to get along with clients when away from the office and with peers when working 100 hours a week." Those who join the firm as full-time investment banking analysts participate in four to six weeks of training in New York. Those who sign on as investment banking associates attend a four-week training program in New York. Analysts in sales, trading or research are in for eight to 12 weeks of training in London; associates can expect either six to eight weeks in New York or eight to 12 weeks in London, depending on the division.

The firm also offers summer analyst and associate positions. Summer positions for investment banking are available in New York, Europe, Singapore and Hong Kong, and last anywhere from six to 10 weeks between June and September.

OUR SURVEY SAYS

Less intense

Insiders describe the firm as being both "less intense" and "less structured" than its Wall Street peers. One insider, formerly of Alex. Brown, speaks favorably of the firm's merger: "Things have moved very smoothly with Deutsche Bank — it wasn't 100 percent seamless, but it was a fluid transition. The firm had a great 1999 and there is a lot of positive sentiment here." Another insider adds, "[The merger] played out well." That source, however, also notes that the firm has become "more bureaucratic since the merger, which was expected, but not necessarily welcome." Another source agrees, nothing, "The firm is going through some of the typical growing pains associated with the integration of various groups or businesses. But the firm is building a great culture, has a great vision and has the potential [and] standing in some areas to make great strides."

Employees in the firm's Baltimore office give the location mixed reviews. One insider says that unlike New York, Baltimore rents are "really cheap." Another insider is less optimistic: "Baltimore is really limited in the number of places where you can live." Insiders in the New York office describe "a typical Wall Street feel" at the firm's offices. Says one associate, "There is a lot of energy here." That source goes on to note, "They have also paid more attention to bankers on the junior level. We weren't on track with the market before, but I think we are now."

Employees at various locations offer praise for the perks. "All the facilities are top-notch," says one analyst, "especially in the San Francisco branch, where the offices are on the top floor of a building that overlooks the city and the bay." Other perks include: overtime meals, taxis and bonuses. "When you travel you stay in the top hotels," notes another source. Bankers in all American locations enjoy a full-time business casual dress policy.

Visit the Vault Finance Job Board — one of the best job boards on the Internet exclusively for finance professionals. Go to www.vault.com.

VAULT   177

Lincoln Plaza
400 P Street
Sacramento, CA 95814
Phone: (916) 326-3000
Fax: (916) 326-3005
www.calpers.ca.gov

DEPARTMENTS

Actuarial and Employer Services
Asset Managment
Benefit Services
Fiscal Services
Health Benefit Services

THE STATS

CEO: James E. Burton
Employer Type: Government
2000 Revenues: $18.8 billion
No. of Employees: 1,500
No. of Offices: 8

KEY COMPETITORS

TIAA-CREF

EMPLOYMENT CONTACT

Human Resources
CalPERS
Lincoln Plaza
400 P Street
Sacramento, CA 95814
Fax: (916) 326-3065

THE SCOOP

A California finance powerhouse

In 1932 a state law was enacted to create CalPERS, the California Public Employees' Retirement System. CalPERS administers investment plans for current and retired state employees. In 1962 CalPERS' scope was expanded to include oversight of health care benefits for state employees and retirees. CalPERS is currently the largest public pension fund in the U.S. (and the third-largest in the world), with more than $160 billion in assets.

Shareholder advocacy

CalPERS has become known for using its power as a shareholder to voice its opinions on how the corporations it invests in should be run. The firm established a corporate governance program in 1984, and has become well known for issuing a list of under-performing companies. Each year, the pension manager combs its investments for 10 of the consistently worst performers and publishes a list of the losers to warn them that they're being monitored. Although the firm still contacts managers at these companies to voice its concerns and to hear how management plans to improve performance, CalPERS has been criticized in recent years for not being aggressive enough in following up with companies on the lists. However, CalPERS still takes action when it deems necessary. In April 2000, the group protested Bank of America Chairman Hugh McColl's $76 million salary by not casting its votes when Bank of America board members were up for re-election. While the protest had no immediate impact, it was noticed. By January 2001, McColl had announced his resignation, in part due to bad press and outraged shareholders who thought the salary was too high. Additionally, CalPERS has made several investments in Relational Investors, a corporate governance fund that invests in under-performing U.S. companies. CalPERS most recent investment in Relational was in June 2001 for $250 million. EDS, Apple, Reebok, Citigroup, Disney and General Motors are just a few of the companies that have faced the brunt of CalPERS' wrath. In 1996 CalPERS expanded its corporate governance program to include international companies.

The firm also has a history of being just as hard on its health care providers. After haggling with Kaiser Permanente about a rate increase, CalPERS agreed to a 10.75 percent hike in June 1998 (Kaiser was asking for 12 percent), but closely questioned the provider on how it planned to trim a proposed $363 million from its operating

Visit the Vault Finance Job Board — one of the best job boards on the Internet exclusively for finance professionals. Go to www.vault.com.

VAULT   179

expenses. CalPERS' reasoning: Kaiser needed to get a grip on its expenses instead of passing those costs along to CalPERS' members. Loyalty to its shareholders was certainly part of the reason for CalPERS' tough stance, but its motives were not totally benevolent. An October 2000 article on the Internet site WebMD noted that the rising costs of health care had taken a bite out of the firm's reserves for claims payments. In February 2001, CalPERS rejected 10 bids from health care providers, citing costs that were too high. The pension manager told the providers to go back to the drawing board and return with some reasonable rates.

The tables turned

Despite its watchdog reputation, CalPERS has also faced its own share of public scrutiny. In 1998, articles in *The Los Angeles Times* detailed trips, meals and campaign contributions given to board members by companies that were in business with or seeking to do business with CalPERS. After the articles appeared, the board voted in February 1998 to change its policies on receiving gifts and contributions.

Up in smoke

CalPERS has also experimented with socially responsible investing. State Treasurer and board member Phillip Angelides has pushed the social agenda, first proposing that the firm sell its tobacco stocks and then advocating investing 2 percent of CalPERS' assets in the state's low-income neighborhoods. Furthermore, Angelides said tobacco stocks are a bad investment because of lawsuits against cigarette makers. But getting this initiative off the ground proved more difficult than CalPERS' foray into corporate governance, partly because socially responsible investments have historically had lower returns. Bills were introduced in the state legislature in 1998 to force a divestiture of the tobacco stocks, but the board opposed it. With the backing of the state legislature again, Angelides convinced CalPERS' board to sell $525 million worth of tobacco stocks in October 2000.

Taking a stand

CalPERS is facing a true test of its right to act independently. Early in 2001, the State Controller, Kathleen Connell, filed a suit alleging that the firm had unlawfully over-compensated board members and portfolio managers, who are considered civil servants. CalPERS disputes the claim, stating that a 1992 amendment to the state constitution gives CalPERS the authority to raise salaries. CalPERS also claims that it is difficult to attract and retain qualified managers because they can go elsewhere and make much more money. An interesting twist: Not only was Connell campaigning to be the next mayor of Los Angeles (CalPERS officials say the suit was an attempt by Connell, who lost the election, to call attention to her campaign), but her position as controller makes her a non-elected member of the CalPERS board.

This isn't the first time Connell and the giant money manager have tangled, although this suit may be their most public battle. Connell's campaign committee filed an earlier suit in 1998 in protest of rules CalPERS passed restricting campaign contributions to elected officials who serve as board members. (She eventually won.) And in 1999, Connell was just one of four board members who voted to allow board candidates to make an expanded statement of their views in mailings sent out to members. After a spat between board president William Crist and candidate Jim McRitchie, other board members voted to only include biographical information about candidates.

New frontiers

CalPERS is considered an innovative investment manager. The firm has even bought stakes in several venture capital firms to ensure it gets in on the ground floor of new companies before they go public. In 1999 the firm purchased a 10 percent stake of merchant bank Thomas Weisel Partners for $100 million. The firm also made an investment of $500 million in Weisel's venture funds and has an option to invest another $500 million pending board approval. In January 2001, CalPERS made two huge VC deals. The firm spent $485 million in a partnership with Texas Pacific Group to establish a technology venture fund investing in early- and late-stage companies. Another $425 million was spent to buy a 5 percent stake in private equity firm Carlyle Group and invest in future Carlyle funds. In May 2001, CalPERS announced investments totalling $475 million in 11 California-based private equity firms. The funds are earmarked to be invested in underserved urban and rural communities throughout the state.

Barry Gonder, one of the senior investment offices at CalPERS, is often credited with drastically improving the firm's private equity investing. Prior to Gonder's arrival, many private equity firms did not want to deal with CalPERS because of its reputation for bureaucracy — doing business with CalPERS required completing an 80-page document and getting past a gatekeeper who decided which equity firms CalPERS would or wouldn't work with.

Visit the Vault Finance Job Board — one of the best job boards on the Internet exclusively for finance professionals. Go to www.vault.com.

V/\ULT   181

GETTING HIRED

The 411

Because CalPERS is a state agency, its employees are civil servants. Therefore, potential employees must take an exam. Tests for most positions are administered by the State Personnel Board, but CalPERS oversees the testing and hiring process itself for some of the banking, actuarial and IT openings. CalPERS offers continuous testing, while the SPB administers tests on an as-needed basis. The firm's web site, www.calpers.ca.gov, provides a link to the State Personnel Board's online application form. The site also provides information on how to contact the SPB and CalPERS regarding employment.

"CalPERS has become known for using its power as a shareholder to voice its opinions on how the corporations it invests in should be run."

Visit the Vault Finance Job Board — one of the best job boards on the Internet exclusively for finance professionals. Go to www.vault.com.

VAULT   183

UBS Warburg

1/2 Finsbury Avenue
London EC2M 2PP
United Kingdom
Phone: (44-20) 7567-8000
Fax: (44-20) 7568-4800
www.ubswarburg.com

299 Park Avenue
New York, NY 10171
Phone: (212) 821-3000
Fax: (212) 821-3285

DEPARTMENTS

Corporate Finance
Credit
Equities
Fixed Income
Interest Rate Products and FX
Sales and Trading

THE STATS

Chairman and CEO: Markus Granziol
Employer Type: Subsidiary of UBS AG
No. of Employees: 39,000
No. of Offices: 66

KEY COMPETITORS

Credit Suisse First Boston
J.P. Morgan Chase
Lehman Brothers
Salomon Smith Barney

UPPERS

- Opportunities for advancement
- Relaxed culture

DOWNERS

- Problems with seniors
- Second-tier image in U.S.

EMPLOYMENT CONTACT

Human Resources
UBS Warburg
677 Washington Boulevard
Stamford, CT 06901

THE SCOOP

Neutral parent

UBS Warburg represents the investment banking operations of UBS, the Swiss-based financial services behemoth with more than 70,000 employees worldwide. Besides investment banking, UBS offers private and corporate banking services through UBS Switzerland and asset management and mutual funds through the aptly named UBS Asset Management. After a tumultuous history of mergers and acquisitions, the firm hopes to become a major player in the U.S. market. In May 2000, the firm listed its shares on the New York Stock Exchange. At the time of the listing, firm representatives made it clear that UBS Warburg had expansion and acquisitions on its agenda and the firm didn't disappoint: UBS later acquired PaineWebber for $10.8 billion.

Multi-mergers

The company's story begins in 1872 with the founding of the Swiss Bank Corporation (SBC). SBC grew internationally (the London office, the bank's first outside Switzerland, opened in 1898) and by the 1990s had established alliances or subsidiaries in the world's financial centers. In the mid-1990s, the firm became a major player in the investment banking world by purchasing the securities business of S.G. Warburg Group, a firm started in London in the 1930s by Siegmund Warburg, a German who was fleeing Nazi persecution. The investment-banking division of the new firm was dubbed SBC Warburg. SBC Warburg expanded into the U.S. with its September 1997 acquisition of Dillon, Read & Co., a New York I-bank founded in 1832. The investment-banking division was then named Warburg Dillon Read. In June 1998, Warburg Dillon Read merged with UBS, taking the name UBS AG. UBS had been formed in 1912 by the merger of two regional Swiss banks, the Bank of Winterthur and Toggenbirger Bank.

Early analysis of the UBS/SBC/Warburg combination was not favorable. The newly combined firm reported a profit of $4.2 billion for 1999; that was nearly double the profits for 1998. However, in 1998 the firm was hit with one-time write-offs (including a $650 million loss due to an investment in hedge fund Long-Term Capital Management) that dragged profits down and made 1999's performance look artificially good in comparison. *The Economist* called UBS "a directionless and unhappy institution" and said the bank's problems resulted from the merger with SBC, which it felt was poorly managed.

Visit the Vault Finance Job Board — one of the best job boards on the Internet exclusively for finance professionals. Go to www.vault.com.

VAULT   185

Things picked up in 2000 as UBS reported profits of $4.8 billion. Insiders say it was because the bumps from the UBS/SBC deal were finally smoothed over. "We now have a range of seamless teams working together, rather than worrying about who's the better guy or who should deal with a particular client," Heino Teschmacher, co-head of European M&A at UBS Warburg, told *The Financial News* in January 2001.

New order for the new millennium

In February 2000, the bank's operations were reordered into its current format, and it was then that the investment-banking arm was renamed UBS Warburg. In May 2000, UBS began trading on the New York Stock Exchange (the first financial services firm based outside the United States to trade on the Big Board). UBS CEO Marcel Ospel told CNBC that the NYSE listing would enable the company to "act in the United States on the acquisition front." Additionally, Ospel emphatically denied the possibility of the firm retreating from the investment-banking business. "These rumors have absolutely no substance; to the contrary, investment banking is very important for our group, we are determined to grow it with a focus to here — North America."

Thank you, PaineWebber

The focus of UBS Warburg's expansion plans turned out to be PaineWebber, the 121-year-old investment bank. In July 2000, UBS announced it was acquiring PaineWebber for $10.8 billion in cash and stock. The purchase connects PaineWebber's considerable U.S. retail presence (the firm was the nation's fourth-largest broker at the time of the deal) with UBS Warburg's growing banking practice. Acquiring PaineWebber added more than 8,000 brokers and 2.7 million clients to the UBS portfolio. "The combination of UBS' international reach and product range, with PaineWebber's leading position in the U.S. market for affluent and high net worth individuals, will create a premier global investment services firm," UBS' Ospel said in the release announcing the coupling.

Analysts were optimistic about the deal, though surprised to a degree. "We thought they would enhance their investment banking," Beat Kaeser, head of Swiss equity research at privately held Bank Darier, Hentsch & Cie, told *The Daily Deal*. "It is a very coherent move for UBS," concurred Oliver Prucheut, an analyst at Natexis Capital. "But it doesn't answer the problem of their investment banking weakness." (UBS reportedly had a plan to address that weakness, according to Bloomberg. The firm held talks with Lehman Brothers in early 2000 to combine UBS Warburg and Lehman into a securities firm co-owned by the two parents.)

However, other observers felt the new firm's increased distribution capabilities will allow for natural growth in I-banking. HSBC Holdings analyst Derek Chambers told *The Daily Deal* that the PaineWebber acquisition "will give [UBS Warburg] a very substantial amount of placing power. It is by having placing power that Merrill Lynch was able to move up the league tables in corporate banking," Chambers pointed out. One potential pitfall for the merger is talent defection, especially since PaineWebber has been known as an aggressive pursuer of talent at other banks. UBS addressed this issue when it reportedly set aside $875 million in incentives for PaineWebber employees; $75 million was reserved for six top executives, including the firm's president. According to *The Daily Deal*, PaineWebber CEO Donald Marron signed a separate contract extension with UBS. Furthermore, industry insiders say mass defections are unlikely because consolidation in the industry means there are fewer banks looking to recruit.

Best at M&A

UBS Warburg's strength is its M&A advisory practice. According to Thomson Financial Securities Data, the firm ranked seventh in announced worldwide M&A in 2000, advising on 291 deals worth $371 billion. Among the firm's biggest assignments: advising Vodafone AirTouch on its $193 billion merger with Mannesmann in February 2000 and advising Diageo plc on the sale of its Pillsbury unit to General Mills for $10.5 billion in July 2000.

GETTING HIRED

UBS Warburg posts recruiting schedules on its web site, www.ubswarburg.com. The firm has instituted a snazzy online application procedure that is required for all candidates outside the U.S. and Switzerland.

Associates at UBS Warburg have in the past warned that a business degree doesn't carry the same weight at UBS Warburg as it does at most American banks, especially in sales and trading. However, the firm is taking steps to emphasize the MBA. For example, the firm has changed its training program to separate undergrads from MBAs in corporate finance, and to initiate undergrads in S&T with a three-week "core training" program before they join the MBAs for training (rather than have undergrads and MBAs go through the exact same program, as they had in the past).

Visit the Vault Finance Job Board — one of the best job boards on the Internet exclusively for finance professionals. Go to www.vault.com.

VAULT   187

On the other side of the coin, insiders note, the firm provides greater opportunity for undergrads. Says one contact: "For undergrads in the analyst position, it's a fantastic place. If you're a Wharton undergrad, it's really ideal. They really love that profile, the really hungry young person." Says one corporate finance analyst, "I worked on a divestiture where I did all the plant tours in addition to the management presentation. On the other side, the most junior person I saw was an associate. That's the opportunity. On the other hand, if you're looking for structure, it's probably not the best place for you."

OUR SURVEY SAYS

Relaxed culture, but issues with senior bankers

"It's hard to make blanket statements for hundreds of people, but overall, in a relative sense, I think this firm has a looser culture than other investment banks," reports one insider about UBS Warburg. Says a contact in Asia: "I would describe the culture at UBS Warburg as relatively loose compared to the U.S. banks." At least one former employee blasts the firm's senior bankers, saying, "When you go to Wall Street you assume you'll be working with the cream of the crop. I was bluntly shocked to see how such low-quality people could occupy high posts at a Wall Street firm. Instead of them teaching us, I was in a position where I wound up editing senior people's text [and] explaining basic concepts."

Insiders appreciate the current aggressiveness the firm is displaying in I-banking, as it means more opportunity personally. "I think that generally, people sense there's a lot more opportunity as far as upward mobility is concerned when compared to other firms," reports one insider, "because we're trying to grow fast." Of course, part of the drive to grow fast means eye-popping salaries to lure lateral bankers, but this doesn't mean UBS Warburg is above the curve at all levels. "If you look at what the average ranges are like, I would say that we are basically smack dab in the middle," reports one insider.

As for the actual offices, Stamford, the American headquarters and site of sales and trading, is a New York suburb in wealthy Fairfield County. The firm's offices are located across the street from the Metro North train station. Reports one Stamford banker: "The younger people tend to all live in New York. People with families tend to live in Connecticut — for them, it's an ideal situation. Anyone who doesn't live in Connecticut better think twice [about joining UBS Warburg]."

Visit the Vault Finance Job Board — one of the best job boards on the
Internet exclusively for finance professionals. Go to www.vault.com.

VAULT   189

Charles Schwab

101 Montgomergy Street
San Francisco, CA 94104
Phone: (415) 627-7000
Fax: (415) 627-8840
www.schwab.com

DEPARTMENTS

Capital Markets
Electronic Brokerage
Retail Services
Retirement Plan Services

THE STATS

Chairman and Co-CEO:
Charles R. Schwab
President and Co-CEO:
David S. Pottruck
Employer Type: Public Company
Ticker Symbol: SCH (NYSE)
2000 Revenue: $7.1 billion
2000 Net Income: $718 million
No. of Employees: 25,800
No. of Offices: 429

KEY COMPETITORS

Alliance Capital Management
E*Trade
Fidelity Investments
T. Rowe Price

UPPERS

- Quarterly bonuses
- Merit-based stock grants
- Free YMCA membership at headquarters
- Great diversity

DOWNERS

- Average base pay
- Some periods of intense work

EMPLOYMENT CONTACT

George A. Rich
Charles Schwab
101 Montgomergy Street
San Francisco, CA 94104

THE SCOOP

The first commander

Charles Schwab got his feet wet in the financial services industry in 1963, founding an investment advisory newsletter with two partners. By the late 1960s Schwab and partners founded First Commander Corp., a San Francisco-based brokerage firm. The company had failed to register correctly with the Securities and Exchange Commission, forcing a temporary shutdown in the early 1970s. The company quickly corrected the error and reopened in 1971. By 1973, Schwab purchased the firm from his partners and named it after himself.

Schwab made its name as the discount brokerage for investors who didn't trust commission-based brokerages. When the SEC outlawed fixed brokers' commissions in 1975, most houses raised commissions drastically, but Schwab, which has always portrayed itself as an unconventional financial services firm, cut its commissions and gained a huge market share. Schwab sold the company to BankAmerica in 1983 for $57 million but organized a leveraged buyout three years later. In 1987 Schwab raised $132 million in an IPO.

King of the 'Net

Schwab has been an extremely hot firm in recent years. The firm now has approximately $806 billion in assets under management from 7.6 million clients. Part of the reason the firm has grown is its alliances with investment banks J.P. Morgan (now J.P. Morgan Chase), Credit Suisse First Boston (CSFB) and Hambrecht & Quist, an initiative begun in 1997. Through these partnerships, the firm offers its clients access to initial public offerings. In 1998 CSFB also began using Schwab to sell debt offerings it underwrites.

But the major reason for Schwab's rapid ascension is its dominance of online trading. According to *The New York Times*, the firm's computing center in Phoenix handles about a third of all Internet trading. And the company is moving quickly toward offering full brokerage services online, dispensing advice and research through its web site. Schwab is also exploring more creative uses of the Internet, such as e-mailing clients with news based on their investment preferences. The firm has gained the lead in online brokering by finding the middle ground between discount brokers like E*Trade and full-service firms like Merrill Lynch.

Show us the money

In January 2000, Schwab announced the acquisition of private banker and investment manager U.S. Trust. While Schwab has long been hailed as the market leader in discount brokerage services, the firm has suffered a reputation as a non-threat to investment management firms that manage accounts for wealthy individuals. So, the marriage of the low-cost brokerage house with a bank that caters to wealthy private clients might seem incongruous. Schwab's strategy is to stay with clients throughout their investing lives — from beginning investing to wealth accumulation and maintenance. The two companies will maintain separate brand identities, but will share processes and services across business lines.

The U.S. Trust acquisition filled a huge void for Schwab by providing the company with an instant base of customers with money to burn and a staff experienced at lighting the fire. But it has also raised some thorny issues for the veteran investment manager. In the past, Schwab has purchased and traded stocks at the direction of its clients, keeping costs low by providing little to no advice on which investments to choose. (Wealthy investors want and expect much more hand-holding and advice from their money managers than that.) Now, some of the independent advisors who had been the foundation of Schwab's business (and who pay a yearly fee to be affiliated with Schwab, while receiving an annual fee from clients for their services) feel betrayed by the U.S. Trust purchase. They worry that Schwab may be more interested in referring clients to U.S. Trust, which would collect annual fees and commissions from clients, than allowing that money to go into advisors' pockets. The firm's challenge it to continue building its wealth management business, while convincing its independent advisors of their value to the firm.

While the U.S. Trust deal brought in stable, long-term investors, Schwab also made moves to attract day-traders, the smaller but more active traders who generate profits for online firms. In February 2000, Schwab purchased CyBerCorp, an Austin, Texas-based electronic trading firm that specializes in day-traders. Schwab paid about $488 million for CyBerCorp, one of the top 10 online firms in terms of trades.

On the same day as the CyBerCorp purchase, Schwab announced it was cutting commissions for their most active traders. Day-traders making more than 30 equity trades in any quarter pay reduced rates, from $29.95 to $14.95 per trade. (Most CyBerCorp clients qualify for the Schwab discounts.) Both moves — the reduced prices and the purchase — were seen as attempts to recapture the online trading market Schwab once dominated. "We've lost online share," Schwab co-CEO David Pottruck conceded after the CyBerCorp deal.

The company's acquisition spree may not be over. Schwab admitted his company is looking to boost its banking capabilities, possibly through merger. The company currently offers limited banking services to customers, including checks and ATM services. However, Schwab is looking to attract customers by building those services, especially since bank products provide a more steady stream of income than brokerage and trading services.

Getting noticed

Schwab made major headlines at the start of 2001 when the company, burned by rising expenses and a decline in fourth quarter earnings, announced that some employees would be given minor pay cuts in the first quarter and have to take three vacation days off without pay. The move was well received by some industry analysts, not only as a sensible solution (more so than massive layoffs) to what may be a temporary problem, but also because Schwab himself and co-CEO David Pottruck agreed to take substantial pay cuts. However, the firm soon had to backtrack on part of the directive — instead, labeling the vacation days as "voluntary" — because of concern that a mandatory time-off policy might be illegal.

The firm has scored kudos from several self-appointed trend-watching publications that compile lists for this, that or the other "best" thing. On its 2000 list of 100 Best Companies to Work For, *Fortune* ranked Schwab No. 5, citing paid employee sabbaticals and business casual dress code, among other perks. Schwab also showed up on *Working Woman*'s Top 25 Companies for Executive Women at No. 2 (the top spot went to Avon). In December 2000 — for the third straight quarter — Gomez Internet Brokerage Scorecard named Schwab "Best Internet Brokerage."

Although Schwab has managed to maintain a fairly good reputation in investment management circles, it has not been immune to the occasional scrutiny. In October 2000, a class action suit was filed against the company in connection with short-term redemption fees the company charged certain customers. The case is pending in a California court.

International growing pains

Though Schwab is firmly entrenched in the U.S., its international operations have gotten off to a slow start. For example, like most U.S. brokers and asset managers, Schwab has had trouble getting on track in Europe. Asset managers and brokers are looking forward to expansion in Europe, where older workers are turning away from state-run pensions and focusing on stocks and mutual funds, similar to the shift to

401(k)s and IRAs in the U.S. However, Schwab has gotten off to a slow start on the continent. According to the *Financial Times*, Schwab has approximately 100,000 online accounts in the U.K., making it the largest online broker in that country. However, besides the U.K., Schwab is currently online only in Switzerland, unlike rival E*Trade, which has online clients in the U.K., Sweden, Norway and Denmark. The company faces identical issues in Australia, where investors have a reputation for being especially savvy. Charles Schwab Australia, which started up without the benefit of the name recognition it enjoys domestically, originally committed to service rather than price, a strategy it was forced to abandon in late 2000 when its competitors slashed prices, some to as low as $4 per trade. The sudden shift in strategy, along with the expensive marketing campaign the firm has launched to build its brand, leave some doubting Schwab's ability to become a major player in Australia. "Schwab is going to have a tough time here," Mara Bun, an analyst at Macquarie Equities, told *BusinessWeek* in April 2001.

GETTING HIRED

Schwab hosts a separate web site for undergraduate and MBA recruiting, located at www.schwabwfd.com. (The WFD stands for Work Force Development.) The site includes the firm's recruiting schedule (Schwab recruited at 61 undergraduate schools and nine MBA schools in 2000-2001), as well as links to descriptions of open positions. According to an insider, the firm "shows up at most Bay Area job fairs, and stages a few of its own from time to time." For MBAs, the firm offers a 13-month Management Associate Program (MAP) that includes an initial classroom-type training program, followed by a series of three-month rotations. Undergrads are hired primarily in Jersey City, N.J., Denver, Colo., Orlando, Fla., Phoenix, Ariz., Indianapolis, Ind., Austin, Texas and San Francisco, Calif. Applicants can submit resumes electronically using the site's online resume submission form, by regular mail or by fax.

Insiders say the company performs a background check, which they run past the Federal Bureau of Investigations before hiring a candidate. However, insiders also call interviews "informal, to get an impression of the person beyond the resume."

OUR SURVEY SAYS

Great diversity

"It is a very eclectic group of people," says one insider about the company. "Schwab prides itself on its diversity and having employees that appreciate how much that enhances a company's performance. There is no old boys network here." Says an employee at the company's headquarters: "There's no 'locker room' talk, even in private, about one race or another. They take harassment very seriously. No one cares if you're straight or gay, and people are pretty liberal and PC." Continues that contact: "If you're going to run afoul of the corporate culture at Schwab, it's most likely going to be in the opposite direction. I think if you made a remark hostile to sex, race, sexual preference or religion, you'd probably get nuked." Schwab has won national renown for making its workplace friendly to gays and lesbians; it was among the first in the industry to extend equal benefits to their partners.

Minorities and women have also fared well at Schwab when it comes to career opportunities. "Many minorities and women are in senior positions and therefore diversity is not an issue," says one insider. Says another: "Some of the women in my department have discussed a glass ceiling, but they are talking about the top 10 positions in the company being disproportionately males. Up to and including the VP level, I'm not aware that there is any disparity."

Women in army boots

Schwab is pretty liberal for a financial-services firm when it comes to dress code, too. While dress is generally described as "business casual," at the company's headquarters, dress varies by department. Reports one insider: "If you have customer contact you have to be presentable, but it's not terribly rigid. I've seen guys that wear dresses, women wearing army boots, body piercings, little cowboy outfits." However, "the VPs and ambitious dress better."

Good perks

Pay at Schwab is considered average, but insiders agree that the benefits the firm kicks in push compensation into quite healthy levels. "Starting salaries won't knock your socks off, but the company match on money put into one's 401(k) is generous. It won't seem like all that big a deal at first, but they keep giving us special grants of stock, which splits all the time, and quarterly bonuses, and lots of little extras and perks along the way." Another insider reports that "pay will always be low to start off with until you get your professional Series 7 license to trade securities." However, says that contact, "the perks are great. It really adds up to a lot of unrealized salary when you have such great health benefits, 401(k) plan and stock options." One contact reports receiving about $10,000 in benefits annually. Says another: "This week there's a guy down in the warehouse who's retiring after only 15 years with the company with about $2.5 million in his 401(k). Not exactly Microsoft millionaires, but this is a pretty low-ranking guy who just did his job a good long while."

For those with heart, Schwab offers nice benefits. "They're quite generous in doing 100 to 200 percent company matches to charitable contributions," reports one insider. "They encourage employees to donate to whatever individual causes they are for, and in some cases donate more than money, like building materials. The longer you stay at Schwab the more you see opportunities to turn your connection to the company into an increased opportunity to participate in more charitable stuff."

Some rough periods

For the most part, working at Schwab means a normal 40-hour week (or maybe a bit more), insiders report. However, this can change during heavy periods. "It is not a job for everybody," reports one Schwab employee. "Financial markets can get very turbulent and we can get very busy. But with hard work comes rewards." Says another contact: "There are a damn lot of demanding, privileged people. If you're in any sort of support role you'll find yourself dealing with people who want everything right away with no concept of what goes into what they're asking for, and if you tell them they can't have it, they're quick to escalate on you." Schwab officially offers comp time for these heavy periods, under which "in theory, you take other time off if you have to work a lot of extra hours." However, says one contact, "I don't see that happen a lot."

"Schwab prides itself on its diversity and having employees that appreciate how much that enhances a company's performance."

— *Charles Schwab insider*

Visit the Vault Finance Job Board — one of the best job boards on the Internet exclusively for finance professionals. Go to www.vault.com.

VAULT   197

Alliance Capital Management

1345 Avenue of the Americas
New York, NY 10105
Phone: (212) 969-1000
Fax: (212) 969-2229
www.alliancecapital.com

DEPARTMENTS

Equity Management
Fixed-Income Management
Research

THE STATS

Chairman and CEO:
Bruce W. Calvert
Employer Type: Public Company
Stock Symbol: AC (NYSE)
2000 Revenue: $2.5 billion
2000 Net Income: $669 million
No. of Employees: 4,400
No. of Offices: 26

KEY COMPETITORS

Fidelity Investments
T. Rowe Price
Vanguard Group

UPPERS

• Excellent pay
• Reasonable hours

DOWNERS

• Bureaucracy
• Tough vacation policy

EMPLOYMENT CONTACT

Human Resources
Alliance Capital
1345 Avenue of the Americas
New York, NY 10105

THE SCOOP

It was a very good year

With about $433 billion in assets under management as of March 31, 2001, Alliance is one of the world's largest investment management firms. Revenues for 2000 reached record highs, breaking $2 billion for the first time, and hitting $2.5 billion, a whopping 35 percent jump from 1999. Most of Alliance's revenues are generated from fees paid by its clients.

Alliance offers institutional account management for corporate and public employee pension funds, and serves money market funds and deposit accounts. The firm manages employee benefit plans for 56 of the Fortune 100 companies in the U.S., and manages retirement funds for public employees in 36 of the 50 states.

Stuck with DLJ

The company was started in 1962 as the investment management department of Donaldson, Lufkin & Jenrette. The department grew, and was spun off into a full-fledged subsidiary of DLJ in 1971. Although DLJ later sold Alliance, the two firms have continued to be intertwined. The Equitable Life Assurance Society of the United States purchased Alliance Capital in 1985. Thirteen years later, Equitable Assurance and AXA Group — which already owned 57 percent of Equitable — together purchased $300 million worth of stock in Alliance's former parent, DLJ. In 2000 DLJ was sold to Credit Suisse First Boston; AXA Group then bought the remaining shares of Alliance's parent, renaming it AXA Financial. There may be more purchases to come. In April 2001, *BusinessWeek* speculated that AXA, which now owns only 53 percent of Alliance, may purchase the remaining shares because it believes Alliance is a strong company in a rapidly consolidating industry

Alliance has made a few purchases of its own. In June 2000, the company announced that it would acquire investment advisor Sanford C. Bernstein for $3.5 billion, and completed the deal in less than four months. The company says that Bernstein's value philosophy was the perfect compliment for its specialty in growth investing. In an effort to stave off the typical post-acquisition defections that many companies face, Alliance developed a retention package for its former Bernstein employees. Other major acquisitions include the purchase of Shields Asset Management in 1994 and Cursitor-Eaton Asset Management Company in 1996. In 1999 Bruce Calvert was named CEO of Alliance, taking over for Dave Williams, who had run the firm

Visit the Vault Finance Job Board — one of the best job boards on the
Internet exclusively for finance professionals. Go to www.vault.com.

VAULT   199

since 1977. Williams remained the company's chairman until Calvert assumed the role in May 2001.

GETTING HIRED

Form an Alliance

Many of the firm's equity, fixed-income analyst, and portfolio manager positions are in its New York offices. Alliance says it looks for "knowledgeable and hardworking" applicants. The extent and type of knowledge required varies by position. Try clicking on the "Careers at Alliance" button on the company's homepage to find out more about openings at Alliance. That button takes potential applicants to a site hosted by HotJobs.com listing open positions at the company. Candidates can also submit a resume and cover letter directly to the company if interested in a position that's not listed as open.

OUR SURVEY SAYS

Hard at work, in uncomfortable clothes

Employees say dress is formal, but "not too conservative," with casual Fridays in the summer, except in New York. Earning "competitive pay," employees are generally expected to work 60-hour weeks, though "hours vary by department." Still, as one insider puts it: "The hours are reasonable, although overtime is expected without pay."

Some criticisms

Some employees say "co-workers are generally okay," but criticize "upper-level bureaucracy" for "slow decision making." Other criticisms include a bad vacation policy, and a great year-end bonus that is based "more on corporate politics than merit." However, not all insiders agree with these assessments. Says one: "The people are extremely open, kind and fun to work with." Continues that contact: "The pay is excellent and commensurate with performance. If you work hard, you get ahead."

"The pay is excellent
and commensurate
with performance.
If you work hard, you
get ahead."

— *Alliance Capital
Management insider*

Visit the Vault Finance Job Board — one of the best job boards on the
Internet exclusively for finance professionals. Go to www.vault.com.

VAULT   201

1 Corporate Center
Rye, NY 10580
Phone: (914) 921-3700
Fax: (914) 921-5392
www.gabelli.com

DEPARTMENTS

Asset Management
Research
Trading

THE STATS

Chairman, CEO and Chief Investment Officer: Mario Gabelli
Employer Type: Public Company
Ticker Symbol: GBL (NYSE)
2000 Revenues: $233.9 million
2000 Net Income: $58 million
No. of Employees: 130
No. of Offices: 6

KEY COMPETITORS

Alliance Capital Management
Franklin Resources
Vanguard Group

EMPLOYMENT CONTACT

Human Resources
Gabelli Asset Management Inc.
1 Corporate Center
Rye, NY 10580
Fax: (914) 921-5392
hr@gabelli.com

THE SCOOP

Starting at the bottom

Gabelli Asset Management (GAM) was founded in 1977 by self-taught stock picker Mario Gabelli. In an interview with *Investor's Business Daily*, Gabelli detailed his humble roots. Gabelli told *IBD* that he learned about the stock market at age 16 while working as a caddie at a golf course in Scarsdale, N.Y. Armed with that experience — and an MBA from Columbia — Gabelli spent several years working as an analyst in the industry. He then went on to found GAM at a time when money managers and research firms were struggling due to changes in the industry. Gabelli credits his company's success to meticulous research techniques that he claims are better able to identify value investments. The firm says it seeks "to identify undervalued companies with dominant industry positions." Investors are apparently convinced of Gabelli's purported bargain-hunting prowess: The firm's assets under managed mushroomed to $24.2 billion in the first of quarter of 2001 from $22.2 billion for the same period in 2000. In addition to its research staff, GAM now manages 25 mutual funds and more than 1,000 pension, trust and individual accounts.

After more than 20 years as an independent firm, GAM went public in February 1999, raising $105 million. Gabelli retained control of the firm with 97.6 percent of the voting shares after the IPO. In fact, Gabelli's control over the firm was seen as a drawback to the offering by some. *Barron's* called the company a "one-man show," and reported that some potential investors were uneasy with the prospect of buying into such a tightly controlled firm. *Barron's* reported that Goldman Sachs pulled out as underwriter of the offering because the bank felt Gabelli's compensation was too high. He reportedly receives 10 percent of the pre-tax profits, plus portfolio management fees. Additionally, Gabelli will get a deferred payment of $50 million in January 2002, plus interest on that payment.

The offering was an initial success, but the shares, which opened at $17, soon began trading at less than $15. Gabelli saw his chance to regain a larger chunk of his company. As of March 1, 2001, Gabelli had bought back up to $3 million worth of shares. The board agreed to a "repurchase of an additional $3 million of stock when the company deems it appropriate," according to *Mutual Fund Market News*. These moves rubbed some investors the wrong way. "It seems to me that Gabelli should have just sold fewer shares in the IPO in the first place," one institutional investor grumbled to the *New York Post* in October 1999. "He's buying back at 15 what I originally bought at 17. I am not a happy camper here." The *Mutual Fund Market*

Visit the Vault Finance Job Board — one of the best job boards on the
Internet exclusively for finance professionals. Go to www.vault.com.
V/\ULT 203

News article states that Gabelli paid an average of $17.38 per share for a little more than a half million shares.

GETTING HIRED

Introduce yourself

Check Gabelli's web site, www.gabelli.com, for a listing of full- and part-time openings. Resumes and cover letters can be submitted directly from the site, and must be sent as plain text files (no attachments). If an opening is not listed on the site for a desired position, interested parties can apply by sending a resume and cover letter directly to the Rye, N.Y., office.

"[Gabelli Asset Management] says it seeks 'to identify undervalued companies with dominant industry positions.'"

Visit the Vault Finance Job Board — one of the best job boards on the Internet exclusively for finance professionals. Go to www.vault.com.

VAULT   205

Robertson Stephens

555 California Street
Suite 2600
San Francisco, CA 94104
Phone: (415) 781-9700
Fax: (415) 248-4110
www.robertsonstephens.com

DEPARTMENTS

Capital Markets
Convertibles
Corporate Finance
Mergers and Acquisitions
Private Client Services
Private Capital
Research
Sales and Trading
Venture Capital

THE STATS

President and CEO: John Conlin
Employer Type: Subsidiary of
FleetBoston Financial
2000 Revenues: $1.6 billion
No. of Employees: 1,200
No. of Offices: 9

KEY COMPETITORS

Credit Suisse First Boston
Deutsche Banc Alex. Brown
Thomas Weisel Partners

UPPERS

• Deal and client exposure for junior
  bankers
• Entrepreneurial spirit
• Friendly, warm culture

DOWNERS

• High turnover and recent layoffs
• Lack of hierarchy can lead to
  disorganization
• Lack of infrastructure and support
  staff

EMPLOYMENT CONTACT

Investment Banking
Leah Lovelace
IB_Recruiter@rsco.com

Research
Laurel Rund
Research_Recruiter@rsco.com

Institutional Sales
Pamela Rattary
Sales_Recruiter@rsco.com

Financial Services Department
Amy DeTolla
FSD_Recruiter@rsco.com

THE SCOOP

Leading the charge

Founded in 1978, Robertson Stephens (affectionately known as Robbie Stephens) is one of the leading underwriters for growth industries and companies, including the technology, Internet, and e-commerce sectors. The firm was the top underwriter of so-called growth IPOs from 1995 to 1998. In 1999 the firm advised on 10 of the 15 largest Internet M&A transactions.

Merger magnet

Like many other San Francisco area boutique banks (Hambrecht & Quist and Montgomery Securities being the two most notable examples), the firm became a merger target in the late 1990s. In 1997 Robbie Stephens chose BankAmerica, then the third-largest bank in the U.S., as its partner. BankAmerica, seeking to take advantage of Robbie's underwriting and M&A capabilities, paid $540 million for Robbie Stephens. BankAmerica's deep pockets enabled Robbie Stephens to expand its staff and to venture outside its high-tech industry base. The ink was barely dry on the BankAmerica/Robbie Stephens merger agreement when the parent decided to merge again. In April 1998, BankAmerica merged with NationsBank, which had previously snapped up its own investment bank — Robbie Stephens' cross-town rival Montgomery Securities. Neither Montgomery nor Robbie Stephens was happy about the prospect of being paired. The two firms had, in the words of a Robertson Stephens spokesman, a "notoriously different approach" to doing business.

To avoid an I-banking death match, BankAmerica agreed to sell off Robbie Stephens' investment banking operations (at the time, Montgomery seemed the far better catch) to BankBoston for $800 million in the summer of 1998. BankAmerica went on to relaunch itself as Bank of America, and renamed its investment-banking arm Banc of America Securities.

Shortly after the acquisition by BankBoston, Sandy Robertson, Robbie Stephens' founder and former chairman, left the firm, along with Misha Petkevich, the head of investment banking. Though such high-level departures usually open up the floodgates, few senior bankers left the firm. The $400 million employee-retention pool was a big factor, but observers say that Robbie Stephens and BankBoston handled the transition well in general, in stark contrast to the BankAmerica/Montgomery combination.

Yet another merger

Try as it might, Robbie Stephens couldn't go a year without being involved in another merger. BankBoston coupled with Fleet Financial Group in October 1999, introducing Robbie Stephens to a third dance partner in less than three years. But Robertson Stephens' independence, which had survived more or less intact throughout the turmoil, remained secure even after the Fleet acquisition. Fleet, which has a reputation for allowing its subsidiary units to function autonomously, restored the Robertson Stephens name. (After being sold off to BankBoston by BankAmerica, the firm was saddled with the clumsy moniker BancBoston Robertson Stephens.) In May 1999, Bob Emery, previously COO and head of investment banking, was named president of Robertson Stephens. Emery stepped aside in April 2001 and John Conlin, a former Credit Suisse First Boston managing director who joined Robertson Stephens in May 1999, was named head of the firm.

Emery's departure was originally met with little fanfare and was regarded as a typical corporate management change. It wasn't until June 2001 that reports surfaced that Emery left amid a dispute about his compensation. According to *The Wall Street Journal*, Emery was paid approximately $25 million for 2001, 20 percent more than his superiors at FleetBoston believed they had approved. Emery received an additional $10 million from previous retention agreements, lifting his total pay for 2000 to $35 million — or, as the *Journal* pointed out, $18 million more than FleetBoston CEO Terrance Murray. FleetBoston asked Emery and CFO Dan Ryan, who also received more than his bosses expected, to resign in April 2001. Neither Emery nor Ryan has been accused of any criminal activity, and the *Journal* reported that both attribute the dispute to a misunderstanding.

Banking prowess

Robbie Stephens rebounded nicely from a sub-par 1998, reappearing on the 1999 league tables in its core industries. The company ranked fifth among advisors of technology M&A transactions and ranked third in the Internet sector. All told, the firm completed more than $60 billion worth of M&A transactions in 1999. Notable clients include WebMD in its $7.5 billion sale to Healtheon, Excite in its $7.2 billion purchase by @Home Network, and CMGI in that company's $2.3 billion purchase of AltaVista. In 2000 Robbie Stephens advised Ask Jeeves on its $507 million purchase of Direct Hit Technologies, E*Trade Group on its $1.8 billion acquisition of Telebanc Financial, and Healtheon/WebMD in a $1 billion investment by News Corp.

In a red-hot tech IPO market, equity underwriting was another booming business for Robbie Stephens. In 1999 the firm lead managed numerous IPOs, including the $98 million December offering by OnDisplay, the $108.8 million offering by IBasis in November, and the $145.5 million IPO for Value America in April. In 2000 the firm lead managed OrphaPharma's $72 million March IPO, as well as the $77 million IPO for Opus360 and the $168 million IPO for DDI, both completed in April 2000. The company was also a co-manager on Palm, Inc.'s $874 million offering in March 2000 and the $180 million IPO of EMachines in June 2000. Robertson Stephens' biggest hit in 2001 was Verisity, which raised $23.3 million in March of that year. By mid-year, Verisity was the top-performing IPO, having shot up 115 percent from its initial offering price.

The company probably would have preferred a little less publicity for what was arguably its most high-profile IPO of 2000. Divine interVentures, a Chicago-based Internet incubator, experienced a trying time getting to the public markets. The company hired Robertson Stephens after founder Andrew "Flip" Filipowski and advisors at CSFB couldn't come to terms on whether to shelve the offering or go forward during the economic downturn. Robbie came on board and soon after encountered a roadblock when Filipowski talked to reporters in what was supposed to be a pre-IPO quiet period. Flip's loose lips meant Robbie had to update the prospectus and re-file for the offering. When the company finally went public, it raised much less capital than Robertson Stephens had hoped for.

Taking stock

Early in 2001, Robbie's parent FleetBoston announced a plan that would give the 400 employees who had attained vice president or above status ownership in the investment bank. The plan has been described as an employee retention tool for executives who stick with the firm for at least the next three years. Talk of a Robertson Stephens spin-off had been bandied about; the employee ownership plan seems to be considered a step in that direction, although Fleet will probably not move too quickly on a spin-off, considering lingering uncertainty about the economy.

As a result of the treacherous economic conditions of early 2001, Robertson Stephens was sending out mixed signals on its hiring strategy. The firm announced plans to boost its European staff by 10 percent over 2001, including an increase of 30 percent in equity research. On the home front, however, Robbie Stephens began reducing headcount, laying off 160 workers, approximately 11 percent of the overall workforce. The layoffs were part of an overall trend among investment banks hurt by the economic slowdown of early 2001 and subsequent dearth of underwriting and

Visit the Vault Finance Job Board — one of the best job boards on the Internet exclusively for finance professionals. Go to www.vault.com.

V/\ULT   209

advisory business. However, some analysts felt that costs leftover from the firm's retention efforts after the numerous acquisitions of years gone by played a part in the layoffs, a charge a Robertson Stephens spokesperson denied.

GETTING HIRED

Picky picky

Like many niche investment banks, Robertson Stephens is fairly selective in hiring. "Robertson Stephens is still 'who you know' and in Boston, Ivy League is almost a must," says one contact. The firm conducts campus recruiting at "top-tier" undergraduate and MBA schools, including Harvard, Penn, Stanford, Columbia and the University of Chicago.

When interviewing, expect to meet with at least five senior-level bankers. "Typically, there is one round of on-campus interviews and a Super Saturday at the office the candidate is interviewing for," reports one insider. "Candidates meet several bankers throughout the process, including informational sessions [and] social events." Another contact reports that "final round interviews take place at corporate headquarters in San Francisco," though the firm says that investment banking recruits interview at field offices and other departments are considering following suit.

Expect a broad range of questions. "Interviewers can usually identify the capabilities of the interviewees by asking them to explain past experiences and course work," says one banker. "The firm also tries to determine the level of interest that the interviewees demonstrate for banking, particularly technology banking." Don't just spout banking buzzwords, though. "We also want to see that the candidate is personable, intelligent and articulate."

OUR SURVEY SAYS

Culture of innovation

Bankers say the culture is "the best part of Robertson Stephens." "The firm does an excellent job of recruiting people who mesh well with the team-oriented environment," reports one insider. "We take our culture seriously," says another contact. "All the analysts in San Francisco work in one area — the bullpen. We pride ourselves on working with each other, helping one another out so that everyone has an easier time with the demands that are placed on us." Analysts in New York and Boston also enjoy the bullpen life. For those in the bullpen, "the firm provides fruit, sodas and snacks."

New Yorkers at Robbie Stephens report a satellite feel. "The New York office is only now rising to the level of the Boston office," says one banker. "As a satellite office, there are unique challenges in staying in the loop. We will never be on par with San Francisco, but our experience here is possibly more humane, and we are in the center of the universe for all things civilized here in the Big Apple. There are trade-offs, of course, but I have been generally happy with my decision to stay in New York rather than relocating to San Francisco." Another New York-based employee adds, "The firm is very laid-back and very much concerned about employees' happiness."

No hierarchy

Relationships between senior and junior bankers are smooth. "We're too busy for people to have big egos," says one source. "I've been very pleased with the senior bankers," says one young contact. "I view them not just as bosses and co-workers, but rather as generally good people. I think there's a pretty good understanding about the pressures on a young banker's life, so they are sympathetic and empathetic." Observes another insider: "The senior bankers at Robertson Stephens treat the younger [bankers] with much more respect than at other banks."

In keeping with the congenial culture, the firm promotes a healthy social environment. "The majority of bankers here have very athletic backgrounds and this carries over into the overall feel of the bank," reports one contact. "Firm-sponsored events are common, with Friday afternoon beer bashes every month, group dinners and lunches, off-sites every quarter, and the occasional firm trip to Colorado for skiing." Insiders feel "the firm is committed to creating a positive social environment that makes the day-to-day enjoyable."

A manageable life with varying pay

Insiders at Robbie Stephens say the firm's compensation packages are "extremely competitive." "Robertson pays as well or better than any other bank in San Francisco," according to one banker in that city. Another banker adds, "[The firm] will pay up for its superstars." In other cities, Robbie Stephens bankers express more

Visit the Vault Finance Job Board — one of the best job boards on the Internet exclusively for finance professionals. Go to www.vault.com.

VAULT   211

concern. "The pay is all over the board," says one Boston banker. "You have to pressure the firm to step up." In New York, the pay is "not the highest, but certainly good compensation. The firm is considering ways to crank up the compensation for junior bankers who currently can't participate in our private investments." Reportedly, the firm recently raised analyst compensation to match Street increases.

Hours at Robbie Stephens are on par with or better than industry average, according to most insiders. One source says M&A analysts can expect 100-hour workweeks, with 80 hours for corporate finance. "Our travel schedule can be a little more demanding than at other firms because of the level of client contact and small deal teams," says another banker. Of course, in the words of one contact, "We do work hard, but it's a trade-off, too. Anything worth doing will require a commitment." Another source concurs: "If you want a nine-to-five job, don't get into investment banking. The hours are long but rewarding."

CFO? Who cares?

"Although the deals may not be the biggest in terms of value or profile, you do benefit from significant participation on transactions," says one banker. One junior banker reports feeling "challenged on a daily basis and [possessing] the ability to bring ideas to the table and act upon those ideas." Says one senior banker: "There are always those days you wish you stayed in bed, but at RS junior bankers get a significant amount of responsibility." Another source claims, "senior bankers realize that this is an apprenticeship business and experience is what makes the difference."

Client contact is the norm at Robertson Stephens. "I have traveled on multiple road shows with senior management and have direct contact with them," brags one banker. "Everyone from MD to analyst has a personal relationship with the executives of all our clients," according to another contact. "I had a two-on-two meeting with Michael Eisner, the CEO of Disney, my first year here," says one lucky source. "I'm not even impressed by the title CFO anymore," says another insider.

Training evolution

"The training program is an ever-evolving thing," says one insider. "It is currently thought that for associates, training should be a refresher, to knock the cobwebs out from the summer. [It's] very focused on teaching the incoming class the Robertson Stephens mode of operation." That contact further notes that "training is composed of several individual assignments focused on analytics and several group projects focused on applying those skills in real banking." The topper is a "final project analyzing an M&A transaction with teams on both sides making presentations to senior bankers."

For analysts, "Robertson Stephens devotes an entire month to analyst training," according to one contact. "After that, much of the training comes from exposure to deals. They do offer the opportunity for continuing education." Still, some feel the firm is a little behind other banks in terms of training. "Robertson Stephens is not as full service an investment bank, so the training is limited to the areas we work in," says an insider. "So I think training is much more extensive everywhere."

Trouble with diversity

While all investment banks have trouble maintaining a diverse work environment, Robbie Stephens seems to be a little worse off than most. "[The firm's] efforts are good," says one source, "but the firm is not extremely diverse." It's not much better for women. "The firm makes a good effort with women, [but] there are few senior women in banking at any firm," says an insider.

Visit the Vault Finance Job Board — one of the best job boards on the Internet exclusively for finance professionals. Go to www.vault.com.

V/\ULT   213

Thomas Weisel Partners

One Montgomery Street
San Francisco, CA 94104
Phone: (415) 364-2500
Fax: (415) 364-2695
www.tweisel.com

DEPARTMENTS

Private Client
Private Equity and Asset
  Management
Research
Institutional Sales and Trading
Investment Banking — M&A and
  Corporate Finance

THE STATS

Chairman and CEO: Thomas Weisel
Employer Type: Private Company
2000 Revenue: $474 million
No. of Employees: 800
No. of Offices: 5

KEY COMPETITORS

Credit Suisse First Boston
Morgan Stanley
Robertson Stephens

UPPERS

- Beautiful offices
- Entrepreneurial atmosphere
- Junior bankers given lots of
  responsibility

DOWNERS

- Hasn't attained bulge-bracket
  status
- Lacks diversity
- Tech focus increases vulnerability
  to market conditions

EMPLOYMENT CONTACT

Recruiting Department
Thomas Weisel Partners
One Montgomery Street
San Francisco, CA 94104
Fax: (415) 364-2876
jobs@tweisel.com

THE SCOOP

A San Francisco "merchant bank"

Thomas Weisel Partners was founded in January 1999 by Thomas Weisel, Frank Dunlevy, J. Sanford Miller, Derek Lemke-Von Ammon and Alan Menkes. The firm bills itself as a merchant bank rather than an investment bank — a reference to the fact that the firm seeks to invest in private companies through several private equity funds which total approximately $2 billion in assets under management. Weisel Partners' growth has been phenomenal; the company advised on 108 investment banking transactions in 1999 worth $23 billion, including 54 IPOs (seven of which the firm lead-managed). The company advised on 140 deals in 2000 (including 42 IPOs and 46 M&A transactions), for total revenues of $474 million. The firm had 630 employees in June 2000, after a little more than 18 months in business; that figure grew to more than 800 employees by February 2001. Additionally, according to *Investment Dealers'Digest*, the bank turned a profit after only four months in business.

Perhaps the company's fast track to success lies in Weisel himself, who has a long history of founding firms. He was a founding partner of Robertson Coleman Siebel and Weisel. However, after a now-infamous falling out with partner Sandy Robertson, Weisel left to form Montgomery Securities. Robertson, on the other hand, went on to establish Montgomery's San Francisco rival, Robertson Stephens.

I'm outta here

Thomas Weisel founded Montgomery Securities in 1978. He sold Montgomery to NationsBank in 1997 for $1.3 billion. (Weisel himself reportedly netted between $100-$120 million from the deal.) Weisel originally intended to remain and run Montgomery after the sale. But Weisel's plan to continue running Montgomery fell by the wayside when NationsBank merged with BankAmerica (now Bank of America).

Weisel clashed repeatedly with NationsBank CEO Hugh McColl after the union with BankAmerica. "At NationsBank, in effect, they were taking the entrepreneurial spirit away," Weisel would later tell *Forbes*. Specifically, after the NationsBank/BankAmerica merger, Weisel felt the bank was trying to fold Montgomery into the combined firm. This, Weisel told *Red Herring*, constituted "a violation of the merger agreement and of my employment contract." (A little history: Montgomery narrowly escaped being merged with Robertson Stephens because BankAmerica had purchased Robbie. Initially, NationsBank and BankAmerica discussed combining the two I-banks when the parents merged, but decided against it. BankAmerica then sold Robbie to BankBoston and proceeded with its merger with NationsBank.) Weisel finally quit in September 1998. He told *Red Herring*: "It was very easy for me to say, 'Fine, see you later.' I had no interest in being around people who don't keep their promises." (It appears Weisel can enjoy the last laugh — McColl announced his resignation in January 2001 because of BofA's lackluster performance.)

You worked at BofA Securities? Me too!

Shortly after splitting from Montgomery, Weisel started assembling a team with the intention of forming an investment bank of his own. Many observers felt Weisel — who was already well-off financially and possessed numerous outside interests — took on the burden of forming an investment bank mainly out of a desire to stick it to his former colleagues at the new Banc of America Securities. This is a charge Weisel denies. "I wish them well," he told *The San Francisco Chronicle* of his former firm. "There's no animosity. I'd like to work with them."

Whatever his motives were, Weisel's actions certainly annoyed the new management of BofA. His new venture took approximately 150 former Montgomery employees, including 36 of the 70 partners currently at Weisel. Weisel took so many employees, in fact, that BofA struck back. In December 1998, a handful of investment-banking analysts resigned from the old Montgomery, shortly after receiving $60,000 bonuses. Nations Bank withdrew the bonuses; after reconsidering, some of the money was restored, minus what NationsBank said were incremental bonuses paid upon promotion to associate — a promotion the analysts refused when they jumped ship for Weisel Partners.

In February 1999, BofA went a step further, filing a lawsuit against Thomas Weisel Partners alleging unfair hiring practices and theft of proprietary information. BofA pointed to the large number of former Montgomery bankers at Weisel and alleged that these employees had not left BofA's offices empty-handed, but had helped themselves to pitchbooks and other sensitive information. According to reports in *Securities Week*, BofA was seeking $500 million in damages in the suit. (Employment law experts said that to win the suit, BofA would probably have to prove that Weisel recruiters knowingly convinced bankers to break employment contracts with BofA.) The case was settled late in 2000, and although the firms did not disclose details, *The San Francisco Chronicle* reported that TWP paid approximately $20 million.

Renaissance man

Weisel is described by those around him as intense and driven. He holds an AB from Stanford and a Harvard MBA and is an accomplished athlete. In fact, he is a five-time speed skating champion who won his first title at the age of 14. (Rumor has it that Weisel just missed making the 1960 Olympic team.) Weisel has also served as chairman of the U.S. Ski Team. More recently, he sponsored Lance Armstrong and the U.S. Postal Service biking team in the 1999 Tour de France. Weisel is also a frequent financial contributor to the San Francisco Museum of Modern Art and a wing at the museum is named after him. His business prowess has also been recognized. He was named "Executive of the Year" in December 1999 by the *San Francisco Business Times* and won a 1999 "Banker of the Year" award from *Investment Dealers' Digest*.

Nasdaq crash claims another victim

In December 2000 Thomas Weisel Partners announced a joint venture with Scudder Kemper Investments aimed at wealthy investors. The partnership, dubbed Scudder Weisel, was meant to give clients access to hedge funds, venture capital funds and exclusive IPOs. The Nasdaq crash, and the subsequent dearth of tech equity deals, made the firms rethink the partnership soon after Scudder Weisel opened its doors. In March 2001 Weisel and Scudder (which changed its name to Zurich Scudder Investments in January 2001) announced that due to a shift in investment strategies for the two firms, the joint venture's fund would be liquidated and the partnership terminated.

New partners

While 1999 was a solid year for the company, 2000 got off to a great start as well. The California Public Employee Retirement System (CalPERS) invested $100 million for a 10 percent stake in the company in January 2000. The investment valued the firm at approximately $1 billion after just a year in business. According to reports in *Investment Dealers' Digest*, CalPERS also agreed to invest $500 million in Thomas Weisel Partners' private equity funds and an additional $500 million "to support new business activity by the firm."

The bank added some new blood in February 2000 when Mark Shafir and Jamie Streator came aboard as partners. Shafir arrived from Merrill Lynch, where he was head of global technology investment banking. He joined Weisel as co-director of investment banking and co-director of the bank's M&A advisory practice. Streator had been a health care banker at Hambrecht & Quist (now J.P. Morgan H&Q) and

Visit the Vault Finance Job Board — one of the best job boards on the Internet exclusively for finance professionals. Go to www.vault.com.

V/\ULT   217

serves as head of the health care investment banking practice at Weisel. In October Weisel lured two new partners into the fold. Bob Kitts, a former managing director at Morgan Stanley Dean Witter, became TWP's co-director of M&A and director of the financial sponsors investment banking, while Gill Sawhney, an ING Barings managing director, joined the firm as a managing director in the health care group. In January 2001, Tony Stais left Goldman Sachs to join TWP as partner and head of sales trading. The firm also poached Credit Suisse First Boston research star Mark Manson as director of research in April 2001.

Quick splash

The firm quickly established itself as an up-and-comer among technology I-banking firms. One of its first transactions was advising Yahoo! on its $4.7 billion acquisition of Geocities in May 1999. The bank also advised REZsolutions on the company's $250 million purchase by Pegasus Systems in April 2000 and SDL on its mammoth $41 billion merger with JDS Uniphase. The firm scored a major coup over larger I-bank competitors by securing the JDS mandate. In speaking about the deal, I-banking co-head Mark Shafir told Dow Jones, "The big firms do not have a monopoly on M&A talent." Other deals that kept TWP bankers busy in 2000: advising Exodus Communications on its $6.5 billion acquisition of GlobalCenter Inc. and Cisco Systems on its purchase of Active Voice Corp.

Thomas Weisel Partners has also been active in the equity markets, though it has not lead-managed many transactions. In August 1999, the bank co-managed the $96.6 million Red Hat IPO. Thomas Weisel Partners was also one of several co-managers for the enormous $10.6 billion AT&T Wireless IPO in April 2000. In June 2000 Weisel led a follow-on offering for Flextronics worth $450 million. The firm also led a $58.9 million IPO for Harvard Bioscience in December 2000. Finally, Weisel was tapped to co-lead an IPO for Tellium in May 2001.

Rough seas ahead?

Despite that phenomenal year, Thomas Weisel Partners wasn't immune to the fluctuations experienced throughout the industry in 2000 and 2001. The downturn in the market for technology firms may have made TWP vulnerable. In January 2001, *Investment Dealers' Digest* published rumors that TWP might be up for sale and that the firm asked its partners to forgo compensation for the fourth quarter of 2000. The article went on to note that the firm "underwrote only one tech equity deal for $51.4 million versus six for $490.7 million in the fourth quarter of 1999, according to

Thomson Financial Securities Data." A spokeswoman for the firm informed *IDD* that TWP is "definitely not for sale." Weisel himself sent a strongly worded letter to *IDD*, denying that the firm had seriously considered a sale or IPO. *IDD* stood by its assertion that the firm's partners were asked to go without pay in the fourth quarter but noted that the firm did pay up, though much less than it paid in the first half of the year.

GETTING HIRED

Growth industry

As at many start-up organizations, insiders report that the hiring process at Thomas Weisel Partners is still being refined. Insiders report a "very quick response [from the firm] if an individual is seen to have strong potential. People take recruiting very seriously. At times, the firm gets carried away with candidate pedigree, but this is changing." The firm's target schools are the "same as most of Wall Street, typically top-20 schools, but we will consider candidates from other [schools]."

Candidates can expect one or two preliminary rounds, either on campus or at one of the satellite offices. After the preliminary rounds, candidates are "flown out to San Francisco or New York for a series of final interviews." Interviewees meet between seven and 10 people who ask "very technical banking skill questions as well as personality questions."

OUR SURVEY SAYS

Near-perfect harmony

Some variation of opinions about working relationships with senior bankers at Thomas Weisel partners seems to exist among junior-level employees. "To your face, people are pleasant, but the knives come out when you turn your back," fumes one employee. "Junior people are used as fall guys for senior people's incompetence," adds the disgruntled worker. Along those same lines, another banker says, "Some senior bankers can show little interest in or respect for younger, developing bankers — unless they are clearly stars." But this contact adds that most senior bankers offer help and encouragement across the board. A third co-worker offers up quite a different opinion regarding his experiences with senior bankers: "They are not tight lipped with the 'thank-yous,' and are respectful of my time commitment."

In general Weisel's environment is considered laid back and its people respectful. "Versus the other firms at which I've worked, the analysts are treated very fairly and given lots of responsibility," says one fairly happy employee. "Senior bankers generally see junior bankers as part of the team — not just resources — and treat them with a high level of respect," echoes another insider.

As for the culture, many employees describe it as "entrepreneurial" and "collegiate." One insider says, "It's not stodgy, but also not laid back. It's young and aggressive and extremely competitive. We work on integrated teams, but there's a feeling that you better carry your share of the load (and then some) or you better find a new job." Typically, the hours are long, but as one employee put it, there's "no face time" required. Another banker explains the work/life dynamic at TWP thusly, "In New York, people wear 100 hours a week like a badge of honor. In California, it is a badge of shame. People work hard, but playing hard is just as important."

Insiders report that diversity at Thomas Weisel Partners is "not very good, but (sadly) we are probably on par for the industry." While contacts are careful to point out that "I don't believe I've seen intentional non-welcoming behavior," and the firm makes an effort to encourage diversity, "there are very few women and minorities at the firm." In the end, the firm's problems with diversity may be a result of its fast growth, which can make maintaining a diverse environment difficult. "When you build a $450 million business in two years," concedes one banker, "it is hard to be as proactive as larger, more established firms."

Class act

If there's one area where there's no disagreement, it's about the offices themselves. As far as aesthetics go, Weisel offices are downright swanky. Employees say custom-designed furniture and beautiful art are staples in all the offices, not just the San Francisco headquarters. "The offices in San Francisco and Menlo Park are extremely posh," reveals an insider. "The New York offices are also very nice and are still undergoing construction. We just put in a very cool state-of-the-art sales and trading floor in our Park Avenue building. No expenses were spared." Don't get too excited, though. Many TWP employees, including principals, share offices.

Right on the money

Compensation is on par with Wall Street firms. "In addition to being competitive with comparable salaries and bonuses, TWP grants options to all employees and enables employees to co-invest in a wide range of venture, private and public equity funds," says one source. Explains another insider: "TWP takes very good care of its employees in terms of salary. They are very aware of where the Street is and meet or exceed" those salaries.

Visit the Vault Finance Job Board — one of the best job boards on the Internet exclusively for finance professionals. Go to www.vault.com.

VAULT 221

Franklin Resources

777 Mariners Island Boulevard
San Mateo, CA 94404
Phone: (650) 312-2000
Fax: (650) 312-5606
www.frk.com

DEPARTMENTS

Asset Management
Portfolio and Trading
Research
Sales and Marketing

THE STATS

President and CEO: Charles Johnson
Employer Type: Public Company
Ticker Symbol: BEN (NYSE)
2000 Revenue: $2.3 billion
2000 Net Income: $562 million
No of. Employees: 6,500
No. of Offices: 45

KEY COMPETITORS

Fidelity Investments
Janus Capital
Vanguard Group

UPPERS

• Tuition reimbursement
• Excellent job training

DOWNERS

• Bureaucracy

EMPLOYMENT CONTACT

Donna Ikeda
Franklin Resources
777 Mariners Island Boulevard
San Mateo, CA 94404
Careers@frk.com

THE SCOOP

A penny saved is a penny earned

An admirer of Benjamin Franklin's business philosophy, "With money and financial planning, prudence comes first," Rupert S. Johnson, Sr., named the company he founded in 1947 in New York after the revered founding father. Hoping to capitalize on Ben's thrifty reputation, (in addition to his name, Franklin's image is used in company literature) Franklin Distributors focused on helping clients build hefty portfolios by investing in value and growth stocks. The firm went public in 1971 and two years later moved its operations to San Mateo, Calif., after acquiring Winfield & Company, an investment management company based in the San Francisco suburb.

Today, Franklin Resources (as Johnson's company is now known) is the largest publicly traded mutual fund concern in the world with $232 billion under management at the end of January 2001. Franklin leads the U.S. in bond funds and was a pioneer of tax-free state bond funds.

Steady growth

While it is possible to buy into Franklin's funds directly, Franklin mostly sells through stockbrokers. Charles Johnson, the son of the firm's founder, has been at the company's helm since 1958, and is largely credited with the firm's impressive growth. The junior Johnson describes his investment style as utilizing "a long-term outlook and intense bottom-up research," meaning that the firm gives much more weight to the strengths of potential and current investments than what is occurring in a particular business sector.

Recent expansion efforts have added a touch of aggressiveness to the firm's traditional conservative investing touch. These include the 1992 acquisition of Templeton, Galbraith and Hansberger, Ltd., a leader in international equity investing known for finding out-of-favor stocks believed to be undervalued. In 1996 Franklin merged with Heine Securities Corporation, strengthening the firm's equity fund offerings.

Recent troubles

Franklin suffered a difficult year in 1998, when income dropped to $68 million, from $130 million in 1997. The firm attributed much of its troubles to the fiscal crisis in Asia. In January 1999, the firm laid off 7 percent of its workforce, cutting 450 employees in its San Mateo headquarters and 560 overall. The business was restructured, resulting in a $58 million charge. The cuts came as the result of a consolidation of clerical operations such as transaction processing; no investment management jobs were lost.

Investors in the firm's Templeton Emerging Markets Investment Trust were upset that the fund fell 6 percent in 12 months. According to a March 2001 article in *Money* magazine, the fund went on to lose a third of its value for 2000. Fund manager Mark Mobius, who is considered a guru on investing in foreign markets, told *The Wall Street Journal*, "We've all woken up to the reality of these markets. We're being a lot more discerning [about the stocks we buy]."

Today, the firm seems to be on the upswing. Franklin's Mutual series of funds suffered heavy losses following the departure of its star manager, Michael Price, in 1998. Franklin's Mutual series of funds struggled in 1998 but showed some improvement in 1999. The funds then rebounded; all six funds in the series beat the S&P 500 Index in 2000, the first time entire series performed that well since 1994. There is some concern, though, that the firm may lose some of the fund's managers in November 2001. Contracts for five of the six managers of the Mutual series will expire then.

Old dog pulls new tricks

Rumors had been circulating for some time that Franklin would be sold, possibly to the German insurance firm Allianz AG, which had expressed interest in Franklin and a couple of smaller U.S. firms. All the while, Franklin CEO Charles Johnson maintained that the firm had no intention of selling out to anyone. Franklin had done a bit of international expanding itself, with the purchase of Canadian management firm Bisset & Associates in July 2000. Still, many industry insiders were surprised in October 2000 when — instead of announcing its own sale — Franklin announced another acquisition. The firm purchased Fiduciary Trust, a New York-based firm specializing in estate planning and asset management for corporations and non-profits, for $825 million in stock. "I think this deal says, with an exclamation point, that we intend to stay independent," Johnson told Reuters when the announcement was made. Franklin plans to market its mutual fund products to Fiduciary customers and sell Fiduciary's estate and trust planning services to its own customers.

GETTING HIRED

Franklin maintains an employment section of its web site, www.frk.com. The page lists job opportunities and contact information for positions at various offices. Franklin offers a two-year development program for entry-level employees, The Futures Program (formerly called Management Training Program). The program is designed to expose employees to different functions, and offers training in a variety of areas including marketing, sales and portfolio management.

OUR SURVEY SAYS

A challenging environment

"When I think of Franklin," says one insider, "a few words come to mind — 'absorbing,' 'high stress,' 'fun,' 'hard work.'" This challenging environment leads to a culture comprised of go-getters. Says one contact: "The people I work with are a great bunch of people — very sharp." Franklin employees note the pay is competitive, and "the experience you can gain is great." Perks include "full medical and dental coverage," and 100 percent tuition reimbursement for employees taking courses related to their work.

Good training

Employees note there is "lots of opportunity" at Franklin. According to one employee, the best route for recent college grads is through the Futures Program: "It is a two-year program where you rotate through various departments every four months, and during the last several months of the program you hope to find a department that you like, and will take you on permanently." Says another insider about the program: "It's well regarded by our competitors who often hire [graduates of the Futures Program] because it's such a cost effective way to get good management material."

Visit the Vault Finance Job Board — one of the best job boards on the Internet exclusively for finance professionals. Go to www.vault.com.

VAULT   225

245 Park Avenue
New York, NY 10167
Phone: (212) 272-2000
Fax: (212) 272-4785
www.bearstearns.com

DEPARTMENTS

Asset Management
Custodial Trust
Derivatives
Equities
Fixed Income
Global Clearing Services
Investment Banking
Merchant Banking
Private Client Services

THE STATS

Chairman and CEO: James Cayne
Employer Type: Public Company
Ticker Symbol: BSC (NYSE)
2000 Revenue: $10.3 billion
2000 Net Income: $773 million
No. of Employees: 11,200
No. of Offices: 21

KEY COMPETITORS

Deutsche Bank
J.P. Morgan Chase
Lehman Brothers
Merrill Lynch

UPPERS

- Responsibility for juniors
- Top of the pay scale

DOWNERS

- Sink-or-swim culture not good for those who can't swim
- Company strives to cut corners

EMPLOYMENT CONTACT

Investment Banking

Undergraduates:
Megan Kelaghan
Recruiting Manager, Investment Banking

MBA:
Abbe Shatles
Recruiting Manager, Investment Banking

Bear, Stearns & Co.
245 Park Avenue
New York, NY 10167
Fax: (212) 272-3052

Private Client Services

MBA:
Robert Benjamin
Senior Managing Director
Bear, Stearns & Co.
245 Park Avenue
New York, NY 10167
Fax: (917) 849-0218

For more contacts, check the career section of www.bearstearns.com.

THE SCOOP

Always profitable

Bear Stearns & Co. is younger than many of its high-profile rivals, but the firm's reputation stands up to those of its competitors. Known as "Bear" to Wall Street players, the venerable institution is one of the nation's top investment banking, securities trading and brokerage firms. With about half a million dollars in capital among the three of them, Joseph Bear, Robert Stearns and Harold Mayer started Bear Stearns in 1923. The firm initially operated with a small staff out of a single office at 100 Broadway. Founded as a partnership, Bear Stearns originally focused on brokerage.

With a gamut of financial services available, Bear Stearns now serves as financial advisor to many of the nation's major corporations and its clearing operations are a top choice of brokerage and other investment firms around the country, including many of its own rivals. After a few years of profit hibernation during the early 1990s, Bear Stearns has bounced back and is outgrowing its office space at a rapid pace. The company is currently building a new headquarters in New York, which is expected to be completed in 2002.

Bear has something of a ferocious reputation for cultivating a sink-or-swim culture and was headed for 15 years by a colorful chairman so thrifty that he reportedly tied broken rubber bands back together. But Bear employees report being satisfied with the relatively small (by Wall Street standards) organization and the entrepreneurial possibilities and sense of responsibility that the firm promotes.

Not at the top (but close)

Despite strong financial performance, highlighted by consistent revenue and profit growth, Bear Stearns has not broken into the upper echelon of Wall Street I-banks. Except for businesses like public finance (underwriting and issuing municipal bonds), in which the firm ranks in the top five consistently, and mortgage backed securities, in which the firm consistently ranks in the top three, Bear Stearns usually hovers at the bottom of the top 10 in the league tables. The firm finished out of the top 10 in M&A advisory and IPO underwriting for both 1999 and 2000.

Deals for Bear

Bear took a step toward growing its business in February 2001 when its announced plans to buy Wagner Stott Mercator, said to be the fifth-largest specialist firm on the

Big Board. (Specialist firms manage trades of specific stocks, as well as the trades of certain firms.) The purchase is being made in partnership with Hunter Partners, the seventh-ranked specialist firm. Bear Stearns will own 49.8 percent of Wagner Stott; Hunter will own the remaining 50.2 percent. Taking less than half interest in the firm means Bear won't have to report Wagner liabilities on its balance sheet; Bear will have to report profit and losses on its income statement, though. Wagner Stott counts Citibank and Merrill Lynch as its major clients, putting Bear Stearns in the unusual position of being in charge of the orders of two competitors. The transaction closed in April 2001.

Deals for clients

Despite its inability to break into the upper echelon, Bear still manages to participate in some of Wall Street's most notable deals. In late 1999, Warner-Lambert retained Bear for its merger discussions with Pfizer. Bear also advised Honeywell on its merger with Allied Signal during 1999. The Honeywell deal was named "Best Strategic Deal of the Year" by *Mergers & Acquisitions: The Dealmaker's Journal*. The firm also senior-managed what was at the time the largest municipal bond issue ever — a $3.5 billion issue for the Long Island Power Authority. Among recent equity deals for Bear was the $75 million IPO for 3-Dimensional Pharmaceuticals in August 2000 and the $80 million IPO for Informax in October 2000. In M&A, the firm advised Adac Laboratories on its $455 million purchase of Royal Phillips Electronics and NH Hoteles on its $900 million purchase of Kransnapolky Hotels.

Alan Greenberg: an "Ace" in the hole

With the odd business guidelines handed down to Bear Stearns employees from the desk of former chairman Alan "Ace" Greenberg, people might think that the investment-banking powerhouse is scraping for pennies. Greenberg earned a national reputation for his humorous (and sometimes biting) memos, which were collected into a book entitled *Memos From the Chairman*. Greenberg's memos have espoused the benefits of reusing rubber bands (if they're broken, simply tie the loose ends) and conserving paperclips. Ace even encouraged employees to inform upon colleagues who might be breaking one of the chairman's rules (this included professionals at all levels).

Ending the year like the big boys

In late 1999, Bear Stearns announced a change in its fiscal year-end date from June 30 to November 30. Most other Wall Street firms have long used November 30 or December 30 as fiscal year-ends. Historically, with Bear's summer year-end, the firm paid bonuses to employees in August. This payment practice made Bear particularly vulnerable to competitors who would try to poach Bear bankers in the early fall. Employees could leave Bear with a full paycheck at the end of August to join a competitor. After Bear paid bonuses in August 1999, the firm lost the co-head of investment banking, two senior managing directors and six health care bankers to other firms. With the new calendar change, bankers will be paid bonuses in January, as they generally are at other firms. Bear is also trying to develop more incentive compensation, handing out some pay in the form of stock options to retain more talent.

Clearing the way

One of Bear Stearns's most profitable divisions is its clearing business. Clearing firms process much of the paperwork that goes along with brokering. The company is hired to execute trades, maintain client records, send out trade confirmations and monthly statements and settle transactions. Close to 2,900 clients employ Bear for clearing, and even rival firms such as Lehman Brothers have employed the department's services. Primarily smaller brokerages use the firm's services; the appearance of Bear Stearns' name on paperwork sent to investors is often a selling point.

Legal troubles

Unfortunately, Bear Stearns' clearing operations have also generated some unwanted attention. One of the many brokerages for which the firm has cleared transactions, A.R. Baron, collapsed after bilking as many as 8,000 investors out of more than $75 million. The government investigated a possible Bear Stearns role in the Baron case — in particular, the ties between former Baron CEO Andrew Bressman and Richard Harriton, Bear Stearns' former chief of clearing. Bear agreed in June 1999 to pay $38.5 million in restitution and penalties to settle the SEC charges. In April 2000, Harriton paid a $1 million fine as a settlement with the SEC without admitting or denying any wrongdoing. Under the terms of his settlement, Harriton paid the fine and was banned for life from the securities industry but did not admit to or deny the charges. In September 2000, a federal judge granted class-action status to a series of lawsuits filed against Bear and Harriton by A.R. Baron customers. The plaintiffs' lawyer told *The Wall Street Journal* that they would be seeking between $50 and $100 million in the lawsuit.

Bear's clearing troubles were not yet behind it. A few weeks prior to Harriton's settlement, Bear was named in a class-action lawsuit by Cromer Finance. Cromer Finance invested in Manhattan Investment Fund, a $400 million hedge fund that lost nearly $300 million. The fund's manager, Michael Berger, was accused by the SEC of covering up these losses. According to the lawsuit against Bear, the company was aware in 1998 that Berger was losing large amounts of investor money but did not act to hinder his activities. The suit also charges that Bear slyly hinted to certain investors, with whom the investment bank had other business relationships, that they should pull out of the fund.

The firm had other legal problems, as well. The bank was ordered to pay a Canadian investor $111.5 million by a federal grand jury in May 2000; the trial judge tacked interest onto the verdict, bringing Bear Stearns' payment total up to $164 million. The wealthy investor claimed his Bear Stearns broker failed to disclose the risks involved in currency trades he made in the late mid- to late-1990s. Bear countered that the client, who at one time had currency positions valued at $6.5 billion, was a sophisticated investor well aware of the risks he was facing. The award, one of the largest against a Wall Street firm, led to a significant drag on the bank's second-quarter 2000 earnings, which were $118.4 million — down from $198.1 million for the same period in 1999.

GETTING HIRED

For investment banking, the firm targets approximately 12 business schools. At these schools, either the co-head of investment banking or another high-ranking official makes a presentation. At about five other business schools, the firm interviews but does not give presentations. Don't worry if your school is not targeted. The firm conducts "in-house interviews for those who write in" from out-of-the-way schools.

Bear Stearns draws many of its associates from its summer programs. The summer hiring process is condensed into a three-week period. The first round is usually an on-campus, two-on-one interview. While students at some schools will travel to Bear's New York headquarters for second rounds, many will simply interview again that evening on-campus. (For example, since the University of Chicago business school does not excuse time off from classes to travel for interviews, Bear conducts both first and second rounds on campus.) The final round in New York is described as "the typical super day format with analyst-level candidates meeting mostly with associate and VP-level bankers and associate candidates meeting mostly with VP and managing director/senior managing director-level people." That source also reports that "one of the two co-heads of investment banking generally interviews every associate candidate."

The firm also generally targets about 40 undergraduate schools each year. It hires about 100 analysts into I-banking worldwide, and about 75 of them work in New York. Although Bear accepts resumes from all undergraduate schools, for summer analyst positions Bear likes to have representation from its core schools — the firm only recruits on campus for summer analysts at Wharton, Dartmouth, Michigan and the University of Virginia.

Insiders say not to look for technical questions. "There is a uniqueness to our culture and we look for people who can both enhance it and excel in it," says one source. "We stay away from the brain teaser questions." Another contact concurs, saying Bear asks "the typical banker questions. 'Why banking,' 'why you' and 'why you with Bear?' Some technical questions for undergrad students with a business degree and MBAs but nothing out of the ordinary — [it] all depends on the interviewer."

The firm doesn't recruit undergrads for sales and trading, although those with BAs who complete the firm's operations training program can go into sales and trading. For associates in sales, trading, research and public finance, the firm recruits on campus at 10 business schools — NYU, Columbia, Harvard, Wharton, Chicago, Kellogg, Stanford, UCLA, Fuqua and Darden. Says a recruiter, "We do very well with Columbia, NYU and Chicago; those are our three best." Associates are hired into one of four departments: fixed income, equity, research or public finance. Candidates in these areas can expect one-on-one interviews, with probably two rounds. "For a full-time hire, you have to have six interviews," according to one insider. Summer hires generally go through an on-campus round and then one callback.

About 50 to 75 percent of the sales trading, and public finance associate class is hired through the summer program. In these departments, the firm hires about 20 to 25 summer associates and about 20 full-time associates. All fixed-income hires complete 12 weeks of rotations, covering six different desks, and are placed after that; the equity division hires students for both specific slots and as generalists. All research positions are hired on an as-needed basis.

OUR SURVEY SAYS

"The culture is broken"

Insiders at Bear Stearns praise the firm as being "entrepreneurial" and "aggressive," though they concede the culture has its downside. Sources say the firm offers "so much responsibility that it automatically becomes a rewarding experience." "You're going to a firm that's large and has its fair share of marquee deals, but you're not going to a factory," reports another insider. One source called the firm "flat," which enables everyone "to make an impact on every level." That autonomy does have its price. "The every-man-for-himself culture and the lack of honesty and fair-mindedness I see in the management outweigh, for me, the early responsibility and challenging, interesting work I have received," rails one insider. "Little effort is made to cultivate junior pros or to instill loyalty in the right kind of people. In short, the culture is broken."

Because "there's very little structure, you have to find your own way" at Bear Stearns. Says one source: "Every place says they're entrepreneurial — this place is entrepreneurial." The firm also allows for "individual stars to shine." Because of Bear Stearns' "thorough commitment to recognizing individual merit, those who perform well can really hold their heads up high." One junior banker explains, "There's an openness here to new ideas. If I do something unique, it's going to get noticed and appreciated."

Sink or swim?

While insiders note the lack of hand-holding that might be present at some other firms, at least one Bear employee says everyone has "the chance to become a star player for the firm." Some employees say the firm has a "survival of the fittest" mentality which "extends into all ranks." Bear is "very much a cowboy culture," continues another source. "[There's] lots of whooping and hollering emanating from the trading floor. A colleague put it best: 'Every man is his own corporation, with his own bottom line.'"

Bear employees are quick to point out that the firm is not a completely sink-or-swim environment, saying that they are provided support from senior employees. "Bear people are, above all else, individuals, and the culture not only accepts but applauds this." Still, the firm makes an effort to encourage teamwork. I-banking associates are assigned a junior and a senior mentor (a VP as the junior mentor and an MD as the senior mentor). There are those who downplay the competitive culture. "The bottom line is to make money," says one associate. "If all that they say about back stabbing and sink-or-swim were true, how the hell would we make any money?" "From a junior banker's perspective, the culture encourages development and rewards those who excel," brags another insider. "It truly is a meritocracy."

Associates, stick to your mentor

Speaking of senior bankers, Bear insiders give their superiors mixed reviews. "Success at Bear Stearns depends partly on good results and partly on patronage," says one source. "There is no formal evaluation process and no institutional method to ensure objective feedback. It is thus crucial to find a good patron to help your career along." Once you find that patron, never let him/her go. "My senior bankers have taken a true interest in my development; I feel that I can sit down in any of their offices at any time and be welcomed. They personally push me to the limits of my ability and are genuinely thankful for the work that I do for them." You'll rarely get stuck doing menial work. "Once in a while you've got to suck it up and work on that random annoying pitchbook that you just don't want to do but the vast majority of the time, work assignments are appropriately assigned to analysts based on their prior experiences and abilities."

Whatever you get from your seniors, don't expect a great deal of formal training. "Come to Bear Stearns already knowing the job you are to do," warns one insider. "Otherwise it will be very difficult. Training simply is not a priority at this firm." Those outside the firm's New York headquarters report that some formal instruction is "offered over video conference."

No paper clips for you

The Bear Stearns support staff has been described by employees as "the best available." Unlike at other Wall Street firms, there are plenty of secretaries to go around, though some offices may have a limited number depending upon their needs. Word processing and data entry services are also available and interns are plentiful and available for all research needs. However, several employees confirm that "the firm does emphasize thrift." The firm distributes a bag of paper clips and rubber bands to each new employee, with a memo from Ace Greenberg that reminds them that "the best poker players leave nothing on the table" (i.e., even in booming markets, watching expenses pays off). Says one banker about the dearth of supplies,

"No joke, if I see a paper clip on the floor or a pen on somebody's desk — if somebody's stupid enough to leave a pen on their desk — I take it."

"Success at Bear Stearns depends partly on good results and partly on patronage."

— *Bear Stearns insider*

Visit the Vault Finance Job Board — one of the best job boards on the Internet exclusively for finance professionals. Go to www.vault.com.

V∧ULT   235

[willing to pay $120K]

[asking for $80K

Vault Finance Channel >

- Company Profiles
- Message Boards
- Finance Member Netv
- Finance Job Board
- Finance Resume Data

THE BEST OF
THE REST

Allen & Company

711 Fifth Avenue
9th Floor
New York, NY 10022
Phone: (212) 832-8000
Fax: (212) 832-8023

DEPARTMENTS

Asset Management
Investment Banking
Sales and Trading
Venture Capital

THE STATS

CEO: Herbert Allen, Jr.
Employer Type: Private Company
No. of Employees: 200
No. of Offices: 1

KEY COMPETITORS

Goldman Sachs
Lazard
Morgan Stanley
Veronis, Suhler & Associates

UPPERS

- Lucrative profit sharing
- No face time
- Schmooze with the stars

DOWNERS

- Bad deals can savage salaries
- Extraordinarily competitive and difficult hiring process
- Must do own research

EMPLOYMENT CONTACT

Human Resources
Allen & Co.
9th Floor
New York, NY 10022

THE SCOOP

Founded in New York in 1922, Allen & Co. is a highly unusual investment bank. Bankers are required to pay their own travel and support expenses and the firm demands that principals at the company do their own research. Despite that, anyone in the industry will tell you that bankers from Allen & Co. are among the most highly regarded in the I-banking universe. That's because the firm, which specializes in media M&A work, carries prestige, an impressive array of media clients and investment opportunities rarely matched by other banks. Besides its M&A prowess, Allen & Co. is probably best known in the industry for its Sun Valley conference, an annual gathering of entertainment and business elite in Sun Valley, Idaho.

Brothers Charles and Herbert Allen founded Allen & Co. as a partnership in 1922. The company provides a mix of investment banking (including securities underwriting and mergers and acquisitions), private equity and venture capital and investment management services.

GETTING HIRED

Allen & Co.'s personnel department does not accept outside calls, does not maintain a job hotline and does not publicize job openings. The firm does, however, accept resumes mailed to its headquarters. Allen hires only MBAs as bankers and typically requires two to three years of experience. Insiders say getting a job directly out of business school is rare, and getting hired right out of college is "next to impossible."

In an exclusive interview with Vault, Allen & Co. Chairman Don Keough had this to say to prospective Allen employees: "My advice to a young person, especially a business school student, interested in Allen & Co. is to be sure you become an interesting person. You should develop a full range of interests and not worry about a career. Secondly, any young person who doesn't put the international world into perspective is a damn fool. Any education in today's world must incorporate some part of it outside the United States."

OUR SURVEY SAYS

Bankers say working at Allen & Co. makes them feel like members of "a very special, secret society." One banker says, "The culture here is one of risk-taking, both on a personal and corporate level. You must have a significant portion of your net worth at risk if you want to work here, and you must be a fee generator soon after arriving." Confides another contact: "There's salary plus a percentage of the fees from deals that you work on. You get paid when a fee comes in — no waiting for year-end bonus.

American Century Investments

4500 Main Street
PO Box 410736
Kansas City, MO 64141
Phone: (816) 531-5575
Fax: (816) 340-7962
www.americancentury.com

EMPLOYMENT CONTACT

www.americancentury.com/careers

DEPARTMENTS

Finance/Accounting
Investment Management
Market/Research Analysis
Retirement Plan Services
Sales
Trading

THE STATS

President and CEO:
William M. Lyons
Employer Type: Private Company
No. of Employees: 3,100
No. of Offices: 4

THE SCOOP

American Century Investments was founded in 1958 by James Stowers, Jr., in Kansas City. Though the company initially offered just two mutual funds, American Century now offers individuals and institutions a variety of investment management options, including IRAs, 401(k)s and 403(b)s, trusts, separate and subadvisory accounts and more than 70 mutual funds. American Century has more than $95 billion in assets under management. Formerly Twentieth Century Investments, the firm changed its name to American Century Investments following a 1995 merger with fixed-income investment firm Benham Group.

Although he's no longer responsible for day-to-day management, Stowers still has an active role in the company, serving as chairman of the board. He and his family retain a controlling interest in the firm. However, financial services giant J.P. Morgan Chase owns a big chunk of the company; the former J.P. Morgan purchased a 45 percent stake in 1998 for $900 million. Although Morgan Chase has two seats on American Century's board Stowers still controls most of the voting stock. American Century plans to leverage the Morgan Chase relationship by marketing its retirement plans to Morgan Chase customers. Another high-profile American Century partnership is with Charles Schwab, which is acting as a distributor of American Century's 529 college savings program. American Century is the administrator of the State of Kansas' 529 plans.

GETTING HIRED

Check out American Century's web site, www.americancentury.com, to search a listing of the company's job openings. Prospective employees can also create a profile based on their area of interest and preferred location. American Century will then e-mail candidates jobs matching the information in their profiles.

The firm says it is committed to providing opportunities for advancement. According to the firm, 52 percent of its job openings in 2000 were filled by people already employed at the firm. New hires go through a two-day orientation. Based on pre-set goals, each employee creates what the firm calls an "individual success plan." Employees can monitor their plans through the company's intranet, complete with links that connect the individual's goals to department objectives. The firm offers additional courses onsite and online. American Century has been named one of the top 100 companies to work for by *Working Mother* and *Fortune* magazines.

Visit the Vault Finance Job Board — one of the best job boards on the Internet exclusively for finance professionals. Go to www.vault.com.

VAULT 241

Banc of America Securities

9 West 57th Street
New York, NY 10019
Phone: (888) 583-8900
Fax: (212) 847-6922

600 Montgomery Street
San Francisco, CA 94111
Phone: (800) 227-4786
corp.bankofamerica.com

DEPARTMENTS

Corporate and Investment Banking
Equity Financial Products
Equity Sales, Trading and Research
Fixed Income Sales, Trading
  and Research
Floating Rate Debt
Global Derivative Products
Global Foreign Exchange
Mergers and Acquisitions
Mortgage Backed Securities
Portfolio Management
Structured Credit Products

THE STATS

CEO: Ken Lewis (Bank of America)
**President, Global Corporate and
Investment Bank:** Ed Brown
Employer Type:
Division of Bank of America
No. of Employees: 9,000
No. of Offices: 60

UPPERS

• More responsibility at junior level

DOWNERS

• Muddled culture due to extensive
  merger history

EMPLOYMENT CONTACT

Ronni Greenberg
Campus Recruiting
9 West 57th Street
New York, NY 10019
Fax: (212) 847-6921

THE SCOOP

Born of complicated merger history, Banc of America Securities is the investment banking arm of Bank of America Corporation, a Charlotte, N.C.-based commercial bank. Banc of America Securities has focused on companies in eight primary industries: technology, consumer retail products, health care, real estate, financial services, media and telecommunications, natural resources, and diversified industries. The investment banking practice has 60 offices worldwide with hub offices in New York and San Francisco.

GETTING HIRED

Insiders report that Banc of America Securities recruits from "Ivy League and larger regional schools." MBAs say candidates can generally expect two rounds of interviews. "The first round is more technical and more 'why do you like us and why do you want to do banking?' The second round is definitely determining whether [the candidate] fits with employees at [the company]," says one associate. The firm hires investment banking MBAs directly into an industry focus or product area.

OUR SURVEY SAYS

Insiders also report a firm culture that is "a little less uptight than the average investment bank" and "entrepreneurial." Says another source, "I think 'teamwork' is a much more important term than it used to be. Ten years ago, the most important characteristic was individual aggressiveness. It was a very small firm, and individuals had to go out and get an account, and they did it by themselves. Now we are much more about working as a team."

Insiders at the firm generally speak highly of co-workers. "Everyone is pretty friendly and good to work with," reports one insider. In terms of diversity, most bankers report that the firm is "fairly diverse for the industry," though at least one contact mentions the firm has "very few females" in the senior ranks. Hours are considered "livable" and one M&A associate estimates an average work week as "ranging from 65 to 75 hours." That contact also reports the quality of work as "decent." He explains, "About 65 percent [of my work] is execution of real deals and 35 percent [is] pitching and prospecting."

Bank of America

100 North Tryon Street
Charlotte, NC 28255
Phone: (704) 386-5000
Fax: (704) 386-6699
www.bankofamerica.com

DEPARTMENTS

Asset Management
Consumer and Commercial Banking
Global Corporate and Investment
   Banking
Principal Investing

THE STATS

Chairman and CEO: Kenneth Lewis
Employer Type: Public Company
Stock Symbol: BAC (NYSE)
2000 Revenue: $57.8 billion
2000 Net Income: $7.5 billion
No. of Employees: 142,700
No. of Offices: 4,500

KEY COMPETITORS

Bank One
Citigroup
First Union
FleetBoston
J.P. Morgan Chase

UPPERS

- Entrepreneurial culture
- Growing in investment banking, asset management

DOWNERS

- Big bank means big bureaucracy
- Following industry layoff trend

EMPLOYMENT CONTACT

Bank of America
Scanning Operations
Attn: WWW
CA4-707-01-37
PO Box 37000
San Francisco, CA 94137
careers@bankofamerica.com

Applications for retail branches and regional offices can be sent to the particular office.

THE SCOOP

Bank of America is certainly living up to its name. Formed by the $43 billion merger of the already large Bank of America and NationsBank, it has approximately 4,500 branches in 21 states and the District of Columbia. Before the merger, which was completed in September 1998, Bank of America (then known as BankAmerica) was the third-largest commercial bank in the country. The combination created the second-largest American bank, in terms of assets. With 8.1 percent of U.S. bank deposits and 29 million households as customers, BofA is the largest in the country in terms of number of accounts under management.

GETTING HIRED

At Bank of America, MBA-level associates are recruited directly by each department. One former employee cautions: "Here's a tip. You can't always choose your city. [The firm] will try, but for example if you want to work in high-yield bonds, you aren't going to be working in San Francisco." The firm also recruits on the undergrad level at UC Berkeley, UC Davis, Stanford, the University of Wisconsin and the University of North Carolina at Charlotte. Candidates from other schools and working professionals can search the company's job listing and submit a resume online.

OUR SURVEY SAYS

Like any company that's grown through merger, Bank of America's culture has gone through some changes. "This used to be an organization where we felt like family," says a manager, but no longer. The company is now "an extremely large retail bank with an extremely large retail bank culture." This shift in the corporate atmosphere has nevertheless fostered an "entrepreneurial" environment in which new employees receive "immediate exposure to clients, upper management and other bank groups." While some feel that the changes have been detrimental to employee morale, others approve of "a new aggressive attitude with an emphasis on teamwork."

Bank of America insiders concur that the culture of NationsBank reflects the personality of former CEO McColl, an ex-Marine known to be hard-charging yet caring. "The exposure to top management is gratifying," says one associate. "The culture involves team work, working hard and playing hard. You will not find many jerks in the organization, as they get culled fast," comments one insider.

Visit the Vault Finance Job Board — one of the best job boards on the Internet exclusively for finance professionals. Go to www.vault.com.

VAULT   245

The Bank of New York

One Wall Street
New York, NY 10286
Phone: (212) 495-1784
Fax: (212) 495-2546
www.bankofny.com

DEPARTMENTS

Asset Management
Corporate Banking
Global Market Services
Global Payment Services
Private Client Services
Retail Banking
Securities Services

THE STATS

Chairman and CEO:
Thomas A. Renyi
Employer Type: Public Company
Ticker Symbol: BK (NYSE)
2000 Revenue: $7.5 billion
2000 Net Income: $1.4 billion
No. of Employees: 18,860
No. of Offices: 400+

KEY COMPETITORS

Bank of America
Citibank
J.P. Morgan Chase

UPPERS

- Job security
- Profit sharing

DOWNERS

- Bureaucracy
- Limited advancement opportunities

EMPLOYMENT CONTACT

Human Resources
One Wall Street
13th Floor
New York, NY 10286

THE SCOOP

The Bank of New York (BNY) was founded in 1784 and is now the oldest bank operating under its original name in the U.S. The company's constitution was written by Alexander Hamilton, founding father and the first Secretary of the Treasury. The Hamilton connection came in handy for BNY; the company made the first loan to the United States, for $200,000 in 1789. When the New York Stock Exchange was founded three years later, BNY was the first stock traded. Now, the company provides a full range of corporate and individual services, including retail and commercial banking services and custodial and trust services (handling of assets for individuals and businesses).

GETTING HIRED

The Bank of New York's web site, www.bankofny.com, has a complete listing of job openings, qualifications and descriptions. The firm posts developmental positions for both MBAs and college grads, as well as for those in computer technology. Expect to meet an HR representative, then several managers in your division including (in some cases) the division head. And be careful not to fib on your resume or in your interviews. "Be aware that HR will check up on the information you provide them — experience, education, salary, etc.," says one source. "If it is discovered that you are dishonest in how you present yourself, you will be asked to leave the firm."

OUR SURVEY SAYS

Bank of New York employees praise the "unwritten policy of permanent job security" and the "collegial" corporate atmosphere. "I think [BNY] has a very stodgy reputation, but the reality is a bit different," reports one contact. For example, "there isn't a whole lot of formality in the office." Insiders say that promotion opportunities are "infrequent" and that the "conservative management" is "slow to implement change."

While this "sluggish" corporate culture is the source of "frustration," employees do benefit from hours that are "not too strenuous," "sparkling" salaries, a profit sharing plan that can be as much as 18 percent of one's salary and performance bonuses.

The firm also gets good marks for diversity. According to one insider: "I'm not sure [BNY] necessarily has a lot of programs that encourage the hiring and retention of certain classes of people," such as minorities or women. "As I look around the firm, however, I recognize that the work force — on all levels — reflects the diversity one expects to see in a place like New York City."

BlackRock

345 Park Avenue
29th Floor
New York, NY 10154
Phone: (212) 754-5560
Fax: (212) 754-3123
www.blackrock.com

DEPARTMENTS

Account Management
Global Operations
Information Technology
Portfolio Management
Real Estate Funds
Risk Analytics
Sales/Marketing

THE STATS

Chairman and CEO:
Lawrence D. Fink
Employer Type: Public Company
Stock Symbol: BLK (NYSE)
2000 Revenue: $476.9 million
2000 Net Income: $87.4 million
No. of Employees: 727
No. of Offices: 6

KEY COMPETITORS

Gabelli Asset Management
PIMCO Advisors
T. Rowe Price

THE SCOOP

For a firm that few people outside the financial industry have even heard of, BlackRock has had a long and successful history. The company was created in 1988 as a unit of leveraged buyout firm Blackstone. Its mastery of the bond market has netted the company more than $200 billion in assets under management. The firm also sells a variety of mutual funds and risk management products to institutional and individual investors. Blackrock runs 700 mutual funds that service approximately 200,000 individual investors and 3,300 institutional clients and is the 13th-largest manager of institutional assets. The company has six offices, including a joint venture with Tokyo-based Nomura Securities.

Blackrock was essentially created in 1988 when Larry Fink, the firm's chairman and CEO, left what was then First Boston to create a fixed-income asset management business for private equity powerhouse Blackstone. Fink and his management group were given a 60 percent stake in the asset management business. Within three years, the team had built up $9 billion under management and a client list of heavy hitters (including Chrysler and GE). But Fink and Blackstone management clashed over strategic planning issues: He wanted to issue more shares with which to entice prospective fund managers; Blackstone didn't want to dilute its equity.

Fink and the firm were at a stalemate, with the only solution being dissolution, so in 1995 Fink and friends left Blackstone, sold to PNC Financial Services for $240 million. Out of an interest in maintaining some connection to the reputation he built at Blackstone, Fink named the fixed-income unit BlackRock. By 1998 PNC had folded much of its asset management services, including its equity and liquidity management businesses, under the BlackRock umbrella. In October 1999, BlackRock went public, selling a 14 percent stake for $126 million, marking the first time a bank had spun off an asset management unit as a public company. The firm is run by an independent management committee that includes Fink and the founders.

GETTING HIRED

The firm offers internships in accounting for juniors and a year-round internship in account administration. BlackRock recruits at more than 20 universities, including Columbia, Cornell, Howard, NYU, Princeton and the University of Virginia. In addition, the company attends several job fairs each year in New York, Washington, D.C., and Chicago. Consult the firm's web site for further details and recruiting schedules. Once a year, BlackRock gives a four-week training program for incoming employees. Other employees are allowed to attend the training, regardless of how long they've been with the firm.

Broadview International

One Bridge Plaza
Fort Lee, NJ 07024
Phone: (201) 346-9000
Fax: (201) 346-9191
www.broadview.com

DEPARTMENTS

Divestitures
Mergers and Acquisitions
Private Equity
Recapitalizations
Refinancings

THE STATS

Chairman and CEO: Paul Deninger
Employer Type: Private Company
No. of Employees: 350
No. of Offices: 5

KEY COMPETITORS

Allen & Company
Dresdner Kleinwort Wasserstein
Thomas Weisel Partners

UPPERS

- Easier hours than bankers on the Street
- Analysts given responsibility at an early stage

DOWNERS

- N.J. headquarters inconvenient for some Manhattanites
- Single-sector focus could hurt firm in market downturn

EMPLOYMENT CONTACT

Justin Kulo
Recruiting Manager
Broadview International
One Bridge Plaza
Fort Lee, NJ 07024
Fax: (201) 346-9191
AssociateRecruiter@Broadview.com
AnalystRecruiter@Broadview.com

THE SCOOP

Founded in 1973, Broadview International has become a major player in the mergers and acquisitions field, especially in middle-market transactions. The firm focuses exclusively on IT, communications and media deals. In 2000 the firm executed 105 M&A transactions with a cumulative value of $32 billion. The company also led 10 private placements worth $951 million over the same period. Broadview's venture capital unit makes early- and late-stage investments and has over $570 million under management. The firm has approximately 350 employees in five offices worldwide. Chairman and CEO Paul Deninger has led the company since 1997. Citing the "industry environment," Broadview cut 50 employees, including analysts and support staff in the M&A advisory division, in June 2001.

GETTING HIRED

Broadview recruits analysts and associates at top U.S. and European schools. Calendars for presentations and on-campus interviews can be found at www.broadview.com. The firm hires undergrads into a two-year analyst program that begins with three weeks of training in the firm's Foster City, Calif., office. Unlike some other investment banks, Broadview prefers one-on-one interviews to two-on-ones. The process for analysts involves an on-campus interview (or one at the firm's headquarters) and then a "super day," usually a Saturday, with four to six interviews. Insiders say you can expect to see at least two senior bankers, typically managing directors.

OUR SURVEY SAYS

Insiders note the firm provides a lifestyle that is characteristic of working for a smaller firm. "The hours [at Broadview] are maybe 60 to 65 a week — that's a week at Club Med compared to Wall Street." Another insider pegs the hours a little higher. "You have the occasional all-nighter, but it's all about a deal cycle. It's minimum 60 or 70." Continues that source, "Still, it's not expected that you'll be there on the weekends."

"Because you're in a small environment, if you're talented, everyone will know," explains one insider. One former analyst recounts leading a six-hour meeting with the CEO of a client. "I'm not saying that's typical, but if you know your shit, you'll get to do some cool stuff," says another contact.

Visit the Vault Finance Job Board — one of the best job boards on the Internet exclusively for finance professionals. Go to www.vault.com.

VAULT 251

The Capital Group Companies

333 South Hope Street
52nd Floor
Los Angeles, CA 90071
Phone: (213) 486-9200
Fax: (213) 486-9217
www.capgroup.com

EMPLOYMENT CONTACT

The Capital Group Companies
333 South Hope Street
Los Angeles, CA 90071-1447
Fax: (213) 486-9035

DEPARTMENTS

Global Institutional Investment
  Services
Global Private Equity
Personal Investment Management
U.S. Mutual Funds

THE STATS

President: Larry Clemmensen
Employer Type: Private Company
No. of Employees: 5,000
No. of Offices: 19

KEY COMPETITORS

Charles Schwab
Fidelity Investments
Vanguard Group

THE SCOOP

Although it may have a lot to crow about, the Capital Group Companies is one of the most low-key firms in the financial industry. Capital Group, a privately held firm formed in 1931, has more than $500 billion in assets under management and 19 offices around the world, but its executives choose to keep a low profile, rarely granting interviews. Founded during a time when the reverberations of the stock market crash of 1929 were still being felt, Capital Group's philosophy of prudent, long-term investing — as opposed to investing in the current hot sector — continues to serve it well today.

The firm was begun by investment researcher Jonathan Bell Lovelace. Lovelace's observance of market conditions led him to believe that many of the stocks on the market were overvalued, but he was unable to convince his partners at E.E. MacCrone & Co. Fearing a market downturn, Lovelace sold many of his personal investments in the summer of 1929. Two years later, Lovelace started the Capital Research and Management, the precursor to the Capital Group. By 1939, Lovelace had reorganized the assets of a former client, The Investment Company of America, creating the firm's first open-end mutual fund. ICA later became the flagship product of American Funds Group, a subsidiary of Capital.

GETTING HIRED

Capital management prefers to call those who work at the firm "associates," rather than "employees." According to corporate literature, the use of the term indicates that everyone who works for Capital Group plays an important role in the company's growth. It should come as no surprise, therefore, that job candidates undergo a thorough interview process. Applicants should be prepared to "meet many people with whom you may interact if you become an associate." Those interested in employment at Capital should search the listing of open positions on the firm's site, www.capgroup.com. Searches can be conducted by location or job function. Resumes can be submitted online; they can also be faxed or mailed to a specific office with an opening.

Capital is known in the industry for having low turnover among associates; the firm claims the annual rate hovers near 5 percent. Benefits may account in part for the low turnover. In addition to the standard health and 401(k) benefits given by most companies, Capital associates receive reimbursements for approved educational programs and gym fees, same-sex partner health benefits and a retirement fund contribution equivalent to 15 percent of annual salary.

CIBC World Markets

CIBC World Markets
425 Lexington Avenue
New York, NY 10017
Phone: (212) 667-7000
Fax: (212) 667-5310
www.cibcwm.com

DEPARTMENTS

Equities
Investment Banking
Leveraged Finance

THE STATS

Chairman and CEO: David Kassie
Employer Type: Subsidiary of
Canadian Imperial Bank of
Commerce
2000 Revenues: $3.1 billion
2000 Net Income: $731 million
No. of Employees: 3,300
No. of Offices: 32

KEY COMPETITORS

Bear Stearns
Lehman Brothers
TD Securities

UPPERS

- High level of deal exposure
- Relaxed working environment

DOWNERS

- Long hours
- Not as well known as other firms
  on the Street

EMPLOYMENT CONTACT

Campus Recruiting
CIBC World Markets USA
1 World Financial Center
36th Floor
New York, NY 10281
Fax: (212) 667-5314

THE SCOOP

CIBC World Markets, the investment banking and brokerage arm of the Canadian Imperial Bank of Commerce (CIBC), provides access to debt and equity markets, leveraged lending, mergers and acquisitions advice and everything else a company could need. Rather than pursuing big clients that have existing relationships with bulge-bracket firms, CIBC serves mid-sized corporations. "We believe that there's a big chunk of companies that aren't served well by bulge-bracket firms," Paul Rogers, CEO of CIBC World Market's U.S. operations, explains.

GETTING HIRED

"On the interview day, it's a half-day, with five or six interviews. The interviews are 30 minutes, one-on-ones with senior-level people." As for the questions, says that contact, "Some people go straight for finance and technical, and some people go for, 'Do you have any sort of life?'" Insiders say interviewers are impressed by those targeting CIBC. "They're looking for someone who, if they can extend an offer, is going to take it. It matters how strong your interest is."

OUR SURVEY SAYS

One second-year analyst typically works 80 to 100 hours a week. "Even though it's a slow market, there have been nights when we're here until 1 a.m.," she says. An associate reports having better hours: "When there are no deals immediately closing, I work about nine to 10 hours a day." But a big deal can mean working "18 hours a day and all weekend."

According to one I-banking associate, CIBC is filled with "fun, intelligent people, without the egos and political battles that dominate many other firms." Insiders say the firm's mid-sized focus creates a less snobby atmosphere than at other Wall Street firms. Says one, "Because we don't chase after the highest-profile clients, we don't have this highfalutin' attitude that we're better than everyone else." The downside, sources say, is that the rest of the Street isn't giving the firm the recognition it deserves. Says one analyst: "I don't think people give CIBC the credit it's due. You say you work here, and people look at you like you have four heads."

Some insiders criticize the firm's lack of diversity, though they note that it is also a function of the industry. "CIBC is still a white male enclave," says one source. One female analyst sums it up this way: "I don't think they make any particular effort to retain, but I know they don't discriminate." The firm reports that 40 percent of the 2000 analyst class is either a minority or female.

Visit the Vault Finance Job Board — one of the best job boards on the Internet exclusively for finance professionals. Go to www.vault.com.

VAULT   255

Dresdner Kleinwort Wasserstein

75 Wall Street
New York, NY 10005
Phone: (212) 429-2000
Fax: (212) 429-2127
www.drkw.com

1301 Avenue of the Americas
New York, NY 10019
Phone: (212) 969-2700

DEPARTMENTS

Asset Finance
Bank Debt
Dresdner Kleinwort Capital
Equities
Debt Capital Markets
Mergers, Acquisitions and Advisory
OTC and Structured Sales

THE STATS

Executive Chairman and Co-Chairman: Bruce Wasserstein
CEO and Co-Chairman: Leonhard Fischer
Employer Type: Subsidiary of Dresdner Bank AG
No. of Offices: 36

KEY COMPETITORS

Goldman Sachs
Lazard
Morgan Stanley

UPPERS

- Friendly colleagues
- High-quality deals

DOWNERS

- Slow workflow/lots of downtime
- Long hours

EMPLOYMENT CONTACT

M&A Recruiting — Analyst, Associate and Lateral Hiring:
Frances A. Lyman
1301 Avenue of the Americas
New York, NY 10019
Fax: (212) 969-7977
Fran.Lyman@drkw.com

Associate — MBA Recruiting, Debt & Equity Sales & Trading, Research, Information Technology and Online Markets:
Jacquelyn Johnson
nymba@dresdner.com

Associate — Lateral Hiring, excluding M&A:
Jeffrey Mann
Fax: (212) 429-2467
Recruitment1@dresdner.com

75 Wall Street
New York, NY 10005-2889

THE SCOOP

In January 2001, Wasserstein Perella combined with Dresdner's London-based investment bank, Dresdner Kleinwort Benson (DKB) to form Dresdner Kleinwort Wasserstein for approximately $1.4 billion. WP Founder Bruce Wasserstein and Dresdner CEO Bernd Fahrholz serve as executive directors, while Leonhard Fischer, DKB CEO, is filling the same role at the new firm. As part of the deal, Dresdner set aside $190 million for retention payments maturing in 2002-2003. "We want to keep the [Wasserstein] people medium-term," a Dresdner spokesman told Reuters.

DKW doesn't transact the same volume of deals as some of its bulge-bracket competitors, but it has advised on some major deals, most notably the Time Warner/America Online merger. The firm also advised UBS on its $12 billion acquisition of PaineWebber and Ernst & Young Global Consulting on its $11 billion purchase by Cap Gemini. The firm provides its clients with access to equity and debt capital market. The Grantchester Securities division of the firm focuses on fixed income sales, trading and research. The primary groups in this division are high yield, distressed securities and private debt.

GETTING HIRED

Dresdner Kleinwort Wasserstein posts information regarding its internship, analyst and associate programs on its web site, www.drkw.com. Resumes and cover letters can be submitted electronically.

OUR SURVEY SAYS

Sources say the workload is characterized by periods of intense work with some lulls. "Sometimes, you could be working until four or five in the morning fairly constantly," reports one source. "But other times, there may not be anything to do." Another contact agrees: "For all the long hours, much of the day is spent waiting for work to trickle down." Candidates should be prepared for all-nighters. According to one employee: "They're definitely looking for people who can work the late hours, people who understand the differences between the small firm and a large firm. It's not a firm where you can sort of hide in the corner and do one small part of a deal."

Insiders report that the firm is a pretty chummy place. "People will typically eat together or watch TV in a conference room," says one former analyst. "People dress down, go to the gym for half an hour or an hour together. At night, it's a different firm: Everyone knows everyone. You're very close with the analyst class."

Federated Investors

Federated Investors Tower
1001 Liberty Avenue
Pittsburgh, PA 15222-3779
Phone: (412) 288-1900
Fax: (412) 288-2919
www.federatedinvestors.com

DEPARTMENTS

Clearing Services
Investment Management
Investment Research
Marketing
Sales

THE STATS

President and CEO:
J. Christopher Donahue
Employer Type: Public Company
Ticker Symbol: FII (NYSE)
2000 Revenue: $680.8 million
2000 Net Income: $155.4 million
No of Employees: 1,900
No of Offices: 7

KEY COMPETITORS

Janus Capital
SEI Investments
Vanguard Group

EMPLOYMENT CONTACT

Employment Services
19th Floor
Federated Investors
Federated Investors Tower
Pittsburgh PA 15222-3779
Fax: (412) 288-6823
resume@federatedinv.com

THE SCOOP

Federated Investors was founded in 1955 by John Donahue, Richard Fisher and Thomas Donnelly. The trio borrowed enough capital to set up shop in Pittsburgh, Pa., where they began selling savings plans and mutual funds door-to-door. The company went public in 1960 and was purchased by Aetna in 1982. The firm claims to have introduced government bond funds, municipal bond funds and high-yield bond funds, as well as the method for valuing money market fund shares at $1.

Federated's management, especially the Donahue family, was reportedly unhappy with Aetna's control; the Donahues bought 75 percent of the firm back from Aetna in 1989 and the rest in 1996. The company is now run by J. Christopher Donahue, the eldest son of founder John. Christopher joined the firm in 1972 and was appointed COO in 1993. He became CEO five years later and led the company through its 1998 IPO. (The Donahue family still owns approximately 20 percent of the company's shares.)

Federated is a lesser-known investment management firm, mainly because the company's 138 mutual funds are targeted to institutional clients. Federated has a reputation for aggressively marketing its services to those institutional clients, including wooing decision makers at the firms. "Millions of shrimp have sacrificed themselves for Federated Investors," Christopher Donahue told *Money & Investments*, referring to the company's penchant for wining and dining potential clients. The strategy has been effective; Federated has approximately $146 billion in assets under management (as of March 31, 2001).

GETTING HIRED

Federated's web site, www.federatedinvestors.com, lists open positions in numerous departments, including investment research, investor services, sales and product development. The web site suggests applicants send resumes to Federated's Pittsburgh headquarters.

The site also details the company's benefits program. Federated offers comprehensive health insurance, profit sharing, 401(k) and employee stock purchase plans, and tuition assistance, among other things.

Visit the Vault Finance Job Board — one of the best job boards on the
Internet exclusively for finance professionals. Go to www.vault.com.
VAULT   259

First Union

One First Union Center
Charlotte, NC 28288
Phone: (704) 374-6565
Fax: (704) 374-3425
www.firstunion.com

DEPARTMENTS

General Banking
Capital Management
Capital Markets
Credit Administration
E-Commerce
Finance

THE STATS

Chairman and CEO: Ken Thompson
Employer Type: Public Company
Ticker Symbol: FTU (NYSE)
2000 Revenue: $24.2 billion
2000 Net Income: $92 million
No. of Employees: 71,300
No. of Offices: 2,600

KEY COMPETITORS

Bank of America
Citibank
FleetBoston

UPPERS

• Excellent benefits
• Fast-growing company

DOWNERS

• Can be political
• Culture in flux due to many mergers

EMPLOYMENT CONTACT

First Union Corporation
ATTN: Resume Scanning
1525 West W.T. Harris Boulevard
Charlotte, NC 28288-0970

THE SCOOP

First Union traces its history back to 1908 with the founding of Union National bank in Charlotte, N.C. The First Union name first appeared in 1958 when Union National merged with Asheville, N.C.-based First National Bank and Trust. The bank expanded throughout the Tar Heel state until the mid-1980s, when deregulation made interstate bank mergers possible. First Union went on a buying spree, expanding throughout the Southeast. In addition to its commercial banking presence (the company has 2,100 banking branches in the U.S.), the company offers securities brokerage (it has 500 brokerage offices in the U.S.), corporate finance services, insurance and mutual funds.

GETTING HIRED

First Union recruits aggressively on college campuses and at job fairs. The company web site, www.firstunion.com, features a thorough listing of employment opportunities, training programs and benefits.

Candidates generally have an interview with human resources, followed by "a full day of interviewing" with a number of people. One contact says "usually you would interview with HR first, then with the department manager and then with the group leader." Those with little or no experience in the industry need not worry; employees say the company "is very interested in 'people' people. You need to be a team player," adding that the interview process is "between moderately relaxed and somewhat stressful."

OUR SURVEY SAYS

Insiders have different takes on the corporate culture at First Union. Says one insider: "The atmosphere is very political, but for a bank, it isn't bad. Not bad for a bank, though, is a hell of a lot worse than anywhere else. I've had government jobs where you'd think politics would be a lot worse, but they are nothing compared to this." Another disagrees, saying "from my perspective, the corporate culture is fairly easygoing with a lot of emphasis on teamwork. There is no need nor room for prima donnas or empire builders, hence, no jealousies, back-biting or in-house political control fights."

Despite the office politics, employees say management at First Union is "better than average in trying to create a good working environment for its employees." Employees applaud the company's efforts to promote a balance between work and family life through flex-time options.

Visit the Vault Finance Job Board — one of the best job boards on the Internet exclusively for finance professionals. Go to www.vault.com.

VΛULT   261

FleetBoston Financial

One Federal Street
Boston, MA 02110
Phone: (617) 346-4000
Fax: (617) 346-0464
www.fleet.com

DEPARTMENTS

Asset Management
Brokerage
Commercial Banking
Investment Banking
Retail Banking
Venture Capital

THE STATS

Chairman and CEO:
Terrence Murray
Employer Type: Public Company
Ticker Symbol: FBF (NYSE)
2000 Revenues: $22.6 billion
2000 Net Income: $3.4 billion
No. of Employees: 53,000
No. of Offices: 250

KEY COMPETITORS

Bank of America
Citibank
First Union
J.P. Morgan Chase

UPPERS

• Tuition reimbursement
• Paid volunteer days
• Job training

DOWNERS

• Excessive bureaucracy
• Long work days

EMPLOYMENT CONTACT

Fleet
Employment Shared Services
111 Westminster Street
Mailcode: RI DE 03314G
Providence, RI 02903

THE SCOOP

FleetBoston Financial is the holding company for one of the top 10 financial services firms in the U.S. and one of the largest banks in the Northeast, where it has 1,250 branches. FleetBoston was formed by the merger of Fleet Financial and BankBoston in October 1999. A year later, the combined firm added Summit Bancorp to the fold, further expanding its base. FleetBoston offers the typical range of commercial and retail banking services, including deposits and loans. The company has a respected investment banking subsidiary (Robertson Stephens) and a discount brokerage (Quick & Reilly).

Fleet Financial and Bank Boston finally came together in a $16 billion merger finalized in October 1999. Terrence Murray, Fleet's CEO, kept that position in the merged company while Charles Gifford, BancBoston's chief, was named president and chief operating officer. Under the merger agreement, Murray is to step aside on January 1, 2002, giving the CEO post to Gifford.

GETTING HIRED

Fleet maintains a large database of resumes at its Rhode Island resume center. Applicants must, however, indicate the "department code" that corresponds to individual job openings listed on the company's job hotline and on its web site, www.fleet.com. Applicants can submit their resumes via regular mail or e-mail. Says one insider: "Most jobs are posted internally at first. Then, if necessary, they will advertise. And sometimes they will hold, or participate in, job fairs."

OUR SURVEY SAYS

Fleet's "explosive" growth has led to the "parallel development of a frustrating bureaucracy." Throughout the company, Fleet employees call the company "meritocratic" and say that "quality work is always recognized." Reports one contact: "As with any large company, management styles can vary greatly throughout the organization. I have been blessed with a fair and flexible manager and a great group of co-workers."

While some say that the bank offers "substandard" pay for the banking industry in exchange for "long workweeks," others say that the "advancement opportunities" and "prestige of working for the region's leading bank" provide adequate compensation.

"We have a 401(k) plan where Fleet matches, dollar for dollar, up to 6 percent of your salary," reports one insider.

Houlihan Lokey Howard & Zukin

1930 Century Park West
Los Angeles, CA 90067
Phone: (310) 553-8871
Fax: (310) 553-2173
www.hlhz.com

DEPARTMENTS

Corporate Alliances
Financial Opinions and
   Advisory Services
Financial Restructuring
Financing
Mergers and Acquisitions

THE STATS

President and CEO: O. Kit Lokey
Employer Type: Private Company
No. of Employees: 500
No. of Offices: 10

KEY COMPETITORS

Banc of America Securities
Broadview International
Wit SoundView

EMPLOYMENT CONTACT

1930 Century Park West
Los Angeles, CA 90067
employment-LA@hlhz.com
Fax: (310) 553-2173

THE SCOOP

Founded in Los Angeles in 1970, Houlihan Lokey Howard & Zukin provides investment banking services to more than 1,000 clients annually. The bulk of Houlihan Lokey's clients are privately held middle-market companies. A well-respected leader in middle-market M&A, in 2000 Houlihan Lokey acted as advisor on 154 deals worth $39.2 billion. The company has 10 offices in North America and Asia, eight of which are in the U.S. Houlihan Lokey has expanded its international presence in recent years through a strategic alliance with British-owned Close Brothers. The company also partially owns Mergerstat.com, an M&A data and analysis company based in Los Angeles.

GETTING HIRED

Insiders say the firm generally has two rounds of interviews. One source says, "The first round was a one-on-one with an HR representative. The second round was a 'Super Saturday'-style round with a series of four interviews in four hours. Two of the interviews during the Super Saturday were rigorous technical interviews. Other interviews were both fit and behavioral to some extent. The bottom line is that if you are not technically inclined, then it will be tough to make it through these interviews."

OUR SURVEY SAYS

While the firm may be small, most insiders give the quality of work a solid rating. One analyst says, "I'd say that I work on live deals 95 percent of the time. I have worked very few pitches. Also, most of our clients are middle market, but they are pretty diverse." One associate says that one of the best aspects of working at HLHZ is "without a doubt the type of work at the firm."

Insiders describe the firm's corporate culture as "fairly laid back" and "less stuffy" than the typical I-bank. According to one banker, "The firm is very open and seeks people who are ready for responsibility. There is a very entrepreneurial feeling within the firm." One analyst says the hours are reasonable at HLHZ and adds, "I feel like I'm fairly compensated." That source continues, "It's not like New York. You work about 65 to 70 hours [per week] and not too much on the weekends."

SG Cowen

1221 Avenue of the Americas
New York, NY 10020
Phone: (212) 278-6000
Fax: (212) 278-6789
www.sgcowen.com

DEPARTMENTS

Corporate Bond Brokerage
Fixed Income
Institutional Sales and Trading
Investment Banking
Private Client Services
Research

THE STATS

President and CEO:
Kim Fennebresque
Employer Type:
Subsidiary of Société Générale
No. of Employees: 1,900
No. of Offices: 16

KEY COMPETITORS

Banc of America Securities
Deutsche Banc Alex. Brown
Robertson Stephens

THE SCOOP

SG Cowen was formed in 1998 when French bank Société Générale acquired Cowen & Co., a New York boutique investment bank. Société Générale paid $540 million for Cowen, which was founded in 1919. The French parent had immediate plans for its new toy. While Cowen had traditionally focused its investment banking operations on three core industries, Société Générale decided to expand to other areas. Another result of the buyout: Cowen's once-robust asset management and mutual fund businesses were scaled down.

SG Cowen underwrote a total of 102 equity deals worth approximately $28.8 billion in 2000. Notable offerings include Vivendi Environement's $2.4 billion IPO in July 2000 and Thomson Multimedia's $2.0 billion follow-on offering in October 2000. More recent engagements include Orange SA's $5.9 billion IPO in February 2001.

GETTING HIRED

SG Cowen says it looks for accomplished and motivated individuals with strong academic backgrounds, and analytical, computer and communication skills. Visit the investment banking section of SG Cowen's web site, www.sginvestmentbanking.com, for job descriptions and contact information. The firm gives presentations to undergraduates at 11 schools, including NYU, Columbia, Yale, Georgetown and Vanderbilt in September and October and holds interviews in October, November and January. For associate (MBA-level) positions, the firm presents in September and October and interviews in October and November at 12 schools. A recent associate hire explains her interview process: "I did a two-on-one for the first round. The second round was a round robin of one-on-ones. I interviewed with four people, and each interview was 30 to 45 minutes."

OUR SURVEY SAYS

With a small- to medium-size company atmosphere, insiders note that each department and office at SG Cowen has its own distinct culture. However, insiders agree that bankers are in general closer to each other at SG Cowen than at bulge-bracket firms. One source praises relationships with the company brass, saying upper management is interested in developing the abilities of its staff and are "even willing to make themselves available to anyone who needs them."

But even though employees are proud that "SG Cowen is a company with a history of success," they acknowledge that "there are drawbacks. You will also perform the mundane tasks that would not be required of you in a larger company. You will do copying, filing — whatever needs to be done."

Visit the Vault Finance Job Board — one of the best job boards on the Internet exclusively for finance professionals. Go to www.vault.com.

VAULT   267

TD Securities

31 West 52nd Street
New York, NY 10019
Phone: (212) 827-7300
Fax: (212) 827-7248
www.tdsecurities.com

DEPARTMENTS

Debt Capital Markets
Derivatives, Money Markets and
  Foreign Exchange
Institutional Equities
Investment Banking
Private Equity

THE STATS

Chairman and CEO:
Donald A. Wright
Employer Type: Subsidiary of TD
Bank Financial Group
2000 Revenues: $2.7 billion
No. of Offices: 20

KEY COMPETITORS

Banc of America Securities
CIBC World Markets
First Union Securities

UPPERS

• Relaxed work environment
  encourages creativity and
  teamwork
• Good work/life balance

DOWNERS

• Pay below Street average
• Reputation not firmly established
  outside Canada

EMPLOYMENT CONTACT

Human Resources: Recruitment
TD Securities (USA) Inc.
31 West 52nd Street
New York, NY 10019-6101
Fax: (212) 827-7248
recruiter@tdusa.com

THE SCOOP

TD Securities is the investment banking unit of Toronto Dominion Bank Financial Group. TD Bank, which reported revenues of $13.2 billion in 2000, also consists of retail bank TD Canada Trust, TD Commercial Banking, TD Asset Management and TD Waterhouse, the world's second-largest online securities broker.

TD Bank was formed in 1955 by the union of the Bank of Toronto and the Dominion Bank. While fairly unknown in the U.S., TD Securities has an excellent reputation in its Canadian homeland. The *Financial Post* called TD Securities the top debt underwriter in Canada for 2001, crediting the firm with 169 deals worth $8.8 billion.

GETTING HIRED

TD Securities' web site, www.tdsecurities.com, advertises for analyst and associate positions in the firm's North American offices as well as in Asia and Australia. The site lists additional positions in sales and trading, research and operations and a mailing address for each of its offices. Applicants should send resumes to the office of interest and keep an eye out for TD Securities' on-campus representatives. Insiders report there are "no crazy questions in interviews." "The types of questions varied, but were less on the technical side, in contrast to other firms." Fit questions — as in "Why are you interested in investment banking and in TD specifically?" — are much more common, sources say.

OUR SURVEY SAYS

Having developed far from the hustle and bustle of Wall Street, TD Securities is "unique in the industry," according to people in the know. More so than other banks, insiders consider TDS to be a "lifestyle firm" where managers and coworkers "give you the time and space that you need to deal with your personal business." One contact describes senior managers as "respectful of all employees" and "very responsive to my requests."

In the industry, there's a "perception that TD's salaries are low, but [that] bonuses have the potential to be higher than at some other firms," says one insider. However, this contact expresses a feeling of uncertainty about how TD really stacks up because "salaries and bonuses are a well-kept secret. So it's difficult to know how your compensation compares to others in the firm and to those outside the firm." Another source seems more certain and straightforward: "Our bases are at least 100 percent below market." On the plus side, the firm has better hours expectations than most Wall Street sweatshops.

TIAA-CREF

730 Third Avenue
New York, NY 10017-3206
Phone: (212) 490-9000
Fax: (212) 916-4840
www.tiaa-cref.org

DEPARTMENTS

Insurance Services
Mutual Funds
Retirement Services
Trust Services
Tuition Financing

THE STATS

Chairman, President and CEO:
John H. Biggs
Employer Type: Not-for-Profit
No. of Employees: 6,358
No. of Offices: 24

KEY COMPETITORS

Fidelity Investments
Vanguard Group

UPPERS

- Reasonable hours
- Responsibility at an early level

DOWNERS

- Bureaucratic culture

EMPLOYMENT CONTACT

TIAA-CREF
HR Staffing
730 Third Avenue
New York, NY 10017
Fax: (212) 916-5883
staffing5@tiaa-cref.org

THE SCOOP

Teachers Insurance and Annuity Association-College Retirement Equities Fund (TIAA-CREF) is a nationwide retirement system that manages the pension plans of two million teachers and staff at colleges, universities and other nonprofit educational and research institutions throughout the U.S. The nonprofit TIAA-CREF serves more than 11,000 educational and research institutions, making it one of the largest private retirement systems in the world. TIAA-CREF is comprised of TIAA, founded in 1918 by Andrew Carnegie to provide retirement services for teachers, and CREF, established in 1952. The firm currently has more than $278 billion invested for employees of higher education institutions and their families.

The company's professionals manage portfolio holdings in nearly every economic sector, with assets spread among private placements, publicly traded bonds, commercial mortgages and real estate. However, the firm is known primarily for its investments in stocks, and is led by its flagship CREF Stock Account, the largest single-managed equity account in the world. The TIAA-CREF group of companies has approximately 50 in-house equity analysts.

GETTING HIRED

The firm's web site, www.tiaa-cref.org, has a searchable list of job openings grouped by state. Send or fax resumes to TIAA-CREF's human resources department at its New York headquarters. Qualifications and requirements vary by position.

OUR SURVEY SAYS

The organization's claims to support diversity are echoed by employees, who describe a "very diverse and women/minority friendly" environment, with "equal opportunity for everybody based on merit." Says one insider: "They are very good at honoring and respecting all people." For employees in finance, the organization offers a "more laid-back atmosphere and more job security" than Wall Street. Says one insider: "Work hours are moderate. Many work 9 to 5 without any problems. Long hours are not needed."

"TIAA will give you a lot of responsibility fairly quickly, but will do it in such a way that you can't cause too much damage to the policyholders or yourself if you are wrong," reports one insider. That contact elaborates: "All investments go through a thorough screening process, so everyone has 'signed on' when the money goes out the door." An investment officer explains the downside to this emphasis on safety thusly, "Overall, the corporate culture is pretty conservative and bureaucratic. It is more important to not make a mistake than to not miss an opportunity."

UBS PaineWebber

1285 Avenue of the Americas
New York, NY 10019
Phone: (212) 713-2000
Fax: (212) 713-4889
www.painewebber.com

DEPARTMENTS

Equities
Financial Planning Services
Fixed Income and Municipal
  Securities
Investment Consulting Services
Private Client Services

THE STATS

President and CEO:
Joseph J. Grano
Employer Type:
Subsidiary of UBS AG
No. of Employees: 20,000
No. of Offices: 390+

KEY COMPETITORS

Merrill Lynch
Morgan Stanley
Salomon Smith Barney

UPPERS

• Fewer hours than most firms
• Relaxed working environment

DOWNERS

• Little interaction among
  departments

EMPLOYMENT CONTACT

Financial Advisor and Branch Manager
UBS PaineWebber
PO Box #549235
Suite 83
Waltham, MA 02454-8533
Fax: (781) 663-8533

Municipal Securities Group Recruiter
UBS PaineWebber
1285 Avenue of the Americas, 15th
Floor
New York, NY 10019
Fax: (212) 713-6051
msg_recruiter@ubspainewebber.com

Private Client Group College Recruiter
UBS PaineWebber
1000 Harbor Boulevard, 10th Floor
Weehawken, NJ 07087
Fax: (201) 583-7180
pcg_recruiter@ubspainewebber.com

THE SCOOP

PaineWebber traces its roots back to 1879, when William Paine and Wallace Webber opened a brokerage house in Boston. The company broke into the big leagues in the 1960s when it moved its headquarters to New York. In recent years, PaineWebber had been the subject of merger rumors. Swiss banking giant UBS finally landed PaineWebber in an $11.8 billion purchase that closed in November 2000.

The firm was renamed UBS PaineWebber in March 2001. PaineWebber's investment-banking and asset-management operations were transferred to UBS Warburg and UBS Asset Management, respectively. The firm now focuses on private clients, especially affluent investors (defined as those with over $500,000 to invest). UBS PaineWebber is the fourth-largest private client business in the U.S. with 8,900 financial advisors serving approximately 2.1 million investors.

GETTING HIRED

UBS PaineWebber's web site has a detailed career section with job openings and human resource contacts. The firm recruits for financial advisors and branch managers year-round. Additionally, UBS PaineWebber recruits on campus for a number of training programs targeted to undergrads. First interviews for these positions occur on campus. Selected candidates make the trip to Weehawken, N.J., for the second round.

OUR SURVEY SAYS

The corporate culture at UBS PaineWebber is said to be much less "stuffy" and "overbearing" than at many of its competitors. Employees praise the firm's top executives for "being so approachable," and insiders generally find that "PaineWebber, despite its size, has a small-business feel."

At PaineWebber, "women and minorities are treated very well, and women constitute a good portion of management. Complaints regarding harassment and discrimination are handled very seriously." While employees think the firm is "relatively liberal" — one contact reports seeing "some long-haired and multi-earringed employees" — and "sensitive, for a place on the Street," some say "the culture is fragmented and people tend to keep to their own divisions."

U.S. Bancorp Piper Jaffray

800 Nicollet Mall
Suite 800
Minneapolis, MN 55402
Phone: (612) 303-6000
Fax: (612) 303-6996
www.piperjaffray.com

DEPARTMENTS

Asset Management
Equity Capital Markets
Fixed Income Capital Markets
Private Advisory Services
Venture Capital

THE STATS

President and CEO: Andrew S. Duff
Employer Type:
Subsidiary of U.S. Bancorp
No. of Employees: 3,600
No. of Offices: 125

KEY COMPETITORS

Banc of America Securities
CIBC World Markets
Credit Suisse First Boston
Robertson Stephens
Thomas Weisel Partners

UPPERS

- High level of job responsibility
- Street-comparable pay for junior bankers

DOWNERS

- Lack of diversity
- Long hours

EMPLOYMENT CONTACT

U.S. Bancorp Piper Jaffray
800 Nicollet Mall
Suite 800
Minneapolis, MN 55402

THE SCOOP

In May 1998, Minnesota-based commercial bank U.S. Bancorp purchased Piper Jaffray, a Minneapolis-based firm founded in 1913 by C.P. Jaffray and H.C. Piper, Sr., for $730 million. The investment banking division was given the cumbersome name U.S. Bancorp Piper Jaffray to distinguish it from the company's other operations. Piper Jaffray provides equity and fixed-income underwriting and venture capital services for companies. Additionally, the firm handles individual investment accounts and asset management.

U.S. Bancorp's operations may not be bulge bracket, but are nonetheless healthy. Lead-managed deals include IPOs for Eloquent and Antigenics in February 2000. As a co-manager, the firm was involved in Therapeutic Systems' $230 million offering in February 2000 and the June 2000 offerings of Handspring ($200 million) and Charles River Laboratories ($224 million).

GETTING HIRED

The company's web site, www.piperjaffray.com, lists job openings and contact information for various positions, including investment banking. Associate recruiting has focused on the top-10 business schools. "They draw a lot from Chicago and Northwestern because they're in the Midwest, but they [also] have a lot of Harvard Business School people," reports one insider.

OUR SURVEY SAYS

Piper Jaffray is unique because "associates don't do any modeling; analysts do all the modeling," reports one insider. "It's great for an analyst because you do all the models, including the complex ones."

The firm offers "healthy salaries" that tend to vary with the performance of the stock market and "some of the best employee benefits" in the industry, including an "unbeatable" employee stock ownership program. When it comes to starting pay, the firm isn't all that different from the big boys back East. According to one insider, "First-year associates can get paid close to what they get paid in New York. Where it gets skewed is after four or five years. Here, people make a million dollars but it's not the rule. But here, people can buy a huge house for $250,000 10 minutes out of town."

Insiders comment that "Piper, like Minnesota itself, is homogenous, with few minorities," though "it is an open environment and the only criteria for advancement is hard work." However, says that I-banking contact: "I think they're very good with the male/female ratio. They're not 50/50 at the top, but they definitely have some strong women there."

Visit the Vault Finance Job Board — one of the best job boards on the Internet exclusively for finance professionals. Go to www.vault.com.

V/\ULT   275

Waddell & Reed Financial Services

6300 Lamar Avenue
Overland Park, KS 66202
Phone: (913) 236-2000
Fax: (913) 236-5044
www.waddell.com

DEPARTMENTS

Accounting/Finance
Insurance
Investment Management
Sales

THE STATS

Chairman and CEO: Keith A. Tucker
Employer Type: Public Company
Ticker Symbol: WDR (NYSE)
2000 Revenue: $521 million
2000 Net Income: $139 million
No. of Employees: 1,340
No. of Offices: 433

KEY COMPETITORS

Liberty Financial Companies
Jones Financial Companies
Van Kampen Investments

EMPLOYMENT CONTACT

Cathie Suchecki
Executive Director — Recruiting
Waddell & Reed
6300 Lamar Avenue
Overland Park, KS 66202
Fax: (913) 236-1545
jobs@waddell.com

THE SCOOP

Chauncey Waddell and Cameron Reed founded Waddell & Reed in 1937. The company provides mutual funds, retirement and other savings plans and life insurance and annuities. W&R has carved out a niche by targeting personal finance products to moderate-income investors, mostly in suburban communities. According to *The Wall Street Journal*, the company's financial advisors are known "to do business across the kitchen table with customers who put an average of $47,000 into its funds." The firm has about 2,600 sales representatives across the country who advise clients about the company's products. These representatives used to only sell funds managed by W&R, but in 2000 the firm began forming alliances with companies such as Nationwide and BISYS Group to market their products.

Waddell & Reed is partially owned by Birmingham, Ala.-based insurance firm Torchmark. Thirty-four percent of W&R was spun off in March 1998 through an IPO that raised $499 million. The remaining 66 percent of W&R shares were later distributed to Torchmark shareholders.

A series of mergers among asset managers fueled speculation during the summer of 2000 that Waddell was interested in being acquired. *Investment News* named American International Group as the potential buyer. The company has sent mixed signals about its willingness to partner with another financial services firm. While the company officially claims to be enjoying its independence, during an August 2000 analyst conference CEO Keith Tucker conceded that Waddell "would not stand in the way of our shareholders deciding" to sell if a good offer came along.

GETTING HIRED

Openings in Waddell & Reed's main office in the areas of accounting, insurance, investment management and sales are posted on the company's web site, www.waddell.com. Additionally, the site contains extensive information on how to become a financial advisor or sales manager in one of W&R's local offices. There's also a quiz designed to assess one's aptitude to be a financial advisor. Financial advisors are based in one of the local offices and work directly with clients, helping them to develop investment strategies based on their life goals. New financial advisors participate in a series of training activities to help them identify sales prospects and hone their marketing skills. During this time, advisors who don't already hold the appropriate licenses must prepare to pass the certification exams required of financial planners. Applicants should contact offices in their area regarding available positions.

Wells Fargo

420 Montgomery Street
San Francisco, CA 94163
Phone: (800) 411-4932
Fax: (415) 677-9075
www.wellsfargo.com

DEPARTMENTS

Commercial Banking
Consumer Banking
Insurance
Investment Services
Venture Capital

THE STATS

Chairman, President and CEO:
Richard M. Kovacevich
Employer Type: Public Company
Ticker Symbol: WFC (NYSE)
2000 Revenue: $27.6 billion
2000 Net Income: $4.0 billion
No. of Employees: 120,000
No. of Offices: 4,300

KEY COMPETITORS

Bank of America
Bank One
Citibank

UPPERS

- Excellent training
- Free and discounted banking services

DOWNERS

- Commercial bankers' pay
- Long hours

EMPLOYMENT CONTACT

Recruitment Services
633 Folsom Street
4th Floor
MAC A0149-047
San Francisco, CA 94107

THE SCOOP

In 1850 Henry Wells and William Fargo were among the New York businessmen who founded American Express, a mail delivery service that was the precursor of the financial services behemoth of today. According to legend, Wells and Fargo were excited about the prospect of expanding west but couldn't convince their partners at American Express. The two started their self-named firm in 1852, providing banking and stagecoach and pony express delivery services. Wells Fargo separated its banking business from its express service in 1905, and has remained with banking since.

Thanks in part to a number of mergers (including First Interstate in 1996, Norwest in 1998 and First Security in 2000), Wells Fargo is now the fourth-largest bank in the U.S. Wells Fargo offers the complete range of financial services, including consumer and corporate banking, investment services and brokerage, insurance and venture capital.

GETTING HIRED

In general, "recruiting is decentralized, so the process varies." For example, one contact in sales reports an interview process with "a group interview that includes role-playing and individual questions regarding customer service and person-to-person interaction. A panel of managers will observe the proceedings." This contact reports two or three rounds before a candidate is made an offer.

OUR SURVEY SAYS

Wells Fargo insiders stress that the firm's culture is a "very entrepreneurial" one, exemplified by Wells' catchphrase, "run it like you own it." Says one contact: "The corporate culture requires that you can change on a dime. Always progressive, Wells Fargo is not an old-boy static network. If it doesn't work, change." Says another insider: "The culture is consistent in that there is a 'run it like you own it' attitude across the bank."

"Pay scale is about average for banking, which is not the most generous industry," reports one source. "Annual salary increases are based on merit and can range up to 10 percent, although the company budgets for average salary increases of 3 percent." Salary, of course, isn't the only compensation Wells employees can earn. "Officers are eligible to earn discretionary bonuses up to about 30 percent of annual salary," reports one insider.

Once employees are hired into Wells, they do not have a hard time getting hired away, insiders say. Says one former employee: "Once you've been trained by Wells, most banks are dying to hire you."

Wit SoundView

826 Broadway
6th Floor
New York, NY 10003
Phone: (212) 253-4400
Fax: (212) 253-4428
www.witsoundview.com

DEPARTMENTS

Investment Banking
Research
Sales and Trading
Venture Capital

THE STATS

CEO: Mark Loehr
Employer Type: Public Company
Ticker Symbol: WITC (Nasdaq)
2000 Revenues: $376 million
2000 Net Income: -$22 million
No. of Employees: 350
No. of Offices: 5

KEY COMPETITORS

Broadview International
Deutsche Banc Alex. Brown
Robertson Stephens
Thomas Weisel Partners

UPPERS

- Exposure to senior bankers and clients
- Relaxed culture
- Responsibility for junior bankers

DOWNERS

- Compensation impacted by low stock price
- Lack of reputation
- Start-up infrastructure

EMPLOYMENT CONTACT

Tiffany Wells
Wit Soundview
826 Broadway
6th Floor
New York, NY 10003

THE SCOOP

Based in New York, Wit SoundView is the investment banking arm of Wit SoundView Group. Wit Capital, the predecessor to Wit SoundView, was founded in 1996 by Andrew Klein, now vice chairman and chief strategist at the firm. In March 1999, Goldman Sachs purchased a 22 percent stake in Wit for approximately $20 million. Wit Capital went public in June 1999, raising $70 million in its offering. In January 2000, Wit acquired SoundView Technology Group, a Stamford, Conn.-based boutique firm, for approximately $310 million. The firm changed its name to Wit Soundview six months later. In May 2000, Wit entered into a strategic alliance with E*Trade. Wit acquired E*Offering, E*Trade's underwriting group, while E*Trade absorbed Wit's retail brokerage accounts. Wit's efforts to boost its equity underwriting prowess has paid off. The company lead- or co-managed 42 IPOs in 2000.

GETTING HIRED

According to insiders, Wit recruits mostly from "Ivy League and top-20" schools. The interview process is typical for the industry. For college and MBA recruits, there's the typical three-round structure, with on-campus interviews, a round at the firm and a Super Saturday. Expect to meet between 10 to 15 people at all levels. The interviews themselves are described as informal and unstructured, with "emphasis on experience, intelligence and cultural fit." "It really depends on the fit of the individual with the firm," says one insider. "We have had candidates get offers from larger bulge-bracket firms who we did not feel were a good fit."

OUR SURVEY SAYS

Wit SoundView's culture, by design, is different from that of most banks. "This is why we all joined Wit," says one banker. "We want to change the way banking is done." Insiders report that the relationships between senior and junior bankers are generally good, though "some [senior bankers] are more traditional in that they expect you to put in the years regardless of your level of relevant work experience."

Though insiders concede the bank tries to pay near the industry average, Wit offers more compensation based on firm performance. Since the company is more like a startup than a typical I-bank, compensation includes more stock options than at most competitors. Wit's bonus structure is a little unusual. A contact reports that "bonus[es are] paid out twice a year in July and January. The first in the summer is sort of liquidity event, enough to keep you going through the year, typically less than 50 percent of bonus, with January being [the] 'real' bonus."

WHY WORK
FOR US?

SPONSORED RECRUITING CONTENT

Northwestern Mutual Financial Network

CONTACT INFO

nmresume@northwesternmutual.com

AWARDS AND KEY FACTS

- Northwestern Mutual has always received the highest possible ratings from the four major rating services: Standard and Poor's, AAA; Moody's, Aaa; Fitch (formally Duff & Phelps), AAA; A.M. Best, A++.

- Voted "Most Admired" company in the life insurance industry, according to a 2001 *Fortune* magazine survey (for the 18th time).

- Ranked "Best Sales Force in the Industry" by *Sales and Marketing Management* magazine in 2000.

- Named "One of America's Top Ten Internships for 2001" by the *Princeton Review*.

NOTABLE BENEFITS

- Comprehensive medical coverage (Flex I & II)

- Two company-funded retirement plans

- Group Life and Accidental Death Benefit

- Disability income plan

- Sponsored Errors & Omissions Insurance Program

- Maternity leave

Why Work For Us?

The Top 5 Reasons to Work for Northwestern Mutu

1. Freedom to manage your own schedule and decide with whom you work. Self-employment means having to make hard decisions. It also means getting to make great choices. As a Financial Representative, some days you might wake up, jog some laps, have breakfast with your family. Or you might be in your office before most are gettin up — preparing to get in front of the markets you want to pursue. That means you work with whom you choose. Enter a business where variety is just one perk.

2. Income that reflects your hard work and efforts. If you're willing to work hard, your income can be a reflection of your energy, commitment and drive, *not* a reflection of someone else's expectations of you and your work. With The Network, your potential isn't stifled with salary caps an glass ceilings. Instead, *your* work is *your* reward.

3. Impact people's lives positively-every day. With The Network, you'll address your clients' concerns with securin businesses, providing legacies to their families or planning comfortable retirements. You'll build relationships in which you'll understand your clients' financial situations, values and goals. And you'll have the financial tools and resource right in front of you — to help your clients' dreams seem ju that close.

4. Support from a network of specialists, mentors and education programs. As a Financial Representative you be in business *for* yourself, not *by* yourself. In Northwester Mutual's 144 years of industry experience, we've learned how to help our representatives make winning skills excellent habits. Our training and mentoring programs will help you help your clients achieve their goals.

5. Reputable financial products and services. We don' expect you to learn it all. Neither will your clients. But you' learn where to turn. Through The Network, you'll have access to knowledgeable specialists of vast products and services. These specialists will provide you and your clien with expertise in areas like retirement planning, estate planning, asset allocation and small business planning. Th expertise is backed up by reputable financial products tha have been built to meet your clients' needs.

Highlights

Excerpted from Vault.com's Independent Research

Since its inception in 1857, Northwestern Mutual has proudly maintained a reputation of excellence — both in products and client service. Northwestern Mutual has always received the highest possible ratings from the four major ratings services: Standard and Poor's, AAA; Moody's, Aaa; Fitch (formally Duff & Phelps), AAA; A.M. Best, A++. Northwestern Mutual Financial Representatives have been ranked the "Best Sales Force in the Industry" by *Sales and Marketing Management Magazine* in 2000. The Network now boasts more than 350 offices and 7,500 Financial Representatives across the United States. Through The Network, these representatives have access to a vast array of products and services from The Northwestern Mutual Life Insurance Company, Northwestern Mutual Investment Services, LLC, Robert W. Baird & Co., Incorporated, Northwestern Long Term Care Insurance Company, The Frank Russell Company, and Strategic Employee Benefit Services (a nationwide marketing program providing employee benefit services exclusively through Northwestern Mutual Financial Network Representatives).

Quote Board

Excerpts from Vault's Independent Surveys

Most of The Network's Financial Representatives rally around Northwestern Mutual, calling it **"an excellent company with a great reputation"** and lauding its **"really top-notch group of associates."** One contact boasts that **"representing a quality company like Northwestern Mutual is a win-win for you and your clients."** Another Financial Representative commented on the career, describing the opportunity as **"good for someone who is self-motivated, looking to be independent, likes to help people, can put up with the ups and downs of dealing with the public and is willing to work hard."**

* Financial Representatives are independent contractors, and not employees of Northwestern Mutual. Northwestern Mutual Financial Network identifies the sales and distribution arm of The Northwestern Mutual Life Insurance Company and its subsidiaries and affiliates.

APPENDIX

Alphabetical Listing of Firms

Finance Glossary

Agency bonds: Agencies represent all bonds issued by the federal government, except for those issued by the Treasury (i.e., bonds issued by other agencies of the federal government). Examples include the Federal National Mortgage Association (FNMA), and the Guaranteed National Mortgage Association (GNMA).

Arbitrage: The trading of securities (stocks, bonds, derivatives, currencies, and other securities) to profit from a temporary difference between the price of security in one market and the price in another (also called risk-free arbitrage). This temporary difference is often called a market inefficiency. Distinguish from risk arbitrage (see below).

Asset management: Also known as investment management. Basically, this is exactly what it sounds like. Money managers at investment management firms and investment banks take money given to them by pension funds and individual investors and invest it. For wealthy individuals (private clients), the investment bank will set up an individual account and manage the account; for the less well-endowed, the bank will offer mutual funds. Asset managers are compensated primarily by taking a percentage each year from the total assets managed. (They may also charge an upfront load, or commission, of a few percent of the initial money invested.)

Beauty contest: The informal term for the process by which clients choose an investment bank. Some of the typical selling points when competing with other investment banks for a deal are: "Look how strong our research department is in this industry. Our analyst in the industry is a real market mover, so if you go public with us, you'll be sure to get a lot of attention from her." Or: "We are the top-ranking firm in this type of issuance, as you will see by these league tables."

Bloomberg: Computer terminals providing real time quotes, news and analytical tools, often used by traders and investment bankers.

Bond spreads: The difference between the yield of a corporate bond and a U.S. Treasury security of similar time to maturity.

Bulge bracket: The largest and most prestigious firms on Wall Street (including Goldman Sachs, Morgan Stanley, Merrill Lynch, Salomon Smith Barney, and Credit Suisse First Boston).

Visit the Vault Finance Job Board — one of the best job boards on the Internet exclusively for finance professionals. Go to www.vault.com.

VAULT   289

Buy-side: The clients of investment banks (mutual funds, pension funds) that buy the stocks, bonds and securities sold by the investment banks. (The investment banks that sell these products to investors are known as the sell-side.)

Chartered Financial Analyst (CFA): A designation given to professionals that complete a multi-part exam designed to test accounting and investment knowledge and professional ethics.

Commercial bank: A bank that lends, rather than raises money. For example, if a company wants $30 million to open a new production plant, it can approach a commercial bank for a loan.

Commercial paper: Short-term corporate debt, typically maturing in nine months or less.

Commitment letter: A document that outlines the terms of a loan a commercial bank gives a client.

Commodities: Assets (usually agricultural products or metals) that are generally interchangeable with one another and therefore share a common price. For example, corn, wheat and rubber generally trade at one price on commodity markets worldwide.

Common stock: Also called common equity, common stock represents an ownership interest in a company. (As opposed to preferred stock, see below.) The vast majority of stock traded in the markets today is common, as common stock enables investors to vote on company matters. An individual with 51 percent or more of shares owned controls a company's decisions and can appoint anyone he/she wishes to the board of directors or to the management team.

Comparable company analysis (Comps): The primary tool of the corporate finance analyst. Comps include a list of financial data, valuation data and ratio data on a set of companies in an industry. Comps are used to value private companies or better understand a how the market values and industry or particular player in the industry.

Consumer Price Index: The CPI measure the percentage increase in a standard basket of goods and services. CPI is a measure of inflation for consumers.

Convertible preferred stock: This is a relatively uncommon type of equity issued by a company; convertible preferred stock is often issued when it cannot successfully sell either straight common stock or straight debt. Preferred stock pays a dividend, similar to how a bond pays coupon payments, but ultimately converts to common stock after a period of time. It is essentially a mix of debt and equity, and most often used as a means for a risky company to obtain capital when neither debt nor equity works.

Convertible bonds: Bonds that can be converted into a specified number of shares of stock.

Derivatives: An asset whose value is derived from the price of another asset. Examples include call options, put options, futures and interest-rate swaps.

Discount rate: A widely followed short-term interest rate, set by the Federal Reserve to cause market interest rates to rise or fall, thereby causing the U.S. economy to grow more quickly or less quickly. More specifically, the discount rate is the rate at which federal banks lend money to each other on overnight loans. Today, the discount rate can be directly moved by the Fed, but maintains a largely symbolic role.

Dividend: A payment by a company to shareholders of its stock, usually as a way to distribute profits to shareholders.

Equity: In short, stock. Equity means ownership in a company that is usually represented by stock.

The Fed: The Federal Reserve, which gently (or sometimes roughly), manages the country's economy by setting interest rates.

Federal funds rate: The rate domestic banks charge one another on overnight loans to meet federal reserve requirements. This rate tracks very closely to the discount rate, but is usually slightly higher.

Fixed income: Bonds and other securities that earn a fixed rate of return. Bonds are typically issued by governments, corporations and municipalities.

Float: The number of shares available for trade in the market times the price. Generally speaking, the bigger the float, the greater the stock's liquidity.

Floating rate: An interest rate that is benchmarked to other rates (such as the rate paid on U.S. Treasuries), allowing the interest rate to change as market conditions change.

Floor traders: Traders for an investment bank located in the firm's offices. Floor traders spend most of the day seated at their desks observing market action on their computer screens.

Glass-Steagall Act: Part of the legislation passed during the Depression (Glass-Steagall was passed in 1933) designed to help prevent future bank failure — the establishment of the F.D.I.C. was also part of this movement. The Glass-Steagall Act split America's investment banking (issuing and trading securities)

Visit the Vault Finance Job Board — one of the best job boards on the Internet exclusively for finance professionals. Go to www.vault.com.

V/\ULT 291

operations from commercial banking (lending). For example, J.P. Morgan was forced to spin off its securities unit as Morgan Stanley. The act was gradually weakened throughout the 1990s and in 1999 Glass-Steagall was effectively repealed by the Graham-Leach-Bliley Act.

Graham-Leach-Bliley Act: Also known as the Financial Services Modernization Act of 1999. Essentially repealed many of the restrictions of the Glass-Steagall Act and made possible the current trend of consolidation in the financial services industry. Allows commercial banks investment banks, and insurance companies to affiliate under a holding company structure.

Gross Domestic Product: GDP measures the total domestic output of goods and services in the United States. Generally, when the GDP grows at a rate of less than 2 percent, the economy is considered to be in recession.

Hedge: To balance a position in the market in order to reduce risk. Hedges work like insurance: a small position pays off large amounts with a slight move in the market.

Hedge fund: An investment partnership, similar to a mutual fund, made up of wealthy investors. In comparison to most investment vehicles, hedge funds are loosely regulated, which allows them to take more risks in their investments.

High grade corporate bond: A corporate bond with a rating above BB. Also called investment grade debt.

High yield debt (a.k.a. Junk bonds): Corporate bonds that pay high interest rates (to compensate investors for high risk of default). Credit rating agencies such as Standard & Poor's rate a company's (or a municipality's) bonds based on default risk. Junk bonds rate below BB.

Initial Public Offering (IPO): The dream of every entrepreneur, the IPO is the first time a company issues stock to the public. Going public means more than raising money for the company: By agreeing to take on public shareholders, a company enters a whole world of required SEC filings and quarterly revenue and earnings reports, not to mention possible shareholder lawsuits.

Institutional clients or investors: Large investors, such as pension funds or municipalities (as opposed to retail investors or individual investors).

Lead manager: The primary investment bank managing a securities offering. (An investment bank may share this responsibility with one or more co-managers.)

League tables: Tables that rank investment banks based on underwriting volume in numerous categories, such as stocks, bonds, high yield debt, convertible debt, etc. High rankings in league tables are key selling points used by investment banks when trying to land a client engagement.

Leveraged Buyout (LBO): The buyout of a company with borrowed money, often using that company's own assets as collateral. LBOs were the order of the day in the heady 1980s, when successful LBO firms such as Kohlberg Kravis Roberts made a practice of buying up companies, restructuring them and reselling them or taking them public at a significant profit

Liquidity: The amount of a particular stock or bond available for trading in the market. For commonly traded securities, such as big cap stocks and U.S. government bonds, they are said to be highly liquid instruments. Small cap stocks and smaller fixed income issues often are called illiquid (as they are not actively traded) and suffer a liquidity discount, i.e. they trade at lower valuations to similar, but more liquid, securities.

The Long Bond: The 30-year U.S. Treasury bond. Treasury bonds are used as the starting point for pricing many other bonds, because Treasury bonds are assumed to have zero credit risk taking into account factors such as inflation. For example, a company will issue a bond that trades "40 over Treasuries." The 40 refers to 40 basis points (100 basis points = 1 percentage point).

Making markets: A function performed by investment banks to provide liquidity for their clients in a particular security, often for a security that the investment bank has underwritten. (In others words, the investment bank stands willing to buy the security, if necessary, when the investor later decides to sell it.)

Market Cap(italization): The total value of a company in the stock market (total shares outstanding x price per share).

Merchant banking: The department within an investment bank that invests the firm's own money in other companies. Analogous to a venture capital arm.

Money market securities: This term is generally used to represent the market for securities maturing within one year. These include short-term CDs, repurchase agreements, commercial paper (low-risk corporate issues), among others. These are low risk, short-term securities that have yields similar to Treasuries.

Mortgage-backed bonds: Bonds collateralized by a pool of mortgages. Interest and principal payments are based on the individual homeowners making their mortgage payments. The more diverse the pool of mortgages backing the bond, the less risky they are.

Municipal bonds ("Munis"): Bonds issued by local and state governments, a.k.a. municipalities. Municipal bonds are structured as tax-free for the investor, which means investors in muni's earn interest payments without having to pay federal taxes. Sometimes investors are exempt from state and local taxes, too. Consequently, municipalities can pay lower interest rates on muni bonds than other bonds of similar risk.

Mutual fund: An investment vehicle that collects funds from investors (both individual and institutional) and invests in a variety of securities, including stocks and bonds. Mutual funds make money by charging a percentage of assets in the fund.

Pitchbook: The book of exhibits, graphs, and initial recommendations presented by bankers to a prospective client when trying to land an engagement.

Pit traders: Traders who are positioned on the floor of stock and commodity exchanges (as opposed to floor traders, situated in investment bank offices).

P/E ratio: The price to earnings ratio. This is the ratio of a company's stock price to its earnings-per-share. The higher the P/E ratio, the more expensive a stock is (and also the faster investors believe the company will grow). Stocks in fast-growing industries tend to have higher P/E ratios.

Prime rate: The average rate U.S. banks charge to companies for loans.

Producer Price Index: The PPI measure the percentage increase in a standard basket of goods and services. PPI is a measure of inflation for producers and manufacturers.

Proprietary trading: Trading of the firm's own assets (as opposed to trading client assets).

Prospectus: A report issued by a company (filed with and approved by the SEC) that wishes to sell securities to investors. Distributed to prospective investors, the prospectus discloses the company's financial position, business description, and risk factors.

Red herring: Also known as a preliminary prospectus. A financial report printed by the issuer of a security that can be used to generate interest from prospective investors before the securities are legally available to be sold. Based on final SEC comments, the information reported in a red herring may change slightly by the time the securities are actually issued.

Retail clients: Individual investors (as opposed to institutional clients).

Return on equity: The ratio of a firm's profits to the value of its equity. Return on equity, or ROE, is a commonly used measure of how well an investment bank is doing, because it measures how efficiently and profitably the firm is using its capital.

Risk arbitrage: When an investment bank invests in the stock of a company it believes will be purchased in a merger or acquisition. (Distinguish from risk-free arbitrage.)

Risk-free arbitrage: When an investment bank buys a derivative or equity for a slightly lower price in one market and resells it in another. For example, if Dell stock were trading at 212 in the United States and 213 in Japan, buying it in the U.S. and reselling it in Japan would be risk-free. Risk-free arbitrage opportunities are infrequent and much more arcane than the example provided.

Roadshow: The series of presentations to investors that a company undergoing an IPO usually gives in the weeks preceding the offering. Here's how it works: Several weeks before the IPO is issued, the company and its investment bank will travel to major cities throughout the country. In each city, the company's top executives make a presentation to analysts, mutual fund managers, and others attendees and also answer questions.

S-1: A type of legal document filed with the SEC for a private company aiming to go public. The S-1 is almost identical to the prospectus sent to potential investors. The SEC must approve the S-1 before the stock can be sold to investors.

S-2: A type of legal document filed with the SEC for a public company looking to sell additional shares in the market. The S-2 is almost identical to the prospectus sent to potential investors. The SEC must approve the S-2 before the stock is sold.

Sales memo: Short reports written by the corporate finance bankers and distributed to the bank's salespeople. The sales memo provides salespeople with points to emphasize when hawking the stocks and bonds the firm is underwriting.

Securities and Exchange Commission (SEC): A federal agency that, like the Glass-Steagall Act, was established as a result of the stock market crash of 1929 and the ensuing depression. The SEC monitors disclosure of financial information to stockholders, and protects against fraud. Publicly traded securities must first be approved by the SEC prior to trading.

Securitize: To convert an asset into a security that can then be sold to investors. Nearly any income-generating asset can be turned into a security. For example, a 20-year mortgage on a home can be packaged with other mortgages just like it, and shares in this pool of mortgages can then be sold to investors.

Visit the Vault Finance Job Board — one of the best job boards on the Internet exclusively for finance professionals. Go to www.vault.com.

VΛULT   295

Short-term debt: A bond that matures in nine months or less. Also called commercial paper.

Syndicate: A group of investment banks that will together underwrite a particular stock or debt offering. Usually the lead manager will underwrite the bulk of a deal, while other members of the syndicate will each underwrite a small portion.

T-Bill Yields: The yield or internal rate of return an investor would receive at any given moment on a 90-120 government treasury bill.

Tax-exempt bonds: Municipal bonds (also known as munis). Munis are free from federal taxes and, sometimes, state and local taxes.

10K: An annual report filed by a public company with the Securities and Exchange Commission (SEC). Includes financial information, company information, risk factors, etc.

10Q: Similar to a 10K, but contains quarterly financial data on a company.

Tombstone: The advertisements that appear in publications like *Financial Times* or *The Wall Street Journal* announcing the issuance of a new security. The tombstone ad is placed by the investment bank to boast to the world that it has completed a major deal.

Treasury Securities: Securities issued by the U.S. government. These are divided into Treasury Bills (maturity of up to 2 years), Treasury Notes (from 2 years to 10 years maturity), and Treasury Bonds (10 years to 30 years). As they are government guaranteed, often treasuries are considered risk-free. In fact, while U.S. Treasuries have no default risk, they do have interest rate risk; if rates increase, then the price of UST's will decrease.

Underwrite: The function performed by investment banks when they help companies issue securities to investors. Technically, the investment bank buys the securities from the company and immediately resells the securities to investors for a slightly higher price, making money on the spread.

Yield: The annual return on investment. A high yield bond, for example, pays a high rate of interest.

Recommended Reading

Suggested Texts

- Burrough, Bryan and Helyar, John. *Barbarians at the Gate: The Fall of RJR Nabisco*. New York: Harper & Row, 1990.

- Endlich, Lisa. *Goldman Sachs: The Culture of Success*. New York: Alfred A. Knopf, 1999.

- Gordon, John Steele, *The Great Game: The Emergence of Wall Street As a World Power, 1653-2000*. New York: Scribner, 1999.

- Lewis, Michael. *Liar's Poker*. New York: Norton, 1989.

- Lewis, Michael. *The Money Culture*. New York: W. W. Norton, 1991.

- Rolfe, John and Traub, Peter. *Monkey Business: Swinging Through the Wall Street Jungle*. New York: Warner Books, 2000.

- Stewart, James Brewer. *Den of Thieves*. New York: Simon and Schuster, 1991.

Suggested Periodicals

- American Banker

- Business Week

- The Daily Deal

- The Economist

- Forbes

- Fortune

- Institutional Investor

- Investment Dealers' Digest

- Investor's Business Daily

- Red Herring

- The Wall Street Journal

Visit the Vault Finance Job Board — one of the best job boards on the Internet exclusively for finance professionals. Go to www.vault.com.

VAULT 297

About the Authors

Chris Prior is the finance editor at Vault. He graduated from Queens College of the City University of New York. Before joining Vault, Chris was a staff reporter at Treasury and Risk Management Magazine, a financial trade publication based in New York.

Tyya N. Turner is a graduate of Howard University. She has worked at several publishing companies, including Pocket Books, McGraw-Hill and Miller Freeman, as both a writer and an editor.

Hans H. Chen, a Pennsylvania native, is a graduate of Columbia University and the Columbia Graduate School of Journalism. He worked as a reporter for Newsday and APBnews.com before joining Vault as a staff writer. He began law school in the fall of 2001.

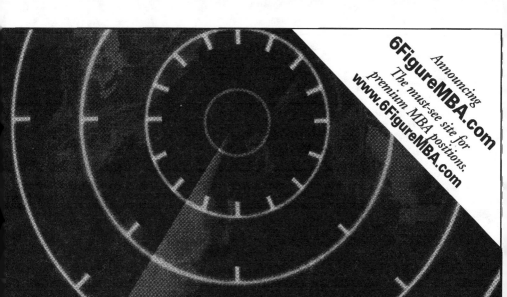

Use the Internet's most targeted job search tools for finance professionals.

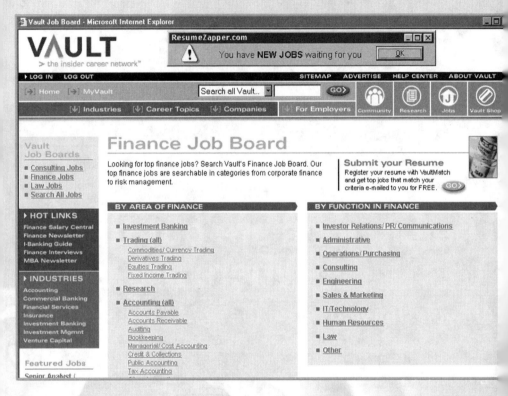

■ Vault Finance Job Board

The most comprehensive and convenient job board for consulting professionals. Target your search by area of finance, function, and experience level, and find the job openings that you want. No surfing required.

■ VaultMatch™ Resume Database

Vault takes match-making to the next level: post your resume and customize your search by area of finance, experience and more. We'll match job listings with your interests and criteria and e-mail them directly to your in-box.

Find out more at
www.vault.com